Indo-Kyrgyz Relations

Challenges and Opportunities

INDO-KYRGYZ RELATIONS

CHALLENGES AND OPPORTUNITIES

Edited by

Ramakant Dwivedi

PENTAGON PRESS LLP

First published in 2023 by

PENTAGON PRESS LLP
206, Peacock Lane, Shahpur Jat
New Delhi-110049, India
Contact: 011-64706243

Typeset in Palatino, 10.5 Point
Printed by Aegean Offset Printers, Greater Noida, U.P.

ISBN: 978-93-90095-77-3 (HB)

www.pentagonpress.in

Contents

	Preface	*vii*
	Acknowledgements	*xiii*
	About the Contributors	*xv*
1.	Potential for Trade between India and Kyrgyz Republic *Amb Ashok Kumar Sharma*	1
2.	Kyrgyz-Indian Trade and Economic Relations: Current Stage of Development *Alybaeva, G.D.*	9
3.	India-Kyrgyz Economic Ties: Retrospect and Prospects *Anil Sharma*	18
4.	Kyrgyz-Indian Cooperation on Regional and International Levels and Perspectives on their Improvement *Nurmatov, T.A. and Orolbaeva, I.A.*	32
5.	Religious Extremism and Terrorism in Central Asia and Afghanistan: A Case Study of Islamic State of Khorasan Province *Dr. Ramakant Dwivedi*	44
6.	Strategic Partnership and India's Evolving Relations with Kyrgyzstan: Examining New Security Realities and Security Governance in the Background of Transforming Geopolitics of the Region *Dr. Anita Sengupta*	52
7.	Russia, USA and China in Central Asia: Cooperation or Competition? *Prof. Ainur Eshimbekovna Jorobekov and Aigerim Turgunbayeva*	64

8. International Terrorism as External Threats to the Regional Security of the Central Asian Countries 76
Prof. Dzhorobekova A.E. and Dr. Abalova N.Zh.

9. Non-Traditional Security Issues in Kyrgyzstan: Concerns and Cooperation 96
Dr. Kamala Kumari

10. State Policy of Kyrgyzstan in the Religious Sphere and the Process of Radicalization in the Context of Globalization 123
Dr. K.K. Malikov

11. An Assessment of the Shanghai Cooperation Organisation: An Indian Perspective 133
Prof. Nirmala Joshi

12. Implications of the Evolving Afghan Situation on Regional Security with Particular Reference to India and the Kyrgyz Republic 144
Pankaj Tripathi

13. Political Processes in Central Asia: A Case Study of Kyrgyzstan 157
Dr. Rashmini Koparkar

14. Situating India in Regional Security and Connectivity in Central Asia 169
Dr. Pravesh Kumar Gupta

15. Impact of COVID-19 Pandemic on Food Security in Kyrgyzstan 185
Dr. Raj Kumar Sharma

16. Cultural Heritage of India and Kyrgyzstan in the Eurasian Region 194
Dr. Kadyrkulova, A.S.

17. Modern Trends in the Development of Intellectual Property Management (International and National aspects) 203
Dr. Alybaev, S.T.

18. Development of Kyrgyz-Indian Relations in the Field of Science 210
Dzhumaliyeva Ryskul Sardarbekovna

19. Expansion of Economic Diplomacy of Kyrgyzstan in the World Community: Prospects for Regional Cooperation 220
Ryskulov, I.A. and Alybaeva, G.D.

Index 228

About the Editor 235

Preface

As part of India's 'extended neighbourhood' and being endowed with a rich historical and cultural legacy, the Kyrgyz Republic is an important country in Central Asia. Additionally, it is rich in hydro-electricity and India's energy needs would make exploring India – Kyrgyz relations in this direction attractive. In regional and international affairs, the Kyrgyz Republic plays an important role; it has good links with the Commonwealth of Independent States.

The political environment in Central Asia has undergone a significant change after the the US withdrawal from Afghanistan and Taliban takeover of Kabul.

Against this backdrop, the present joint study on India - Kyrgyz Republic relations attempts to present a coherent perspective of social, economic and political developments in Kyrgyz Republic, along with the play of religious extremism and terrorism in Central Asia and the role of major powers in the geo-politics of Central Asia. The potential for enhanced engagement in a wide spectrum of areas of common interest is addressed. The potential role of India in promoting long-term stability in Central Asian is described.

Management and resolution of issues like international terrorism and religious extremism are of critical importance to both New Delhi and Bishkek. Hence, assessing the current status of international/regional extremist movements/groups/parties/ and their new linkages forms another important part of the joint study.

We hope it would be of interest to scholars, technocrats, entrepreneurs, diplomats and decision makers in both countries as well as those with an interest in Central Asian matters.

Coverage of Topics

This volume is a collection of 19 papers written by scholars from India and Kyrgyz Republic.

An Indian perspective of Indo-Kyrgyz economic ties and potential for trade between the two countries is provided by Amb Ashok Kumar Sharma. He argues that the two countries have not been able to realise the full potential and suggest a mechanism to achieve the said potential.

Alybaeva, G.D. provides Kyrgyz view on the bilateral trade between Kyrgyz Republic and India and the possibilities for improving Kyrgyz-Indian cooperation in various areas of the economy.

Anil Sharma provides an in-depth analysis of economic cooperation between New Delhi and Bishkek. It also identifies areas which have potential for enhancing bilateral economic cooperation.

Amb Irina Orolbaeva and Nurmatov examine bilateral cooperation between Kyrgyz Republic and India in modern conditions. They analyze the prospects for enhancing the interaction of the parties and takes into account the emerging alignments on a regional and global scale.

Central Asia faces numerous non-traditional challenges to its security as well. The most prominent is the threats from religious extremism and terrorism. Ramakant Dwivedi provides a detailed and systematic analysis of the Islamic State of Khorasan Provinces (ISKP) which espouses extremism and terrorism. The decline in living standards, corruption, a sense of injustice and lack of sufficient democratic space are among other important factors that attract persons to extremism and terrorism. He argues ISKP's operational capability in the Central Asian region and Afghanistan remains limited. Its initial gains and territorial claims have waned significantly. Lack of effective control by the security forces will provide space for the ISKP in the said region. It cannot function in Central Asia and Afghanistan without the support of entities based in Pakistan and West Asia.

Dr. Anita Sengupta paper's focuses on changed geopolitical realities in the Eurasian region and transformation of India's own security perceptions. This article examines the essential components of India's engagement with the region in general and with Kyrgyzstan in particular, given its proximity to areas of conflict and instability and convergence of interests as far as security governance is concerned.

Ainur Eshimbekovna Jorobekov and Aigerim Turgunbayeva critically examine the role of Russia, USA and China in Central Asia. It evaluates the possible trajectory of their engagement in the region.

Professor Dzhorobekova A.E. and Dr. Abalova N.Zh. provide detailed analysis of the groups, parties and movements responsible for international terrorism in the region. They further examine the various factor responsible for the terrorism and extremism.

Kamala Kumari provides an in-depth study of the non-traditional security issues being faced by in Kyrgyz Republic. With the changing dynamics of security, geo-strategy, and international politics, it is necessary to look at an individual state's overall development and progress from time to time. The paper highlights the non-traditional security issues, particularly, the rise of the drug-narcotics business and trafficking apart from looking at major concerns and responses and the potential prospects of cooperation particularly, with India.

Dr. K.K. Malikov's article examines the state policy of the Kyrgyz Republic in the religious sphere in the context of globalization. The author substantiates the importance of regulating the religious sphere in the Republic by forming a new layer of normative legal acts. The classification of those convicted for crimes of terrorism and extremism is presented. The tendencies of the threat of radicalization, which are embodied in the al-Qaeda and ISIS, interests of Russia, China, Turkey, India, Iran, KSA, the proximity of Afghanistan, and the Fergana Valley as a centre of religious activity in Central Asia are considered. Further, external labour migration, the Civil War in Syria, the crisis of liberal and democratic reforms in Central Asia, the insufficient level of education of the population, and radical information related to modern technologies have also been considered.

Prof. Nirmala Joshi's contribution has focused on Shanghai Cooperation Organization (SCO) led by its 'locomotives drivers', Russia and China. The SCO is poised to play an important and increasing role in this region. SCO's role has been critically examined with a detailed description of challenges and prospects for the success of this Organization.

Pankaj Tripathi critically examines situation in Afghanistan post Taliban takeover. Afghanistan has been a country ravaged by near continuous conflict during the past four decades. High levels of violence and fighting have been the norm during this long period. Taliban takeover of Kabul came about within a year of the start of the intra-Afghan talks between the Ashraf Ghani-led Afghan government and the Taliban that started on 12 September 2020. These talks, in turn, flowed from the US-Taliban deal of 29 February 2020, titled, 'Agreement for Bringing Peace to Afghanistan' outlining a timetable for a full US troop withdrawal from Afghanistan. He examines the reasons for the sudden collapse of the Afghan national security forces in 2021, after the withdrawal of the USA and NATO forces.

Dr. Rashmini Koparkar focuses on the political processes in the Kyrgyz Republic. The country has been a part of the larger Central Asian geo-politics, and has experienced similar trends of political transition. It has also met with similar economic and security challenges. Despite this, it stands out as a unique instance in Central Asia. She argues that this distinctiveness comes from a variety of reasons. Geographical complexities, economic hardships, North-South dichotomy, and strained ethnic entanglements add to the existing political intricacy.

Dr. Pravesh Kumar Gupta focuses on how India and the Central Asian republics can find convergence in the regional security and connectivity in the region. Based on the findings, the paper makes some recommendations.

Dr. Raj Kumar Sharma examines the impact of the COVID-19 pandemic on the food security situation in Kyrgyz Republic. He highlights the concept of food security and the relationship between food security and national security on the one hand and food security and political stability on the other.

Kadyrkulova A.S., provides analysis of cultural heritage of India and Kyrgyz Republic in detail bringing out the salient points of number of epic works of both the countries.

Dzhumaliyeva Ryskul Sardarbekovna provides Kyrgyz perspective on enhancing mutually beneficial cooperation in the field of science between New Delhi and Bishkek. The article underlines the need of finding common ground for exploitation and channelization of the available resources to achieve the said objectives.

Alybaev, S.T. provides an analysis of modern trends in the development of intellectual property management from the perspective of the international experience of Kyrgyzstan.

I am happy to offer this volume to scholars, policy makers, diplomats, entrepreneurs, academicians and decision makers in both countries – as well as those with a similar interest in the foreign policy of India and Kyrgyz Republic and Central Asian affairs.

I hope that this book would contribute towards a greater and enlightened appreciation of Indo - Kyrgyz relations.

New Delhi
March 13, 2023

Ramakant Dwivedi

Acknowledgements

I would like to record my appreciation of the support extended by Late Dr K Santhanam, Prof Nirmala Joshi, Director, India Central Asia Foundation, New Delhi, Prof Chinara Adamkulova, Rector, Dikambayev Diplomatic Academy, Ministry of Foreign Affairs, Kyrgyz Republic, Professor BB Kumar, Former Chairman, Indian Council of Social Science Research (ICSSR), New Delhi, Mr Evgeny Kahlukov, and Dr Anita Sengupta. The enthusiastic support given by Kyrgyz Republic Embassy in New Delhi and Eurasia Division, Ministry of External Affairs, Government of India needs to be especially acknowledged.

I would like to thank all the contributors of the papers published in the book. Without their dedication and persistent hard work, this book may not have seen the light of the day. Gratitude to Prof Mamidala Jagadesh Kumar, Chairman, University Grants Commission and Amb K Raghunath, Former Foreign Secretary, Ministry of External Affairs, Government of India.

Emotional support and love of my wife Renu Dwivedi and daughters Ramanshi Dwivedi and Ramya Dwivedi are of immense value and source of encouragement.

I would also like to record my appreciation of the efforts made by Dr Pradeep and his team in translation of the Russian papers.

I would like to thank Pentagon Press LLP for copy-editing and publishing the book in record time. The publisher Rajan Arya Ji's patience needs to be especially appreciated and acknowledged.

New Delhi
March 13, 2023

Ramakant Dwivedi

About the Contributors

Amb Ashok Kumar Sharma, Indian Foreign Service (Retd), currently, is Vice President of the India Central Asia Foundation (ICAF), New Delhi. He was India's ambassador to Kazakhstan and Finland spent 12 years in the former Soviet Union Republics in different capacities. He retired as Secretary to Government of India. *e-mail: pikusharma@hotmail.com*

Alybaeva G.D. is a faculty at the K. Dikambayev Diplomatic Academy, Ministry of Foreign Affairs, Kyrgyz Republic. *e-mail: dipacadem@kmet.kg*

Anil Sharma, is a Chartered Accountant by profession. He is a Member of National Financial Reporting Authority, Ministry of Corporate Affairs, Government of India and an Adjunct Faculty with the Indian Institute of Corporate Affairs. He was an Independent Director with UCO Bank for 2016-19. He is actively associated with various NGOs working in social Sector. *e-mail: anil54@gmail.com*

Dr Nurmatov T.A., Associate Professor, Department of International Relations and Law, K. Dikambayev Diplomatic Academy, Ministry of Foreign Affairs, Kyrgyz Republic. *e-mail: dipacadem@kmet.kg*

Orolbaeva I.A. is a former Kyrgyz Ambassador to India and currently Professor at the Department of International Relations and Law, K. Dikambayev Diplomatic Academy, Ministry of Foreign Affairs, Kyrgyz Republic. *e-mail: dipacadem@kmet.kg*

Dr. Ramakant Dwivedi has a PhD from the Central Asian Studies Division of the School of International Studies, Jawaharlal Nehru University, New

Delhi. Dr. Dwivedi was a Visiting Research Fellow at the Al-Beruni Institute of Oriental Studies, Tashkent (1998-2001). He was Associate Fellow at the Institute for Defence Studies and Analyses (IDSA), New Delhi (2003–2007). He has been working with Government of India since last 16 years. He has looked after a variety of domains assigned to him during the service. His major areas of research are national security, foreign policy, ethnic issues and religious extremism in Eurasian region (Russia, Caucasus and Central Asian countries). He holds a Diploma in the Russian Language from the University of World Economy and Diplomacy, Tashkent and a Diploma in the Uzbek Language from the Tashkent State Institute of Oriental Studies, Uzbekistan. He has widely travelled in the Eurasian region. Dr. Dwivedi was awarded Nehru Memorial Scholarship for Doctoral Studies by Jawaharlal Nehru Memorial Fund, Teen Murti House, New Delhi. He has represented India in 14 countries as domain expert and part of official delegation for scholarly presentations. His published works include 41 research papers in national/international journals, edited books. He co-edited *India and Central Asia: Advancing the Common Interest*, *India-Tajikistan Cooperation: Perspectives and Prospects*, *India- Kazakhstan Perspectives: Regional and International Interactions*, *India-Turkmenistan Relations*, *Indo-Uzbek Perspectives on the Environment and Sustainable Development*, *India-Kyrgyz Relations: Perspectives and Prospects* and *Contemporary Indo-Uzbek Perspectives on Bilateral and Regional Issues*. *e-mail: ramakantdwivedi2012@gmail.com*

Dr. Anita Sengupta is an area studies specialist engaged with the study of the Eurasian region. Her areas of interest include issues of identity politics, migration, gender, borders, critical geopolitics and logistics. She is a regular commentator on debates on Asian affairs. She has been Fellow, Maulana Abul Kalam Azad Institute of Asian Studies, Kolkata, Senior Fellow, Indian Council of Social Science Research, New Delhi and Director, Calcutta Research Group, Kolkata. She is currently Director, Asia in Global Affairs, Kolkata. *e-mail: anitasengupta@hotmail.com*

Prof Ainur Eshimbekovna Jorobekov, currently, is Head, Department of International Relations and Law, K. Dikambayev Diplomatic Academy, Ministry of Foreign Affairs, Kyrgyz Republic. *e-mail: dipacadem@kmet.kg*

Aigerim Turgunbayeva, Lecturer, Department of International Relations and Law, K. Dikambayev Diplomatic Academy, Ministry of Foreign Affairs of the Kyrgyz Republic. *e-mail: dipacadem@kmet.kg*

Prof Dzhorobekova A.E. is currently working with K. Dikambayev Diplomatic Academy, Ministry of Foreign Affairs, Kyrgyz Republic.
e-mail: dipacadem@kmet.kg

Dr Kamala Kumari has been teaching at the University of Delhi. HShe has completed Ph.D. fom the Centre of Russian and Central Asian Studies, School of International Studies, Jawaharlal Nehru University, New Delhi. Her areas of interest include foreign policy and security issues of Central Asia. *e-mail: kamala2003@gmail.com*

Dr. Malikov K.K. is working in the Department of International Relations and Law, K. Dikambayev Diplomatic Academy, Ministry of Foreign Affairs, Kyrgyz Republic. *e-mail: dipacadem@kmet.kg*

Prof Nirmala Joshi is Director of the India-Central Asia Foundation New Delhi India. She was professor at the Centre for Russian, Central Asian and East European Studies, School of International Studies, Jawaharlal Nehru University, New Delhi. Prof. Joshi has been the member of the Indo-Russian Joint Commission for Cooperation in Social Sciences. She is member of the Standing Committee of the University Grant Commission of India. Her major areas of research are foreign and security policy, democratisation and energy security of Russia, Central Asia and South Caucasus. She is the author of *Indo-Soviet Relations: Unofficial Attitudes and Contacts 1917-47* and has edited *Central Asia the Great Game Replayed: An Indian Perspective.*
e-mail: nirmalajoshi2002@hotmail.com

Pankaj Tripathi is currently Principal Consultant with the Sarojini Damodaran Foundation's Vidyadhan program that supports the education of students from economically disadvantaged families. He was serving with the Government of India for 25 years (1993-2018) in different capacities within India and in Indian Diplomatic Missions abroad, including in Bishkek, Islamabad and Frankfurt. His writings on India-Central Asia relationship have been published by the Indian Council of World Affairs (ICWA), New Delhi. *e-mail: tripspankaj@gmail.com*

Dr Rashmini Koparkar is Assistant Professor at the Centre for Russian and Central Asian Studies, School of International Studies, Jawaharlal Nehru University (JNU), New Delhi. She has formerly worked as Research Fellow at the Indian Council of World Affairs (Aug 2019- Feb 2020) and as Research Associate at the Vivekananda International Foundation (2016-18). She has published a monograph on 'Issues and Dynamics of the Fergana

Valley: Regional Implications' with the Vivekananda International Foundation. Her research interests include Politics and Foreign Policies of Central Asian states, India's engagements in Eurasia, and issues of Identity and Nation-Building. Dr Koparkar was awarded PhD in 2016 from the Center for Russian and Central Asian Studies, JNU. Her PhD thesis was titled, 'Nation-Building in Post-Soviet Central Asia: A Case Study of Uzbekistan'. She has completed M.A. and M. Phil in International Relations from JNU. Dr Koparkar is proficient in Russian language. She has participated in various international and national conferences, and has written number of research papers and articles.

e-mail: rashmini.koparkar@gmail.com

Dr. Pravesh Kumar Gupta is a Research Associate at Vivekananda International Foundation (VIF). He has a doctoral degree in Central Asian Studies from Jawaharlal Nehru University, New Delhi. His primary interests of research are society and politics of Central Asian Republics, geopolitics of Central and South Asia, Energy Security and trans-regional energy linkages between Central and South Asia.

Dr. Raj Kumar Sharma is currently teaching at the Indira Gandhi National Open University (IGNOU), New Delhi.

Dr. Kadyrkulova A.S. is a faculty at the Department of International Relations and Law, K. Dikambayev Diplomatic Academy, Ministry of Foreign Affairs, Kyrgyz Republic. *e-mail: dipacadem@kmet.kg*

Alybaev S.T. is a faculty at the Department of International Relations and Law, K. Dikambayev Diplomatic Academy, Ministry of Foreign Affairs, Kyrgyz Republic. *e-mail: dipacadem@kmet.kg*

Dzhumaliyeva Ryskul Sardarbekovna, Senior Lecturer, is a faculty at the Department of the State Institute of Foreign Languages, K. Dikambayev Diplomatic Academy, Ministry of Foreign Affairs, Kyrgyz Republic.

e-mail: dipacadem@kmet.kg

Ryskulov, I.A. is a faculty at the K. Dikambaeva Diplomatic Academy Ministry of Foreign Affairs of the Kyrgyz Republic.

e-mail: dipacadem@kmet.kg

Alybaeva, G.D. is a faculty at the K. Dikambaeva Diplomatic Academy Ministry of Foreign Affairs of the Kyrgyz Republic.

e-mail: dipacadem@kmet.kg

1

Potential for Trade between India and Kyrgyz Republic

Amb Ashok Kumar Sharma

Foreign trade plays an important role in the economy of Kyrgyzstan. In 2019, the foreign trade volume (in goods only) of Kyrgyzstan amounted to 103.1 per cent of GDP according to World Bank figures. India-Kyrgyzstan bilateral trade has remained at a low level because of several factors, difficulties associated with transportation being the most important impediment. In recent years, both sides took some steps to boost the trade relations but these efforts suffered a big setback due to the COVID-19 pandemic in 2020-21.

As per the statistics published by the Ministry of Commerce (Govt. of India), the trade volume between the two countries has been as follows in recent years. (Table 1)

Trade Data from Government of Kyrgyzstan Sources

As per the data available on the website of the National Statistical Committee of the Kyrgyz Republic, during 2019, imports from India to Kyrgyzstan amounted to US$ 42.017 million whereas exports from Kyrgyzstan to India during the same year amounted to US$ 3.104 million. There will always be some discrepancy in the trade statistics of the two

Table 1: Trade Data from Ministry of Commerce (Government of India)

Year	*Exports from India (India's official Financial Year) (US$ million)*	*Imports by India to Kyrgyzstan (US$ million)*	*Total Bilateral Trade from Kyrgyzstan (US$ million)*
April 2013-March 2014	34.54	0.64	35.18
April 2014-March 2015	37.76	0.77	38.53
April 2015-March 2016	25.11	1.79	26.90
April 2016-March 2017	30.44	1.48	31.92
April 2017-March 2018	28.59	30.94	59.53
April 2018-March 2019	30.02	2.59	32.61
April 2019-March 2020	29.13	1.33	30.46
April 2020-Nov. 2020	24.33	0.11	—

Source: Comtrade.

countries due to the difference in their financial years, different practices of calculating the value of exports and imports (FOB or CIF), sale on the high seas, trans-shipment, time lag between export and its arrival in the importing country, etc. The main point to be noted here is that the bilateral trade between the two countries is very low given the fact that the total imports of Kyrgyzstan in 2019 were US$ 4,989 million and exports amounted to US$ 1,986 million.

Table 2: Main Trade Partners of Kyrgyzstan (2019)

Total Exports in 2019: US$ 1,986 million Main Countries of Exports		*(in Million US$)*	*Total Imports in 2019: US$ 4,989 million Main Countries of Imports (in US$)*	
1.	U.K.	833.23 (41.96%)	1. China	1.73 billion (34.68%)
2.	Kazakhstan	347.07 (17.48%)	2. Russia	1.40 billion (28.06%)
3.	Russia	281.25 (14.16%)	3. Kazakhstan	649.33 million (13.02%)
4.	Uzbekistan	138.88 (6.99%)	4. Turkey	222.84 million (4.47%)
5.	Turkey	89.85 (4.52%)	5. Uzbekistan	200.89 million (4.03%)
6.	China	81.47 (4.12%)	6. USA	90.26 million (1.81%)
7.	Tajikistan	57.21 (2.88%)	7. Germany	70.78 million (1.42%)
8.	Lithuania	17.13 (0.86%)	8. Ukraine	48.47 million (0.97%)
9.	Iran	15.43 (0.78%)	9. Belarus	46.48 million (0.93%)
10.	Ukraine	13.63 (0.69%)	10. India	42.02 million (0.84%)
11.	Belarus	13.14 (0.66%)	11. France	37.67 million (0.76%)
12.	U.A.E.	10.23 (0.52%)	12. South Korea	33.15 million (0.66%)

Source: Comtrade.

Table 3: Main Items of Export from Kyrgyzstan (2019)

1.	Gold, including gold plated with platinum (unwrought)	41.9% ($ 832 million)
2.	Precious metal ores and concentrates	8.2% ($ 162 million)
3.	Petroleum oils and oils from bituminous minerals	3.2% ($ 75 million)
4.	Dried leguminous vegetables	3.8% ($ 74 million)
5.	Waste and copper scrap	3.2% ($ 62 million)
6.	Women's garments	1.9% ($ 38 million)
7.	Cotton (raw)	1.8% ($ 35 million)
8.	Parts and accessories for tractors and motor vehicles	1.7% ($ 33 million)
9.	Cement including cement clinkers	1.6% ($ 31 million)
10.	Float glass	1.4% ($ 28 million)

Source: Comtrade.

Table 4: Main Items of Import by Kyrgyzstan

1.	Petroleum oils	12.3% ($ 612 million)
2.	Footwear	4.1% ($ 205 million)
3.	Electrical apparatus for telephone lines/infra	3.7% ($ 186 million)
4.	Pharmaceuticals	3.4% ($ 172 million)
5.	Woven fabrics (synthetic)	2.1% ($ 103 million)
6.	Cigars, cigarettes & tobacco products	1.5% ($ 77 million)
7.	Base metal mountings, furniture, doors, fittings, etc.	1.3 % ($ 63 million)
8.	Iron and steel bars, rods, etc.	1.2 % ($ 60 million)
9.	Petroleum gases and other gaseous hydrocarbons	1.1 % ($ 56 million)
10.	Knitted or crocheted fabrics	1.0 % ($ 50 million)

Source: Comtrade, latest available data.

Analysis of Bilateral Trade between India and Kyrgyzstan

As is obvious from the statistics in the previous paragraphs, bilateral trade between India and Kyrgyzstan is limited. The biggest impediment has remained the transportation of goods. Most items with volume/weight become unviable because of high transportation costs and transit time. Hence, high value and low volume/weight items will have to be identified to increase bilateral trade.

Existing Items of Export from Kyrgyzstan to India

Kyrgyzstan's exports to India are limited to a few items only. These include beans (mainly kidney beans) and other edible vegetables, dry fruits (walnuts), gums and raisins (mainly asafoetida), some dress materials to be used in garments to be imported from India and small quantities of items like raw leather (wet blue), mercury, liquorice, shilajit (mumijo), etc.

Potential Items of Export from Kyrgyzstan to India

There are several items in Kyrgyzstan which could be considered for export to India. However, some value addition may be required to make them commercially viable due to high transportation costs. Moreover, the items that could be sent through air cargo may also be identified.

Beans and lentils may still be commercially viable. If good quantities are available, exports to India could be increased. India is a large consumer of asafoetida. Efforts may be made to process it and export to India in larger quantities. Similarly, dry fruits (especially walnuts and almonds), shilajit (mumijo), liquorice, honey (white mountain honey), etc., may find a good market in India.

India needs high quality leather for manufacture of leather garments and accessories. Import of wet blue has been attempted but not found viable due to high transportation costs and transit time. If the leather is tanned and processed in Kyrgyzstan before exporting to India, it could be commercially viable.

Kyrgyzstan produces high quality grapes and berries. These are good to produce high-quality wines. Indian companies may look into the possibility of setting up joint ventures for wine making in Kyrgyzstan, some of which could find a market in India as well as in other countries. In addition, Kyrgyz raisins (both big and small) have a good potential in India.

India needs rare earths for its growing electronics, telecommunications, space and nuclear power industries. India has to secure its supply of rare earths which are crucial in the new electronic age. It is estimated that Kyrgyzstan has about 20 rare earths sites, of which (reportedly) only one (Kutesay-2) in the Chu Region is operational. More geological studies are required. Indian companies and organisations like the Geological Survey of India and Indian Rare-Earths Ltd. could look into the possibility of collaboration in this field. There are environmental issues in such mining and the potential for joint studies could be explored. High quality tantalum is available in Kyrgyzstan which is an important metal for electronics.

India has been importing mercury and antimony in small quantities from Kyrgyzstan. The possibility for joint ventures in this regard for import of value-added items could be explored. At present, India does not produce antimony and its entire requirement is imported. Kyrgyzstan can become a good source for it. Kyrgyzstan can also be a good source for copper and beryllium.

India imports stearic acid from various sources. Kyrgyzstan exports high quality stearic acid. Kyrgyz exporters may also try to explore possibilities of export to India. Similarly, unwrought and refined lead can be exported to India if found competitive.

Indian companies are reluctant to set up joint ventures for gold mining and processing. This field is controlled by a few big multinational companies. However, with the entry of Indian companies in mining activities (especially coal) abroad, gold mining and processing in Kyrgyzstan may also interest them.

Potential Items for Export from India to Kyrgyzstan

Indian exports to Kyrgyzstan have remained static around US$ 30 per annum for many years. Apparel (garments) and pharmaceuticals have accounted for over 75 per cent of the total exports. There is a need to diversify India's export basket. India imports many manufactured and consumer items and it is more difficult for Indian products to compete with imports from China in the Kyrgyz market due to high transportation costs and other limitations like inability to reach economies of scale due to low volumes. However, there are some areas where India has some advantage and exports to Kyrgyzstan could be augmented.

Tea and coffee have been traditional export items of India to Kyrgyzstan. They face tough competition from other countries like China and Sri Lanka. Some quantities of Indian tea are also imported from Kazakhstan and the UAE. Because of lack of economies of scale, Indian exporters do not find it viable to set up packing and branding facilities in Kyrgyzstan and try to export via neighbouring countries. There is still some scope for increasing Indian tea exports due to its distinct quality and aroma.

Indian spices can also be acceptable in Kyrgyzstan. Indian cumin seeds are already being exported. Indian basmati and parboiled rice have potential for increased export volumes.

Kyrgyzstan imports most of its apparel from China. Indian exporters may also identify the items in which they can compete. The Indian share is very small at present. India also produces good quality knitwear and a comprehensive market survey could help. Indian terry towels have good potential.

In pharmaceuticals, India's share is about 8.5 per cent which is half that of Russia. According to the Comtrade Database of the UN, Kyrgyzstan imported pharmaceuticals worth US$ 189.17 million in 2019, of which India's share was US$ 26.57. This does not match with the figures of the Ministry of Commerce (Government of India) database which shows much lower amounts of exports. This includes vaccines, bandages and other related items. Because of low volumes, joint ventures in the pharma industry may not be viable.

Kyrgyzstan adopted a new law in 2017 on the procedure of registration of drugs and other medical products, medical devices and medical equipment as per the norms of the Eurasian Economic Union (EAEU). Some Indian medicines may also be coming to Kyrgyzstan via other EAEU countries. However, efforts should be made to register more products, especially vaccines and other medical items to augment India's share. Many Indian exporters find the procedures of registration and approval in Central Asian countries very cumbersome and expensive, given the small size of the market. However, the procedure is the same for other exporting countries too and this should not deter Indian companies from this market.

India manufactures good quality surgical and medical equipment and consumables. Small quantities are exported to Kyrgyzstan and there is potential for more. Export of veterinary drugs may also be promoted.

Footwear is another area worth exploring. In Kyrgyzstan, over 99 per cent of rubber footwear is imported from China. Import of leather footwear is over 60 per cent from China followed by Turkey (over 17 per cent) and Italy (over 8 per cent). Textile footwear is also imported mainly from China (over 95 per cent). India manufactures many of these items at competitive prices.

Export of sports goods may be looked into. The quantities may be small but there are some items which can be promoted. Jewellery (including artificial jewellery) is a potential area of export from India. At present, over 96 per cent of these items are imported from Turkey.

There are many other items that have been tried for exports from India like essential oils and cosmetics, leather items (garments and accessories), floor coverings, construction fittings, furnishing fabrics, mattresses, household utensils, books and stationery items, bathroom fittings, colours and pigments, paints and varnishes, tableware, ceramic items, tanning material for leather, stones and granites for monuments, mica (insulation items), etc. Efforts may be made to promote the export of these items in an organised manner.

Project Exports

There is enough scope for project exports (especially in projects funded by international financial institutions or Indian lines of credit), dairy machinery and equipment, printing machinery, agricultural implements including tractors and textile machinery. Indian auto-parts and accessories are exported to many countries and may also find a good market in Kyrgyzstan.

Services Sector

Tourism between India and Kyrgyzstan has good potential. Many tourists from Kyrgyzstan come to India. Medical tourism is also picking up. One can find Kyrgyz patients coming to India for affordable medical treatment. However, tourism from India to Kyrgyzstan needs a major push. Tourist places like Issyk Kul Lake, Ala-Archa Gorge, Altyn Arashan, etc., could become major attractions for Indian tourists. Absence of direct flights between the two countries makes it difficult to develop tourism between India and Kyrgyzstan. In the post-COVID era, the potential in this sector will have to be studied afresh.

Civil Aviation

Due to low volumes, airline companies do not find it commercially viable to operate regular scheduled flights on this route. However, frequent charter-flights could be considered during the tourist season.

Computer Software

Due to the rapid development of Information Technology (IT), a new culture of work-from-home and advances in communication technology worldwide, medium-sized Indian IT companies may explore the possibility of joint ventures in Kyrgyzstan. Similarly, potential for collaboration in the financial sector could also be explored.

New Possibilities for Bilateral Economic Collaboration with an Indian Credit Line

India's Prime Minister, Mr. Narendra Modi, paid an official bilateral visit to the Kyrgyz Republic during 13-14 June 2019, when he announced a line of credit of US$ 200 million for financing development projects in Kyrgyzstan. Several joint projects are likely to be financed with this credit line which will open new areas of bilateral trade and collaboration. Indian companies may use this opportunity to get a foothold in this market. Kyrgyz companies can also avail of this facility to strengthen their export competitiveness. Several joint projects are likely to be financed with this credit line.

Collaboration through Joint Ventures

There are around 20 Indian companies in the Kyrgyz Republic but they are relatively small. Large and medium Indian companies should explore business opportunities with the Kyrgyz Republic in sectors such as mining, agri-food (food processing), pharmaceuticals (for Eurasian markets), textiles and garments, gems and jewellery (utilising local resources) and agricultural implements. There is sufficient scope for cooperation in health, information and communication technology and education. A large number of Indian students go to Kyrgyz medical colleges for degrees. There is a need to modify their syllabus as per the requirements of the Indian Medical Commission (formerly Medical Council of India). These students have to pass an exam conducted by the Indian Medical Commission before their degrees are recognised. These medical colleges may consider the possibility of collaboration with Indian medical colleges, including faculty exchange.

Latest Developments at Bilateral Level

A five-year road-map for trade and economic cooperation between the two countries was adopted during the visit of the Prime Minister of India, Mr. Narendra Modi, to Bishkek in June 2019. It envisaged diversification of products of trade and increase in foreign investment. Addressing the Business Forum during the visit, Prime Minister Modi highlighted the opportunities for investors from India in areas of medicine, textiles, railways, hydro-power, mining and minerals and tourism. On this occasion, business delegations from both countries agreed to explore joint collaborations and cooperation in the fields of textiles, handicrafts, fabrics and arts. The pandemic had put some brakes but the momentum has to be revived in the post-COVID era.

2

Kyrgyz-Indian Trade and Economic Relations: Current Stage of Development

Alybaeva, G.D.

ABSTRACT

This article examines export-import flows between Kyrgyzstan and India, as well as issues of Kyrgyz-Indian cooperation in various areas of the economy.

Keywords: *trade turnover, investments, trade and economic cooperation, strategic partnership.*

Kyrgyz-Indian relations are deep in nature, encompassing active interaction on international issues, and trade and economic cooperation, and ties in many other areas.

The most important component of the Kyrgyz-Indian partnership is trade and economic cooperation. Kyrgyzstan and India have all the prerequisites for the further expansion of ties in the economic sphere. This is not only significant human and raw material resources, a developed scientific and technical base and the activity of business circles, but also the course of the governments of both countries towards reforms.

Trade and economic cooperation between Kyrgyzstan and India has recently been developing quite dynamically and does not slow down, despite the global financial and economic crisis. Among the main obstacles to building up bilateral trade and economic cooperation are usually called insufficient awareness of the parties about mutual opportunities, complex bureaucratic procedures, underdevelopment of credit and financial mechanisms and transport infrastructure, difficulties in the selection of qualified personnel, national peculiarities of doing business and the language barrier.

Table 1: Trade Turnover of Kyrgyzstan with India in 2015–2019 (in thousand US$)

Goods turnover	*2015*	*2016*	*2017*	*2018*	*2019*	*Growth/Decline 2018/2019*
Export	1,239.0	2,325.3	3,478.9	5,766.1	3,103.8	–47%
Import	22,613.9	22,660.3	28,813.8	31,447.6	42,017.1	+33.6%
Balance	–20,924.9	–2,535.0	–25,334.9	–2,568.5	–3,891.3	—

Source: Compiled by the author based on the data "Foreign and Mutual Trade of the Kyrgyz Republic 2015-2019: Statistical Book," NSCKR, Bishkek, 2020, p. 96.

At the moment, statistical data for 10 months of 2020 are available for this study. The volume of mutual trade between Kyrgyzstan and India for 10 months of 2020 amounted to US$ 35.5 million, having decreased by 3.2 per cent when compared to January-November 2019. Trade turnover between the countries in January-November 2020 amounted to US$ 35.4 million.

The volume of imports from India to Kyrgyzstan for 10 months of 2020 amounted to US$ 30.7 million, while exports from Kyrgyzstan to India for the same period amounted to only US$ 4.7 million; mainly, coffee, tea, pharmaceuticals, chemical products and much more are supplied from India to Kyrgyzstan. For 10 months of 2020, pharmaceutical products were imported from India to the Kyrgyz Republic for US$ 21.3 million, chemical products for US$ 3 million, coffee, tea, for US$ 223 thousand. The range of Indian imports is over 180 items. The data of Diagram 1 "Structure of imports from India to Kyrgyzstan" clearly shows that 92 per cent of the total volume is occupied by pharmaceutical products, the second most important group of goods is "Articles of clothing and clothing accessories", which make up 4 per cent.

Diagram 1: Structure of Imports from India to Kyrgyzstan for 10 Months of 2020

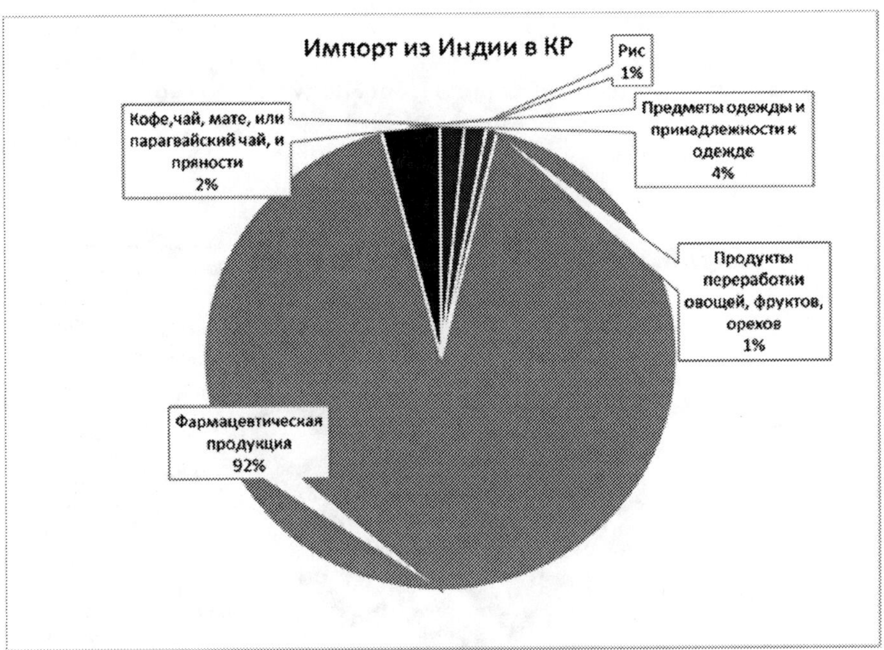

Russian	*English*
1. Импорт из Индии в КР	1. Import from India to the Kyrgyz Republic
2. Кофе, чай, мате, или парагвайский чай и прятности 2%	2. Coffee, tea, or Paraguayan tea and sweeteners 2%
3. Рис 1%	3. Rice 1%
4. Предметы одежды и принадлежности к одежде 4%	4. Articles of clothing and clothing accessories 4%
5. Фармацевтическая продукция 92%	5. Pharmaceuticals 92%
6. Продукты переработки овощей, фруктов, орехов 1%	6. Products of processing vegetables, fruits, nuts 1%

In the structure of Kyrgyz exports to India for 10 months of 2020, mineral fuel, oil and products of their distillation accounted for 41 per cent (US$ 637.9 thousand) of the total supply, vegetables and some edible root crops and tubers, 30 per cent (US$ 5 thousand), meat and edible meat offal, 17 per cent (US$ 168 thousand), other prepared or canned meat, meat offal or blood products, 3 per cent (US$ 26.6 thousand), edible fruits and nuts, 8 per cent (US$ 74.7 thousand). The rest of the commodity items of export supplies of Kyrgyzstan have a specific weight of less than 1 per cent (for example, natural honey), which is not reflected in Diagram 2.

The range of Kyrgyz exports is no more than 10 items, which indicates the limited opportunities for Kyrgyz to actively develop bilateral trade cooperation with India.

Diagram 2: Structure of Exports from Kyrgyzstan to India for 10 Months of 2020

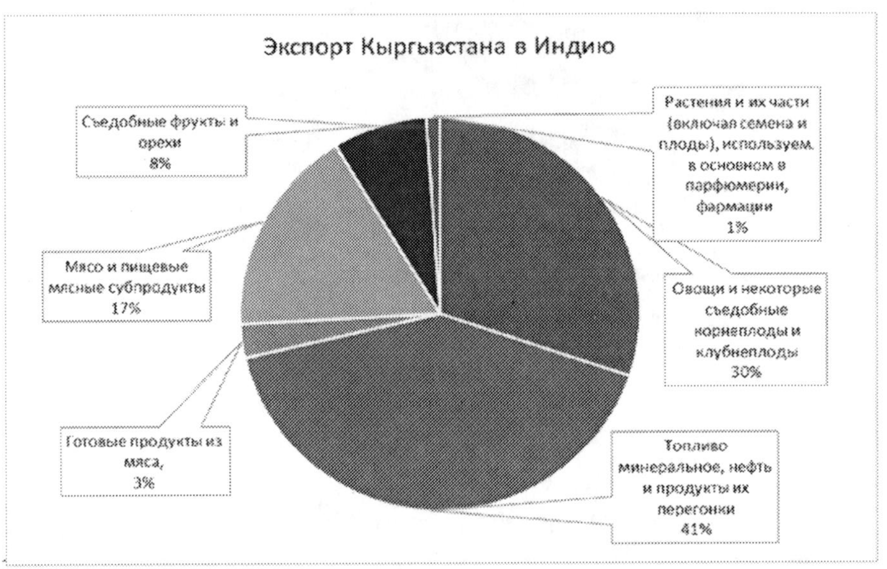

Russian	*English*
1. Экспорт Крыгызстана в Индию	Export of Kyrgyzstan to India
2 Съедобные фрукты и орехи 8%	Edible fruits and nuts 8%
3. Мясо и пищевые мясные субпродукты 17%	Meat and edible meat offal 17%
4. Готовые продукты из мяса, 3%	Prepared meat products, 3%
5. Растения и их части (включая семена и плоды), используем в основном в парфюмерии, фармации 1%	Plants and their parts (including seeds and fruits), for use mainly in perfumery, pharmacy 1%
6. Овощи и некторые съедобные коренплоды и клубнеплоды 30%	Vegetables and some edible roots and tubers 30%
7. Топливо минеральное , нефть и продукты их перегонки 41%	Mineral fuel, oil and products of their distillation 41%

To widen Kyrgyz-Indian cooperation, mechanisms of interaction in the field of economics have been created and debugged. The key role here is played by the Intergovernmental Commission on Trade, Economic, Scientific, Technical and Cultural Cooperation. To date, nine meetings of the Kyrgyz-Indian intergovernmental commission have taken place. The ninth meeting was held on 15-16 November 2018 in New Delhi. The co-chairmen of the Kyrgyz-Indian intergovernmental commission were the Minister of Health of the Kyrgyz Republic K. Cholponbaev and the Minister of Commerce and Industry of India Suresh P. Prabhu. This was an important event for the activation of Kyrgyz-Indian trade and economic relations, following which the protocol of the ninth meeting of the Kyrgyz-Indian Intergovernmental Commission on trade, economic, scientific and technical cooperation was signed.

During the meeting of the Intergovernmental Commission, issues of mutual cooperation in the field of trade and investment, agriculture, health care and pharmaceuticals, information technology and electronic government, environmental and technical safety, culture, information, tourism, textile and clothing industry, entrepreneurship, banking, and labour were discussed, along with social development, mining, and standardization, metrology and certification.

The parties agreed to take necessary measures to increase the interaction of exporters and importers of Kyrgyzstan and India and expand the trade basket, and agreed to increase the supply of agricultural products to the markets of the two states. The Kyrgyz side initiated the issue of creating joint food and processing enterprises, and crop and livestock products for export to the markets of the EAEU member-countries.

The parties expressed their readiness to cooperate jointly on telemedicine issues. The Kyrgyz side initiated cooperation in a number of areas in the healthcare sector, including the implementation of PPP projects, creation of joint ventures, and provision of benefits for treatment of citizens of the Kyrgyz Republic who need to carry out operations using high-tech equipment.

The Parties agreed to hold the tenth meeting of the Kyrgyz-Indian Intergovernmental Commission on Trade, Economic, Scientific and Technical Cooperation in Bishkek. However, due to the corona virus pandemic in the world, the date has not been set. Thus, the main results of interaction in priority areas were summed up and tasks for the next year were outlined. In addition, contacts between the chambers of commerce and industry and industrial associations of our countries are being actively pursued.

On the initiative of the Embassy of the Kyrgyz Republic in India, on 18 November 2016, the Indo-Kyrgyz Business Council was formed as an association of business persons, currently consisting of 22 members representing Indian business companies.

The goals and objectives of the Business Council are to promote and develop mutual interest in economic relations between India and Kyrgyzstan, hold business meetings, conferences, seminars and meetings, organize trips for business delegations, as well as other activities that may be useful for the development of bilateral relations.

On 26 March 2019, a symposium was held to promote Indian-Kyrgyz trade and economic relations with active assitance of the Chamber of Commerce and Industry of the Kyrgyz Republic and the Embassy of India in Kyrgyzstan. The main purpose of the meeting was to establish business contacts between entrepreneurs of the two countries. Five investment projects of the Naryn region and a report on the benefits of investing in the Bishkek Free Economic Zone were presented to the participants of the symposium.

More than 70 people took part in the event. Representatives of the Embassy of India in Kyrgyzstan informed about the priority areas of the Indian economy. At the same time, it was emphasized that the Indian leadership views Kyrgyzstan as a strategic partnership and intends to intensify mutually beneficial partnerships in a number of sectors of the economy.

One of the weak links in our bilateral cooperation is the insignificant presence of investors from India in our economy. On the part of the state, the creation of favourable conditions for investors was identified as a priority area and a number of measures were taken in this direction. Today, the most favourable conditions for doing business have been created in Kyrgyzstan.

Investors' assets and their private property are reliably protected by the state. They are inviolable; the Kyrgyz state guarantees this. In order to protect the interests of private entrepreneurs and investors, for the first time in the country the institution of a business Ombudsman was created. New enterprises are exempted from inspection for a period of three years. Kyrgyzstan has the most liberal tax regime in the region with the lowest tax rates.

For example, value added tax is 12 per cent, and income tax is 10 per cent. Agricultural producers, and trade and logistics centres are exempt from income tax. Value added tax for enterprises processing agricultural raw materials produced in Kyrgyzstan is only two-and-a-half per cent. Import of technological equipment is exempt from customs duties.

Tariff and non-tariff restrictions have been removed, which means that products manufactured in Kyrgyzstan will have an advantage over products manufactured in third countries.

Foreign investors can benefit from inexpensive and skilled labour and cheap electricity. In Kyrgyzstan, the electricity tariff is very low; its cost for legal entities is about three cents, and for individuals, only about one cent.

There is a free exchange rate regime in our country. There are no restrictions for buying and selling foreign currency on the territory of Kyrgyzstan. Kyrgyzstan is a member of the Eurasian Economic Union. More than 183 million people live on the territory of the Union. In addition, in 2016, Kyrgyzstan received the status of the European Union GSP+.

In our opinion, we have good opportunities for a significant improvement in Kyrgyz-Indian trade relations. The Kyrgyz side is ready to increase the volume of exports of environmentally friendly organic products that will find consumers in the expanding Indian market.

In general, bilateral trade and economic cooperation between the Kyrgyz Republic and the Republic of India is developing progressively and systematically.

In addition to bilateral Kyrgyz-Indian economic relations, multilateral relations are actively developing in Central Asia. On 8 October 2020, the Chamber of Commerce and Industry of the Kyrgyz Republic took part in the second online meeting of the India-Central Asia Business Council, which was established in February 2020 in New Delhi under the chairmanship of a well-known business organization in India, the Federation of Indian Chambers of Commerce and Industry (FICCI). It includes such countries as: Kyrgyzstan, Kazakhstan, Tajikistan, Turkmenistan, and Uzbekistan. All the participants expressed their readiness and desire for sustainable economic cooperation and development using existing economic opportunities.

Dr. Sangita Reddy, President of FICCI and Managing Director of the Apollo Hospitals Group, as well as Mr. Adarsha Svayki, Secretary of the Eurasia Department, Ministry of Foreign Affairs of India, spoke to the participants of the Business Council—heads of the Chambers of Commerce and Industry of Kyrgyzstan, Kazakhstan, Tajikistan, Turkmenistan, and Uzbekistan—, who noted the importance of building favourable and transparent conditions for long-term partnerships between the industrial sectors of our countries.

FICCI is one of the leading business associations in India and has vast experience in various fields. The meeting resulted in the creation of four working groups that will work in four areas: agriculture, energy, health and pharmaceuticals, education and skill development. In addition, the participants signed a joint declaration on the development of trade relations between the countries of Central Asia and India.

The Kyrgyz side expects that the India-Central Asia Business Council will contribute to the development of small and medium-sized businesses in all states. It will serve to strengthen interconnections to provide an opportunity for the further development of economic cooperation and the establishment of new forms. It will give priority to the development of the agricultural, energy, textile sectors, as well as in the field of health and tourism. Kyrgyzstan has favourable conditions for the export of ecologically clean agricultural products to India. We can note with satisfaction the success of the partnership in the field of health. It was India that provided humanitarian assistance to our country during the pandemic and provides support in the treatment of cancer.

The level of trade and economic relations between Kyrgyzstan and India does not correspond to the existing potential. Kyrgyzstan is interested in filling this gap. Our countries have held a number of business events that should serve as an impetus for the further development of economic relations.

Trade, economic and partnership relations between Kyrgyzstan and India are gradually strengthening, as seen by the regular official visits of the delegations of both countries on a reciprocal basis. Among the latest steps is the holding of a business forum in 2019 with the participation of the President of the Kyrgyz Republic, as well as the Prime Minister of India.

India is a reliable trading partner for the Kyrgyz Republic since the beginning of WTO membership, India has positioned itself as a country firmly adhering to the course of liberalization of the multilateral trading system and WTO rules.

In addition to bilateral cooperation, the Kyrgyz Republic and India maintain close cooperation on a multilateral basis within the framework of international organizations and initiatives, such as the UN, the Shanghai Organization and the WTO. Currently, the Eurasian Economic Union and India are engaged in a dialogue on the possibilities of further cooperation,

In conclusion, we can summarize that the Kyrgyz-Indian relations, despite the current low level of economic relations, have great prospects. The main locomotive of our relations is traditionally the state authorities of the two countries. Kyrgyzstan and India officially recognize that cooperation is beneficial to both parties and strive to maintain a high level of mutual understanding.

REFERENCES

1. Foreign and mutual trade of the Kyrgyz Republic 2015-2019: Statistical compilation, National Statistical Committee of the Kyrgyz Republic, Bishkek, 2020.
2. Embassy of the Kyrgyz Republic in the Republic of India. https://mfa.gov.kg/ru/dm/posolstvo-kyrgyzskoy-respubliki-v-respublike-indiya/menyu-inostrannoe/-uslugi/torgovo-ekonomicheskoe-sotrudnichestvo/osolstvo-kyrgyzskoy-respubliki-v-indii
3. Embassy of the Republic of India in the Kyrgyz Republic. https://indembbishkek.gov.in/pages.php?id=364

3

India-Kyrgyz Economic Ties:
Retrospect and Prospects

Anil Sharma

Regional Economic Environment

Kyrgyzstan, one of the Central Asian countries, is surrounded by Kazakhstan, Tajikistan, Uzbekistan and China. It is a mountainous country but deserts and plains surround it from the north, west and southeast. It is a unitary multiparty republic with one legislative house. Three-fourths of its population is Kyrgyz. Uzbek, Russians, Tajiks, Uyghur and some other ethnic groups constitute the remaining population. About two-thirds of its total population is rural and engaged in farming. Hydroelectric power and mining of gold, coal and other non-ferrous metals are major sources of revenue for the country. Cultivation of cotton, fruits, grains, meat, wool and tobacco are major agricultural activities. Light machinery for food processing and electronic components is predominantly visible in the manufacturing sector.[1]

Kyrgyzstan's GDP for 2018 was US$ 8,093 million and GDP per capita was US$ 1,204 in that year. Its merchandise exports and imports for the year 2018 were US$ 1,765 million and US$ 4,907 million, respectively. Its current account balance as percentage to GDP in 2018 was (–) 9.8 per cent.

The business environment in Kyrgyzstan is improving. In the World

Bank's Doing Business 2020 report, the Kyrgyz Republic has been in to among the 20 most improved countries in the world.

Real GDP growth in the first three quarters of 2019 has accelerated to 6.1 per cent from 3.5 per cent in 2018 due to substantial gains in the manufacturing and mining sectors. Due to fiscal consolidation, the deficit also declined to 1.3 per cent of GDP in 2018 from 4.6 per cent in 2017. Rule of law, inadequate protection of property rights and corruption, which were major obstacles in doing business, have been addressed by setting up a Business Ombudsman by the Government in 2019 as well as amendments made in the legal framework for anti-money laundering and combating financing for terrorism. Average annual inflation decelerated to 1.5 per cent in 2018 from 3.2 in 2017 due to falling food prices. Strong loan growth was witnessed in 2018 and the same continued in the first quarter of 2019 also. GDP growth was expected to reach 4.3 per cent in 2019 due to higher gold production and higher remittances by expatriates.[2]

Bilateral Economic Ties

The main commodities exported by Kyrgyzstan were agricultural products (primarily dried leguminous vegetables and cotton) and gold, precious metal ores and women's apparel are major non-agricultural exports. The main destinations of exports are the European Union, Russia, Kazakhstan and Uzbekistan. The main imports are petroleum oils, footwear, medicaments and cigars, chocolates and edible oil. A substantial part of imports is from China and Russia.[3]

Foreign investment in Kyrgyzstan is governed by the 'Law of the Kyrgyz Republic on Investment in the Kyrgyz Republic' which was enacted in March 2003 and has been amended on various occasions subsequently. All the important provisions which are relevant to foreign investors are appropriately included in the statute. Article 2 provides that in case of any amendment or modification made to investment, tax customs legislation of the Republic, the investor shall be allowed to choose the most favourable conditions during the first ten years of investment activity. Article 6 provided guarantees of protection from expropriation of investment and reparation of damages to investors. Article 5 guarantees export or repatriation on income in the form of dividends, interest, investment, property or information outside the Republic by the investors. Article 8 provides that any amendments in Kyrgyz laws restricting foreign currency transfers to and from the Republic shall not apply to foreign investors except when preventing terrorism financing and laundered money derived income. Article 16 provides freedom to the investor to freely hire employees other than Kyrgyz citizens in accordance with Kyrgyz laws and any salary, compensation and other reimbursements paid by investors to employees shall be freely transferable outside the Republic.[4]

The Law on State Registration of Legal Entities, Branches and Subsidiaries in Kyrgyz Republic provides for single window system for registering companies as well as branch/representative offices in the Republic by foreign investors. The corporate income tax rate is 10 per cent. However, enterprises carrying on mining and processing of gold are charged zero per cent income tax. Tax benefits are also available for specified preferential industries set up in specified territories for a period of 5 to 10 years and they are also entitled to sales tax, land tax and property tax exemptions for the specified period.[5]

However, FDI inflow showed a deep fall in 2017. FDI inflow was US$ 255.6 million and US$ 668.6 million in 2006-08 and 2014-16, respectively. It was US$ 93.8 million in 2017. However foreign remittances have shown an increasing trend. Remittances which were US$ 800.1 million during 2006-08 have reached US$ 2,485.8 million in 2017. Official development assistance inflows during2017 was US$ 544.9 million.[6]

India-Kyrgyz Economic Ties

Since the independence of the Kyrgyz Republic on 31 August 1991, India was among the first to establish diplomatic relations on 18 March 1992. The resident mission of India was set up on 23 May 1994. Since the establishment of diplomatic ties, the two countries have signed several framework agreements including on culture, trade and economic cooperation, aviation, investment promotion and double tax avoidance convention. Two MOUs on cooperation in the field of textiles and hydropower were signed in November 2018 in New Delhi under the forum of the India-Kyrgyzstan Inter-Governmental Commission (IKIGC). A joint statement on strategic partnership and a five-year road map for trade and economic cooperation was adopted in June 2019. The India-Kyrgyz Business Forum was inaugurated. A line of credit of US$ 200 million for financing for financing development projects in the Kyrgyz Republic was announced by India. Technical assistance is being provided by India to Kyrgyzstan under the Indian Technical and Economic Cooperation (ITEC) Program particularly in terms of human resource development. The Government of India contributed US$ 2 million to Kyrgyzstan for holding the SCO Summit in Bishkek in June 2019.

India-Kyrgyz Republic bilateral trade during 2018-19 was only US$ 32.6 million. India's exports to the Kyrgyz Republic, mainly comprising readymade garments, pharmaceutical products, tea, coffee, spices, electric motors, etc., was US$ 30.02 million, while the Kyrgyz Republic's exports to India, mainly comprising fruits and nuts, raw hides, woollen products, was US$ 2.59 million. There are around 20 Indian companies in Kyrgyzstan Republic. There are about 100 Indian nationals apart from around 8,000 students in Kyrgyzstan.[7]

It was acknowledged in the joint declaration by the two countries on establishing a Strategic Partnership, signed on 14 June 2019, that the current level of Kyrgyz-India cooperation in the trade and economic sphere does not correspond to the potential that exists between the two countries. It was decided to develop cooperation in the industrial sphere particularly in textiles, garments, mining and information and communication technology. They noted the importance of regional road and railway connectivity and agreed to explore possibilities of cooperation in developing mutually beneficial projects to improve connectivity. Both sides also agreed to jointly explore opportunities of training and capacity building and development in tourism, eco-tourism and wildlife conservation. It was also declared that 2021 would be observed as 'Friendship Year' between the two countries.[8]

In addition to the joint declaration, 14 other important documents were exchanged which include: (a) Road map on Trade and Economic Cooperation between the Republic of India and the Kyrgyz Republic for the Five-Year period (2019-2024), (b) Bilateral Investment Treaty (BIT) between India and the Kyrgyz Republic, (c) Protocol to Amend Article 26 of India-Kyrgyzstan Double Taxation Avoidance Agreement (DTAA), (d) Memorandum of Cooperation between Export-Import Bank of India and the Investment Promotion and Protection Agency of the Kyrgyz Republic, and (e) MoU between India and the Kyrgyz Republic on cooperation on Information and Communication Technology.[9]

A bilateral investment treaty between the governments of the Kyrgyz Republic and the Republic of India was entered into to promote bilateral cooperation between the two countries by promoting and protecting the foreign investments of investors of one country in the territory of the other. This treaty replaces the agreement between the Government of the Kyrgyz Republic and the Government of India for the Reciprocal Promotion and Protection of Investments signed on 16 May 1997. The treaty is forward-looking and relevant to the present times and, therefore, would be helpful in cross-border investments between the two countries.[10]

Other Initiatives to Enhance India-Kyrgyz Economic Relationship

(a) India is developing its contacts with the Central Asia region not only through strengthening bilateral relations but also as a member of the Shanghai Cooperation Organization (SCO) and on the issue of connectivity projects. The SCO is a Russia and China-led eight-member economic and security bloc. Other members of the grouping are Kazakhstan, Kyrgyzstan, Russia, Tajikistan and Uzbekistan. India and Pakistan were admitted to the grouping in 2017. The SCO now consists of approximately 42 per cent of the world population, 22 per cent of its land area and it contributes 20 per cent to the global GDP. In its 19th Head of State Council Meeting in Bishkek during 13-14 June, 2019, a number of important themes/issues were discussed. It is considered that improvement and advancement of connectivity with the SCO will boost economic cooperation and integration in the SCO space. The Central Asian countries and regional multilateral initiatives are trying to synergize their development plans with the BRI of China. However, in recent times, concerns have been raised over the Chinese model of investment and the financial repayment capacity of the recipient countries, particularly, Tajikistan, Kyrgyzstan and Pakistan.[11]

(b) For strengthening India's economic relations with five Central Asian countries, namely, Kyrgyzstan, Kazakhstan, Tajikistan, Turkmenistan and Uzbekistan, the India-Central Asia Business Council was launched in New Delhi on 7 February 2020. At that occasion, External Affairs Minister S. Jaishankar highlighted the formation of the council as a significant step in exploring the investment opportunities and examining the viability of establishing air corridors between India and Central Asia. At the same, he also expressed concern over India's low level of trade with the Central Asian Republics "despite excellent bilateral relations".[12]

(c) India has successfully agreed to the renovation of Chabahar port, development of the International North-South Corridor (INTSC) and membership of the Ashgabat Agreement.

(d) The Eurasian Economic Union (EAEU) is an international organization for regional economic integration and established by the Treaty on the Eurasian Economic Union. The member-states of the EAEU are the Republic of Armenia, the Republic of Belarus, the Republic of Kazakhstan, the Kyrgyz Republic and the Russian Federation. India and the EAEU are discussing the possibility of signing a Free Trade Agreement (FTA) and in this connection the FICCI has conducted two surveys to obtain Indian industry feedback on the status of trade between the two and the advantages that Indian industry can reap from the FTA.[13]

The absence of direct land connectivity to the Central Asian region acts as a constraint in India's economic engagement in the region. The unfriendly investor, unfriendly environment along with a strict visa regime in Central Asian countries proves to be another major obstacle in strengthening economic contacts.

Chinese products enter Central Asia with relative ease and provide a tough competition to India with China catering to a wide range of products from oil and gas to mobile phones. India's trade relations are limited to high-end products. India has the potential to revitalize the economic relations not just through connectivity and energy security but in the spheres of knowledge transfer, enterprise, innovation, pharmaceuticals, tea industry, and spices.

Chinese Impact on Regional Economic Environment

Central Asia's economic growth largely depends on China, though the situation varies from country to country. Since the Belt and Road Initiative (BRI) was announced in 2013, China's expanding economic, geopolitical, and business presence around the world demonstrates its eagerness to play a more significant role in the systems of international governance and law. Central Asia, and Kazakhstan, in particular, has strategic relevance for the BRI.

For Central Asia, BRI projects look highly promising, allowing regional countries to increase connectivity, expand regional trade, and modernize their obsolete transport infrastructure. From China's perspective, the BRI is the way to deliver public goods, promote global connectivity, and portray itself as a responsible stakeholder.

China, being economically more powerful, is one of the most prominent investors and trade partners for Central Asia. This deep economic engagement allows Beijing to exert some pressure on Central Asian governments to ally with China's plans and policies. However, these same investment inflows, fuelled by low transparency around BRI projects, contribute to the existing "Chinese threat" sentiment among the population in Central Asia. As a result, despite China's desire to export its development model by promoting the BRI, it is perceived by the local community as inconsistent with civil society, liberal values, and national interests. It raises particular doubts that China's model and legal system would facilitate further institutional progress in the region.

For some academics, the BRI represents the evolution of China's role in global governance from being a rule-taker to an active rule-maker. Like China, Central Asian countries, to a large extent, are authoritarian states. They share similar political values and seek to defend themselves from human and civil rights criticisms and the call for political reforms, which they often label as interference in domestic affairs.

The public, academics, and experts should get a chance to exercise more scrutiny over BRI projects to assess possible risks and minimize corruption. An open and well-informed discussion over the protection of domestic interests, fairness, governance, and business opportunities can build trust and address legitimate concerns over BRI projects.[14]

According to data from China's customs service, in 2018, the trade turnover with the five Central Asian countries was more than US$ 41.7 billion. While Central Asia accounts for 0.8 per cent of Chinese imports and 0.9 per cent of Chinese exports, the region's dependence on China is growing. China is now the destination for about 22 per cent of all Central Asian exports, and the source of 37 per cent of their imports. The countries of Central Asia are in an asymmetrically dependent trade relationship with China.

According to data from the Chinese Ministry of Commerce, in 2018 the volume of foreign direct investment in the five countries of Central Asia reached US$ 14.7 billion (1.2 per cent of all Chinese investment in Asian countries).

The main symbol of Chinese soft power is the Confucius Institute and its China studies classes. The organization has 37 branches in Central Asia. The career opportunities that knowledge of the Chinese language opens up make it a magnet for young people in Central Asia.

In addition, China's Education Ministry and the Chinese Language International Council have not skimped on issuing grants for students who wish to obtain their degrees in China. In 2010–2018, more than 5,000 study grants were given to applicants from Central Asia, and, as of 2017, there were nearly 30,000 students from Central Asia studying in China.

China's economic inroads into the region are leading to an increasing number of conflicts and scandals. China's growing influence on the region's economy, which has raised concerns among the public and elites, has combined with corrupt practices and the incidence of unsuccessful projects involving the Chinese to lead to an outburst of anti-Chinese sentiment.

In November 2019, thousands of people protested against contraband and corruption at the border with China. The protests were sparked by the publication of a joint research by the Organized Crime and Corruption Reporting Project (OCCRP), Radio Azattyk (RFE/RL's Kyrgyz service), and the Kyrgyz news site Kloop.kg. The report described in detail a complex scheme for doctoring documents on the Kyrgyz-Chinese border. According to the journalists, those profiting from the criminal schemes included public officials' right up to the now former deputy chair of Kyrgyzstan's State Customs Service, Raimbek Matraimov (aka Raim-Million).

China is a key investor in the region, but along with the growth in joint projects, Central Asia's debt is growing too. The countries most at risk are Kyrgyzstan and Tajikistan. Forty-five per cent of Bishkek's external borrowing (worth US$ 1.7 billion) is from China, along with 52 per cent of Dushanbe's foreign debt ($ 1.2 billion). The debts of both countries to China are greater than 20 per cent of their GDP.

The issue that has caused the most damage to China's reputation in Central Asia is, however, the Chinese Communist Party's policy in the Xinjiang Uyghur Autonomous Region. The persecution of Muslims there particularly angers impoverished and strongly religious segments of the population. They believe that the Chinese see all Muslims and Turkic peoples as nothing more than a source of terrorism and extremism. The lack of an independent media and public policy in Central Asia creates an ideal environment for spreading rumours and false information via social media and messaging apps.

Although anti-China protests periodically flare up in various cities in Kazakhstan and Kyrgyzstan, it is too early to speak of universal Sinophobia. In Kyrgyzstan, the protests were led by nationalist groups whose demands included the expulsion of all Chinese migrants from the country.

Within the region itself, the public does not want to see their country become too dependent on China. Protests there increasingly lead to real consequences; in Kazakhstan, following riots over land in 2016, the authorities introduced a moratorium on selling land to foreign nationals and legal entities with a foreign component, while protests in Kyrgyzstan in February 2020 prompted a Chinese company to cancel its plans to invest US$ 280 million in the construction of a trade and industry logistics centre in the Taryn region.

There are other important players also in Central Asia. Many people see Russia as China's main rival in the region. Moscow's political influence is undeniably large, as it has shown during various events in the region. At the very least, local elites keep the Kremlin abreast of what is going on there, or ask for help during conflicts among the elites. Nor should Russia's economic influence be ignored: Kazakhstan and Kyrgyzstan are members of the Eurasian Economic Union (EEU), and the region's joint trade turnover with Russia is in excess of US$ 25 billion.

Central Asia has always felt the need to maintain a balancing act between the various external players, and has tried to achieve that. Today, many countries have their own format of cooperation with the region: there is the C5+1 (the five Central Asian nations and the USA), the EU strategy on Central Asia, India's Connect Central Asia policy, the Central Asia plus Japan dialogue, South Korea's Eurasia Initiative, and the Turkey-based Turkic Council.

The EU countries and the USA are not in a position to play the role of an alternative to China in terms of either trade or investment, although the EU is currently one of the main investors in the economy of Central Asia; but that balance is gradually shifting in China's favour.[15]

EAEU and Regional Economic Development

The EAEU was created for the purpose of comprehensive modernization, cooperation and increasing the competitiveness of national economies and creating conditions for stable development in the interests of improving the living standards of the population of the member-states.

The process of concluding trade agreements between the EAEU and its partner-countries is proceeding rapidly. Vietnam became the first EAEU partner in May 2015; Iran signed an agreement in 2018. The Agreement on Trade and Economic Cooperation between the EAEU and China, signed in May 2018, is another such agreements to improve the access of domestic goods for the Chinese market by simplifying trade procedures and increasing the transparency levels. The EAEU is negotiating similar agreements with Israel, India, Serbia and Singapore.[16]

The EU does not recognise the EAEU and prefers to deal with each member-country separately. It views the EAEU as a Russian-dominated geopolitical instrument to re-establish its hegemony in the post-Soviet space. The EU has restricted its relations with Russia and strongly preferred to deal with the other EAEU member-states on a bilateral basis. Comprehensive cooperation agreements with Kazakhstan and Armenia concluded in 2015 and 2017, respectively, are witness to that approach.

Currently, bilateral trade between India and EAEU member-countries is around US$ 9 billion and the potential export growth is estimated at around 18 per cent if a free trade agreement is in place between India and the EAEU. The Joint Feasibility Study Group Report published in early 2019 has shown potential bilateral trade up to US$ 37.62 billion.[17]

Russia has pushed for India's entry into the EAEU. The EAEU member-states have approved a document defining the strategic goals for developing Eurasian integration until 2025. A decision to hold talks on drafting a preferential EAEU trade agreement with India has been made.[18]

However, EAEU member-states and Russia are presently facing an increasingly strong Chinese push for a wider Eurasian integration, serving primarily Chinese geopolitical and geo-economic interests.[19]

Kyrgyzstan in South-South Cooperation

South-South cooperation is built on the principles of mutual interests through an exchange of knowledge, experience, technology, investment, information and capacity building amongst developing nations. South-South cooperation and its agenda have to be set by countries of the South and should continue to be guided by the principles of respect for national sovereignty, national ownership and independence, equality, non-conditionality, non-interference in domestic affairs and mutual benefit. On the other hand, North-South Cooperation is based on more liberalised type and influence-based diplomacy. The EAEU is based on more of a traditional North-South Cooperation framework than South-South Cooperation. Kyrgyzstan, being a developing economy, should have preferred a South-South Cooperation framework.[20]

Perspective for India-Kyrgyz Economic Ties

(a) India has to adopt a country-specific trade strategy instead of engaging with Central Asian countries as a whole. India has immense potential in developing small and medium scale industries in the region which is presently being provided through India's program of ITEC (Indian Technical and Economic Cooperation). Indian companies can actualise their share in the market through joint ventures and setting up manufacturing units in Kyrgyzstan.

(b) From Kyrgyzstan, cumin, saffron, pepper, etc., and from India's side, tea has immense potential to boost the trade volume between the two countries. Central Asia has a vast potential of an untapped service market and India can bridge the gap of rise in demand and lack of services. India, being a major hub of the information technology sector, has vast scope for collaboration with these economies for strengthening their Information Communication Technology (ICT) sectors. Pharmaceuticals, processed food, agri-produce and defence are the main product lines whereas financial services, legal services, IT and mining are services that require focus by Indian investors in Kyrgyzstan.

(c) India is required to change its focus from an import-dominant business relationship to establishing manufacturing base in Central Asia independently or through joint ventures. India needs to establish the base of a special manufacturing zone with a tax-free zone for the goods. Central Asian countries, and particularly Kyrgyzstan, would be mutually interested in manufacturing bases as it will save their industries from Chinese dominance, facilitate better prices for their raw materials and provide jobs to the local workforce.[21]

(d) Financial issues, which constitute the major impediments to trade and investment between the two countries, are required to be addressed on government level.

(e) India needs to take steps to enhance the image of 'Brand India'. Participation and organisation of exhibitions displaying products and services, and better visa regime are other important steps where government authorities have an important role to play.

(f) Indian public sector undertakings such as NHPC have the potential to tap the export of hydel power from Kyrgyzstan to other countries in the region including China. They have to look for suitable private players as well as local partners.

(g) Due to geopolitical reasons and keeping in view the presence of China in Kyrgyzstan through it 'Belt and Road Initiative', India has to increase its visibility in Kyrgyzstan and for that reason, the Government of India may have to incentivise Indian players to scale up/enhance their investments in trade and services in Kyrgyzstan.

(h) India also needs to promote Chabahar as a transit hub for trade. India should also invest in the Chabahar Free Trade Zone.[22]

(i) UNIDO, in its Report in 2018, after reviewing of existing databases on investment, found differing evaluations regarding the quality and the ability to implement legislative frameworks for investment in Kyrgyzstan. The report found that weaknesses in legislative frameworks contribute to factors that jeopardize investment in Kyrgyzstan. Investors may be forced to resort to litigation that tarnishes the country's image and has detrimental effects on the investment climate. The Kyrgyz leadership realized the importance of investment. The president himself identified reducing corruption, reform to the judicial system, introduction of information technologies and electronic government services as drivers of investment. According to data from the World Economic Forum's Global Competitiveness Report 2017-2018, Kyrgyzstan is at the 112th place out of 137 in Quality of overall infrastructure, 122nd out of 137 in Road quality, and 102nd out of 137 in Quality of electricity supply ranking Another major obstacle in infrastructure development is the difficulties of business to get connections to the electric grid, rolling blackouts and growing indebtedness of energy companies. Kyrgyzstan has to make some serious effort in these areas.[23]

(j) As recommended in the Transition Report 2019-20—Better Governance, Better Economies, Kyrgyzstan should work harder on sustainability of municipal infrastructure, tariff reforms, fiscal consolidation, effectiveness of a business ombudsman, risk-oriented supervision of the banking sector and adoption of international standards on combating money laundering.

(k) The public in Central Asian countries, especially Kyrgyzstan, is deeply fears Chinese expansion and would like to know whether their country's relationship with China is really built on a win-win principle or the cooperation is in China's favour. The leadership of Central Asian countries are trying to address these questions and behind-the-scenes discussions are going on as to how to counterbalance the Chinese influence. The EU countries and the USA are not in a position to play the role of an alternative to China in terms of either trade or investment in Central Asia.[15] (ibid.)

Under these circumstances and due to geopolitical necessity, India must increase its presence in Kyrgyzstan and other Central Asian countries with the help of Russia as well as the USA.

REFERENCES

1. Britannica Online Encyclopaedia.
2. Transition Report, 2019-20—- Country assessments-Kyrgyz Republic.
3. WTO Trade Profile of Kyrgyzstan.
4. Law of the Kyrgyz Republic on investment in the Kyrgyz Republic (No. 66, 27 March 2003, as amended up to 30 April 2009, No. 141.
5. Tax and Investment Guide-Kyrgyz Republic prepared and published by Deloitte in 2019.
6. Aid for Trade-At a Glance 2019: Economic Diversification and Empowerment–OECD, WTO 2019.
7. Website of Embassy of India in Bishkek (accessed in September 2019).
8. Joint Declaration, 15 June 2019.
9. India and Kyrgyzstan Now Strategic Partners:India.com, News Desk, edited by Kunal Gaurav, 14 June 2019.
10. Bilateral Investment Treaty dated 3 June 2010.
11. Dr. Sanjeev Kumar and Dr. Athar Zafar. SCO 2019 Summit: A view from India, Indian Council of World Affairs, 11 July, 2019.

12. Affairs Clouds, 7 February 2020.
13. India EAEU FTA Survey Report, FICCI, www.ficci.in, cis@ficci.com
14. Roza Nagozhayeva. How is China's Belt and Road Changing Central Asia?, *The Diplomat*, July 2020.
15. Temur Umarov. China Looms Large in Central Asia, Carnegie Moscow Centre, Carnegie Endowment for International Peace, 30 March 2020.
16. Maria Shilina., Analyst, Eurasian Studies, National Research University, Moscow, 26 January 2019.
17. India EAEU FTA Survey Report, FICCI, www.ficci.in, cis@ficci.com
18. Russia pushes India's entry into EAEU strengthening third country coop, *The Economic Times*, E-paper, 3 September 2020.
19. Ton Van Der Togt. Senior Research Associate, EU and Eurasia Economic Union, A Common Chinese Challenge, 30 April 2020.
20. Asel Azhykulova. Kyrgyzstan in South-South Cooperation, *Development Cooperation Review*.
21. Akanksha Meena. Strengthening India's Economic Engagement in Central Asia, 19 May 2020.
22. Summary of Discussions, VIF Roundtable on India Central Asia Relationship, Vivekananda International Foundation, 2020.
23. Industrial Development of Kyrgyzstan: Investment and Financing, Working Paper, 18 October 2018. International Institute for Applied System Analysis, Austria.

4

Kyrgyz-Indian Cooperation on Regional and International Levels and Perspectives on their Improvement

Nurmatov, T.A. and Orolbaeva, I.A.

ABSTRACT

This article examines bilateral cooperation between Kyrgyzstan and India in modern conditions, analyzes the prospects for enhancing the interaction of the parties, and takes into account the emerging alignments on a regional and global scale.

***Key words:** foreign policy; cooperation between Kyrgyzstan and India; Free trading zone; Eurasian Economic Union; international treaty.*

The Foreign Policy Concept of the Kyrgyz Republic clearly defines benchmarks for the coming years and foreign policy goals, which are defined as multi-vector. At the same time, the Asian region remains a priority, including relations with India.

For India, the collapse of the Soviet Union and the emergence of new republics in Central Asia opened up new prospects in the foreign policy sphere. With a new look at Central Asia in a changed context, it was found that India's historical ties with the region are more than 2500 years old. It is obvious that events and processes on the Eurasian continent were of decisive importance for most of India's political history.

In the last decade, a new system of interaction between the countries of Central Asia has developed according to the 5 + 1 formula, and these are Kazakhstan, Kyrgyzstan, Tajikistan, Turkmenistan and Uzbekistan (5) + USA, 5 + Japan, 5 + Republic of Korea, 5 + European Union. As a rule, these platforms are also used to discuss bilateral issues. The "Connect Central Asia Policy"[3] formula announced by India, that is, the connection with Central Asia, indicates that one of the leading countries of Greater Asia has shown an interest in more active participation in the affairs of the Central Asian region.

India's full participation in the Shanghai Cooperation Organization (SCO) strengthens its position for a more effective presence in the regiont. This may be due to both general involvement in solving problems associated with the unstable situation in Afghanistan and the need to develop economic projects and allocate capital. An important factor is the fact that a more active presence of India can counterbalance the influence of China, which has strengthened in Central Asia.

"India is firmly convinced that by combining economic multilateralism and building up their national potential, the SCO countries will be able to get out of the crisis caused by the pandemic of economic losses. Moving forward with a vision of a "Self-sufficient India" in a post-pandemic world, "Independent India" will prove to be a force multiplier for the global economy and accelerate the economic progress of the SCO region, Prime Minister N. Modi said at the last SCO summit in November 2020, thereby confirming India's intention to take a leading position in the region.

Against this background, the Kyrgyz Republic is very interested in developing ties with India, a country that historically the peoples of Central Asia treat with interest and love. The bilateral relations between India and Kyrgyzstan are based on feelings of mutual sympathy. The joint history is not overshadowed by conflict memories, which creates an excellent basis for mutually beneficial cooperation.

In recent years, cooperation between India and Kyrgyzstan has begun to gain momentum. This can be clearly seen in the level of relations and the frequency of meetings of representatives from both sides. So, over the past five years, mutual visits have been made at the level of heads of state and government. In 2019, the President of Kyrgyzstan took part in the inauguration of the Prime Minister of India Narendra Modi, and in June of the same year, Bishkek received the Indian Prime Minister on an official visit. All this shows the success of the work on a bilateral basis. Our diplomatic mission in India, as well as the Indian embassy in Kyrgyzstan, are working with maximum efficiency for the benefit of the two peoples.

Thus, in the entire history of the establishment of diplomatic relations between the Kyrgyz Republic and the Republic of India, a number of high level mutual visits took place. The presidents of Kyrgyzstan visited India in 1992, 1999, 2002 (transit working visit) and 2003, during which the foundations for the development of cooperation in the political, trade, economic, cultural and humanitarian fields were laid. The Minister of State for Foreign Affairs of India, S. Khurshid (1994), Prime Minister of India N. Rao (1995), Vice-President of India K.R. Narayanan (1996), Vice-President of India K. Kant (1999), similarly played an important role in the development of political cooperation between the two countries.

On 2-5 May 2013, the visit of the First Deputy Prime Minister of the Kyrgyz Republic, J. Otorbaev, took place within the framework of participation in the 46th annual meeting of the Asian Development Bank (ADB).

On 12 September 2013, the Minister of Foreign Affairs of India, S. Khurshid, paid an official visit to the Kyrgyz Republic in the framework of his participation as the Head of the Indian delegation to the SCO CHS (12-13 September 2013 in Bishkek). During the negotiations, the parties discussed the current state and prospects for the development of Kyrgyz-Indian relations.

On 22-23 October 2013 in Bishkek, an Indian delegation headed by Deputy General-Director of Forestry of India. S. Garbyal, took part in the International Forum on the Protection of the Snow Leopard.

On 13-15 February 2014, on the invitation of the Minister of Foreign Affairs of India S. Khurshid, the Minister of Foreign Affairs of the Kyrgyz Republic E. Abdyldaev paid an official visit to India. This visit is the second of the Head of the Foreign Ministry of Kyrgyzstan in the 22-year history of Kyrgyz-Indian relations. Within the framework of the visit, a meeting was also held with the State Minister of Trade and Industry of India.

On 12 July 2015, the Prime Minister of India Narendra Modi paid an official visit to Kyrgyzstan. In November 2015, in Islamabad, within the framework of the participation of the Kyrgyz delegation headed by the Minister of Foreign Affairs of the Kyrgyz Republic E. Abdyldaev in the 5th ministerial conference of the Heart of Asia / Istanbul Process on Afghanistan, a bilateral meeting was held with the Minister of Foreign Affairs of India, Sushma Swaraj.

The first official visit of the Prime Minister of India, Mr. Narendra Modi, to Kyrgyzstan in July 2015, followed by the state visit of the President of Kyrgyzstan to Delhi in December 2016 were significant milestones in the revival of friendly ties with India that have existed since the independence of Kyrgyzstan. The official visit of Mr. Narendra Modi to Kyrgyzstan on 14 June 2019 as part of his participation in the SCO summit in Bishkek, can be called historic, as it opened up new horizons for cooperation.

As noted in the Joint Declaration of 14 June 2019, the Parties share "similar values of freedom, democracy, fundamental human rights and respect for the rule of law", and it was on this basis that they "decided to bring bilateral relations to the level of strategic partnership." This means not only raising the status of bilateral cooperation, but also the level of mutual trust. With Kazakhstan, a strategic partnership with India was announced back in 2009, so this should be perceived as a strengthening of the Indian presence in the region as a whole.

As part of the visit of the Prime Minister of India, a Kyrgyz-Indian exhibition of textile and handicrafts and a large Business Forum was held, where the President of Kyrgyzstan and the Prime Minister of India noted in their speeches that countries do not largely use the existing potential that will contribute to creating favourable conditions for business, including various mechanisms for coordination and removal of existing barriers between the two countries.

During the official visit, a number of memorandums of understanding and cooperation between various departments were signed. Among them is the Memorandum between the Ministry of Education and Science of the Kyrgyz Republic and the Indian company "INFINITY" on cooperation in the field of education. In my opinion, the Kyrgyz side makes little use of the opportunities for cooperation through the Indian Council for Cultural Relations (ICCR), which is an important instrument of Indian cultural diplomacy. Every year, India accepts up to 4,000 students from different countries for training in 25 specialties through this Council. The number of students enrolled in leading universities in India, in particular, the University named after Jawaharlal Nehru in Delhi has dropped significantly. We could cooperate in this matter with the Embassy of India in Bishkek.

The Indian Centre has been operating in the National Library under the Culture and Arts Sector of the Information Department since 2014, where books in English, Russian and Hindi are presented. This is a real opportunity for students to learn more about the culture of India.

Kyrgyzstan and India are democracies and partners who share common fundamental values such as freedom, democracy, human rights, and the rule of law.

Political cooperation between the two countries can be characterized as partnership, progressive, on an equal basis.

India and Kyrgyzstan share the basic principles of modern international relations. Thus, they note the challenges associated with terrorism and extremism in the world, especially on the Asian continent, and emphasize the importance of ensuring a stable and secure environment for peaceful economic development. Positions on global issues on the UN agenda coincide to a greater extent.

Also, the two countries support:

- adoption by the UN of the UN Comprehensive Convention on Counteraction to International Terrorism;
- ratification of the Paris Agreement on climate change under the UN Convention by individual countries;
- the need to use renewable energy sources to combat climate change and much more.

Kyrgyzstan supported India's candidacy for the seat of a non-permanent member of the UN Security Council for the period 2021-2022. Today India is a non-permanent member of the UN Security Council for a specified period.

It is important to note that when discussing issues related to UN reforms, the Kyrgyz Republic expressed support for India to replace the permanent member of the UN Security Council and the quantitative expansion of the UN Security Council.

Kyrgyzstan twice received active support from India for its candidacy to the UN Human Rights Council. India also supported draft UN General Assembly Resolutions initiated by Kyrgyzstan.

In modern conditions, it is necessary to further deepen cooperation in priority areas, such as medicine, IT-technologies, agriculture, culture, etc. That is, bilateral relations should be built around specific projects and plans. For example, Soviet-Indian relations have been building up in the field of military cooperation, nuclear energy, etc. As we can see, these areas in Russian-Indian relations remain strategic and fruitful to this day.

Kyrgyz-Indian relations have great development prospects in the coming years. Thus, the result of the long-term work of the parties was that Kyrgyzstan and India announced their entry to a new level of strategic relations. The year 2021 was declared as the Year of Friendship and Culture of Kyrgyzstan and India. Unfortunately, the intervention a pandemic postponed the implementation of the planned measures.

The legal framework includes 46 interstate, intergovernmental and interdepartmental treaties and agreements. Some of them require updating and revision, but it should be emphasized that the existence of a contractual framework provides a basis for cooperation. The foundations of bilateral cooperation were laid in 1992 and were reflected in the "Joint Declaration on the Principles and Directions of Cooperation between the Kyrgyz Republic and the Republic of India" dated 18 March 1992. The first decade was generally distinguished by fairly high activity in the field of political cooperation; in the period from 1992 to 1999, the foundations of multifaceted relations in all spheres of cooperation were laid. The activity of bilateral reciprocal visits, distinguished by a high level of mutual trust, contributed to the creation of an atmosphere of friendship in mutual relations.

It was in the period 1996-1999 that inter-parliamentary relations were established and then further developed. So, in June 1997, a visit of a parliamentary delegation of the Jogorku Kenesh, headed by the speaker of the Legislative Assembly, to India took place. Then, Kyrgyz parliamentarians visited India on several occasions, both to hold bilateral meetings and to participate in multilateral events. At the same time, the Deputy Friendship Group for Cooperation with India was created. Currently, such a group also operates in the Jogorku Kenesh. This group includes India, Bangladesh and Sri Lanka.

With the support of the Government of the Republic of India, the Kyrgyz-Indian Centre for Information Technologies at KSUCTA, the Mahatma Gandhi Centre at the Bishkek Humanitarian University, and the

Mountain Medical Centre at the National Centre have been opened and operate in Kyrgyzstan.

There are many more different projects being implemented with the assistance and participation of the Indian side.

For the Diplomatic Academy of the Ministry of Foreign Affairs of the Kyrgyz Republic, the possibility of strengthening cooperation in the field of training diplomatic service specialists is of particular interest. In April 2007, a Memorandum of Understanding was signed in Delhi between the Diplomatic Academy of the Ministry of Foreign Affairs of the Kyrgyz Republic and the Foreign Service Institute (FSI), and although the tasks of these two educational institutions differ, we find common areas of cooperation. Over the years, over 30 Kyrgyz diplomats have been trained in internships organized by FSI. With great gratitude, we accepted the assistance provided at the time to the Diplomatic Academy in the form of equipping our language laboratory; we still use the equipment.

I would very much like the interaction between the diplomatic educational institutions of Kyrgyzstan and India to contribute to the expansion of information exchanges in order to further strengthen the diplomatic, scientific and educational ties of the two countries. Ways of informing the broad masses of the population, the public of our countries about everyday life, culture, traditions, political structure, etc., are of great importance in creating a positive reflection of bilateral relations.

The noticeable activity of bilateral ties at the highest political level gives educational institutions the opportunity to realize the potential of cooperation with the support of government agencies.

In order to fill the inter-parliamentary and political dialogue with content, specific measures were initiated in the area of cooperation between the central electoral structures of the two countries. India's experience in the development of parliamentary democracy is of great interest to the Jogorku Kenesh of the Kyrgyz Republic. In 2017, India hosted a group of parliamentary deputies and employees of the Parliament of Kyrgyzstan for training courses at the Indian Agency for the Study of Parliamentarism and Professional Development. In July 2017, a parliamentary delegation of the Kyrgyz Republic visited India to participate in training courses. Back in 2014, a working trip to India of the Chairman of the Central Election Commission for Elections and Referenda of the Kyrgyz Republic took place.

The experience of parliamentary and party building in India can help Kyrgyzstan to develop democratic institutions. The distrust of parliament that arose in Kyrgyz society resulted in a complete rejection of the parliamentary system of government, and at the republican referendum held in January 2021, the majority of those who took part spoke in favour of a return to the presidential form of government.

At the last stage, Kyrgyzstan developed along the path of parliamentary, and the path and experience of India in the democratic, parliamentary arrangement of the country are very important and interesting for us. Democracy with a population of one billion, where more than a hundred languages are used; all religions of the world are represented; a huge number of ethnic groups are developing so dynamically, while maintaining the identity of cultures—all this cannot but arouse admiration and interest. The Diplomatic Academy is ready to become a platform for expert discussion, including issues of party and parliamentary building in the interest of peace and prosperity.

One of the dynamically developing spheres of Kyrgyz-Indian relations was military-technical cooperation. On an annual basis, representatives of the defence sector of Kyrgyzstan took short-term courses at military educational institutions in India and at the Academy of the General Staff of the Armed Forces of India.

With the aim of close coordination and cooperation of the defence departments of Kyrgyzstan and India, since October 2013, the Institute of the Military Attache has been opened at the Embassy of India in Kyrgyzstan.

In 2013, the Minister of Defence of Kyrgyzstan paid an official visit to India. Following talks, the parties decided to continue cooperation in the construction and improvement of the military infrastructure of the Kyrgyz Republic, providing military-technical assistance in the form of medical equipment, creation of a joint venture for the production of military products in the territory of the Kyrgyz Republic, conducting joint exercises and training of special forces, etc., etc.

The visit to India of a delegation of the General Staff of the Armed Forces of Kyrgyzstan in 2017 confirmed the plans for mutual cooperation.

Unfortunately, the return visit of the Minister of Defence of India has been cancelled several times for an indefinite period. On an annual basis, study visits to Kyrgyzstan are conducted for students of the National Military College of India.

Military-technical cooperation is also carried out through the OJSC TNK "Dastan" with the Ministry of Defence of India.

In July 2011, the opening ceremony of the Kyrgyz-Indian Mining Biomedical Scientific Centre was held with the participation of high-level representatives of both sides. At present, it has been expanded and an additional field station has been created, where medical research on human physiology in high altitude conditions is carried out.

As part of the state visit of the President of Kyrgyzstan to India, the Government of India allocated humanitarian aid in the form of Bhabatron-2 radiation equipment for the treatment of cancer patients. During the visit of the Minister of Foreign Affairs of India, S. Swaraj, to the Kyrgyz Republic in August 2018, the parties agreed on the provision of the second "Bhabatron-2" in Osh by India on a grant basis.

Cultural and humanitarian cooperation is developing very successfully. More than 9,000 Indian students are currently studying in Kyrgyzstan in medical universities in Bishkek, Osh, Jalal-Abad, Kant.

In preparation for the parliamentary elections in the JK of the Kyrgyz Republic in October 2010, the Government of India provided technical assistance to the CEC of the Kyrgyz Republic in terms of 25 new generation computers and 25 multifunctional devices. In August 2012, with a grant from the Government of India on the basis of the Diplomatic Academy, a language laboratory for learning English for 15 places was created and is functioning.

Political statements about friendship and the desire to develop relationships for mutual benefit, however, do not find resonance and support from the business community. Despite the fact that small enterprises have been created and operate in the republic with the support and participation of Indian entrepreneurs, they have no influence on the development of private entrepreneurship in the country. Given the weak logistics capabilities and Kyrgyzstan's lack of access to ports, trade relations are rather low. At the same time, the capacity of the Central Asian market with a possible access to Russian space demonstrates other ways of interaction, when it would be more profitable to create joint ventures on the territory of Kyrgyzstan with the attraction of capital from Indian companies for increased sale of products in the region and in the countries of the EAEU, of which Kyrgyzstan is a member. A key step in achieving this goal should be the creation of a Free Trade Area (FTA) between the Eurasian Economic Union (EAEU) and India. For India, the FTA with the EAEU is one of the many trade agreements that New Delhi has readily signed with various countries and blocs since the mid-1990s. In the Indian expert and political community, the prevailing idea is that any trade agreement helps the development of the Indian economy.

For the development of a successful business, it is necessary to promote a favourable image of the country, and broader familiarization with the culture and mentality of the people. The generation that has grown up on evincing interest and love for Indian history, culture, films, and household items is being replaced by a new one that is unfamiliar with Indian traditions. Sometimes the systematic introduction of the values of the Arab world of an exclusively religious persuasion has a significant impact on the youth of Kyrgyzstan, which creates a threat of the emergence of religious fanaticism. Kyrgyzstan needs the experience of a multi-confessional India that has endured its painful moments of collision of extreme religious views. The presence of a contingent of medical students becomes an irritant among a part of the population that does not have proper education and no idea about the country from which young people come to study. In fact, this is a separate big problem, and it requires the intervention of trained media to disseminate knowledge among the widest sections of the population.

Bilateral trade between Kyrgyzstan and India is characterized as not meeting the existing potential of the two countries, which is carried out by small private entrepreneurs; the trade structure is variable.

The trade turnover of the Kyrgyz Republic with India for the period from 2011 to 2016 decreased by 1.9 times, including exports that decreased by 7.95 times, and imports by minus 1.24 per cent.

In 2018, trade between the Kyrgyz Republic and India amounted to US$ 37.2 million and increased by 15.2 per cent in comparison with 2017, including import receipts that amounted to US$ 31.4 million and increased by 9.1 per cent; export supplies amounted to US$ 5.8 million and increased 1.7 times.

In order to promote trade, economic, scientific, technical, cultural and humanitarian cooperation, the Kyrgyz-Indian Intergovernmental

Commission on Trade, Economic, Scientific and Technical Cooperation is functioning.

For the first time in the history of bilateral relations, Kyrgyzstan became a focal country at the International Indian Trade Fair-2017 and a partner country at the Surajkund Mela-2018 International Fair.

In order to increase investment cooperation and implement projects of interest to both countries:

1. The Indian restaurant "Salam Namaste" by the Indian company "ADM Hospitality & Services LTD" was opened in Bishkek;
2. The Indian company "RÊ Infrabuild Pvt. Ltd." completed the construction of the hotel "Altyn Taj" on the southern shore of lake Issyk-Kul in village Kajy-Sai;
3. A gypsum plant is successfully operating in the Aksu district of the Issyk-Kul region;
4. Passed—approval and certification of agricultural products for introduction to the Indian market: walnuts. Memorandums were signed between cooperatives of the two countries for the supply of agricultural products (7 items) to India. Kyrgyz honey is sold in the Amazon online store;
7. Large-scale participation of representatives of Indian business associations at the Green Investment Economic Forum, which was held within the framework of the International Snow Leopard Conservation Forum;
8. Opening of a joint haemodialysis centre at the KRSU Centre, with the provision of equipment for the amount of 16,000 US dollars.
9. Investment in a dairy plant in Tokmok.

We would like to end this article with a quote from the congratulatory speech of the Prime Minister of India on the occasion of the election of S. Japarov as President of the Kyrgyz Republic, which says that "the Indian-Kyrgyz strategic partnership is based on common democratic values, as well as on historical and cultural ties". Based on historical ties and modern realities, Kyrgyzstan and India will strengthen and expand bilateral cooperation.

REFERENCES

1. Decree of the President of the Kyrgyz Republic, 11 March 2019, UP No. 37 "On the Foreign Policy Concept of the Kyrgyz Republic". http://cbd.minjust.gov.kg/act/view/ru-ru/43 0044? cl = ru-ru.
2. Stobdan P., India and Central Asia. The Strategic Dimension, New Delhi, 2020. // https://idsa.in/system/files/book/ book-india-and-central-asia.pdf
3. Dr. Jyoti Prasad Das. India's "Connect Central Asia" Policy. *Foreign Policy Journal*, 29.10.2012. URL: foreignpolicyjournal.com/2012/10/29/indias-connect-central-asia-policy
4. D. Efremenko. A new stage in the development of the Shanghai Cooperation Organization. China in world and regional politics—History and modernity, 2019, No. 24, URL: https: //cyberleninka.ru/article/n/novyy-etap-v-razvitii-shanhayskoy-organizatsii-sotrudnichestva (date of access: 22.02.2021).
5. Speech by the Prime Minister of the Republic of India Narendra Modi at the meeting of the Council of Heads of the SCO Member-States in 2020, http://rus.sectsco.org/news/20201111/690543.html
6. Dynkin A., Telegina E., and Halova G. The role of the Eurasian Economic Union in the formation of Greater Eurasia, World economy and international relations, 2018-T. 62.-No. 4.- S. 5-24. //https: //www. imemo.ru/index.php?page_id=1248&file=/https://www.imemo.ru/files/File/magazines/meimo/04_2018/0005_0024_ (1) _Dynkin_ID17817.pdf
7. Joint statement of the Kyrgyz Republic and the Republic of India on partnership, solidarity and the development of multifaceted cooperation between democratic states. State visit of the President of the Kyrgyz Republic to the Republic of India, 18-21 December 2016.

5

Religious Extremism and Terrorism in Central Asia and Afghanistan:

A Case Study of Islamic State of Khorasan Province

Dr. Ramakant Dwivedi

ABSTRACT

The Islamic State of Khorasan Provinces (ISKP) entry into Central Asia and Afghanistan was first noticed in early 2014. By September 2014, Abdul Rahim Muslim Dost, a former Taliban commander from Kunar province of Afghanistan, was named as the Emir of ISKP. In October 2014, five regional emirs from Tehreek-e-Taliban Pakistan (TTP), namely, Hafiz Dolat Khan, Hafiz Saeed Khan, Maulana Gul Zaman, Mufti Hassan Swati and Khalid Mansoor, along with Shahidullah Shahid pledged formal allegiance to Islamic State (IS) and Abu Bakr al-Baghdadi. The ISKP has been taking the help of Pakistan-based entities for recruitment, training, weapons transfer and kidnapping of civilians in Central Asia and Afghanistan. In Central Asia, the ISKP and Afghanistan are supported by disaffected terrorists from Tehreek-e-TTP, Islamic Movement of Uzbekistan (IMU), Hezb-e-Islami, Afghan Taliban and local cross-border drug smugglers and criminals. Salafism ideology is providing a fertile ground for the ISKP to grow. It will continue to sustain its activities in Central Asia and Afghanistan as it has been receiving funds, both externally (West Asia) and internally. Disaffected terrorists from like-minded organisations will continue to fight for the ISKP as they can be easily bought. The ISKP's operational capability in the Central Asian region and Afghanistan remains limited. Its initial gains and territorial claims have waned significantly. Lack of effective control by the security forces will provide space for the ISKP in the said region. It cannot function in Central Asia and Afghanistan without the support of entities based in Pakistan and West Asia.

Security Situation in Central Asia

Sergei Lavrov, Russian Foreign Minister, arrived in Dushanbe, Tajikistan, to attend a meeting of the Commonwealth of Independent States (CIS) Council of Foreign Ministers on 13 May 2022. He discussed the issues related to the security of Central Asia. Analysts predict that Tajikistan could become another flashpoint if the threats from Afghanistan are not contained. Russia and the USA allocated US$ 100 million and US$ 60 million, respectively, to Dushanbe to strengthen the Tajik-Afghan border[1] on May 12 2022. Sergei Lavrov speaking at a meeting of Afghanistan's neighbours in China in March 2022 said that the activities of international terrorist organizations such as ISKP, Al-Qaeda, Jamaat Ansarullah, and others remain a serious threat to the peace and security of Central Asia and Afghanistan. Radical groups and their supporters are planning to destabilize the Central Asian states and export instability to Russia. This is a serious matter of particular concern to Central Asian. An alarming signal is the build-up of ISKP and Jamaat Ansarullah detachments in the region of the Afghan-Tajik border.

The 'Taliban' return to power in Afghanistan has emboldened the ISKP to incentivize recruits from Central Asian countries. The ISKP has intensified and broadened its regional propaganda campaign to target Central Asia and Afghanistan post the Taliban takeover of Kabul in August 2021. Its Al-Azaim Foundation for Media Production has evolved a coordinated strategy to propagate its ideas in the region. It has carried out rocket attacks against Uzbekistan in April 2022 and Tajikistan in May 2022.

Deployment of US and NATO military forces or the employment of Central Asians and Afghans by them on the territory of neighbouring states of Russia, primarily in Central Asia and Afghanistan, is unacceptable to Moscow. Both, the USA and Russia, have been financing the strengthening of the Tajik-Afghan border. Russia will provide Dushanbe with a grant of more than US$ 100 million to build an outpost on the Tajik-Afghan border. Meanwhile, Washington will spend more than US$ 60 million on Tajikistan's security over the next two years, as per US Ambassador to Tajikistan John Mark Pommersheim. As part of this assistance, the US government will supply Tajikistan with Puma reconnaissance drones to monitor the country's airspace in the border areas. At the same time, he stressed that the USA did not intend to create a military base on the territory of Tajikistan.

ISKP's Footprints in Central Asia and Afghanistan

The Islamic State of Khorasan Province's (ISKP), also known as Wilayat Khorasan (the historical name of the region comprising areas from today's Afghanistan, Iran, Pakistan, and Central Asia) entry into Central Asia and Afghanistan was first noticed in early 2014 when fighters from the TTP were encouraged to defect to the ISKP. Abdul Rahim Muslim Dost, a former Taliban commander from Kunar province was named as the Emir of the ISKP in September 2014. Muslim Dost focused on recruiting fighters from the Salafi concentrations in eastern provinces of Kunar, Nangarhar and Nuristan. In October 2014, several TTP commanders defected to the ISKP after the declaration of Mullah Fazlullah as leader following death of Mullah Hakimullah Mehsud in 2013. Muslim Dost attracted mid-level commanders from the Afghan Taliban and fractured Movement of the TTP. In October 2014, TTP's five commanders from Pakistan—Hafiz Dolat Khan from Kurram Agency, Hafiz Saeed Khan from Orakzai Agency, Maulana Gul Zaman from Khyber Agency, Mufti Hassan Swati from Peshawar and Khalid Mansoor from Hangu Tehsil of Orakzai Agency, along with Shahidullah Shahid, the former TTP spokesman, pledged allegiance to the ISKP and the leader of the Islamic State of Iraq and the Levant (ISIL), Abu Bakr al-Baghdadi. ISKP fighters comprised disaffected terrorists from TTP, Afghan Taliban, IMU, Hezb-e-Islami and local cross-border drug smugglers and criminals along with some foreign fighters.

Hafiz Saeed Khan utilized his established terrorist networks to recruit fighters from Central Asia and Afghanistan, where many terrorists had settled following the Pak military operation, 'Zarb-e-Azb', in North Waziristan Agency, Pakistan. Deputy Governor Mullah Abdul Rauf Khadim did the same in Afghanistan. Disaffected and under-resourced militants were prime targets for recruitment by the ISKP in Central Asia and Afghanistan. Many Taliban defectors to the ISKP appear to have been persuaded by the group's generous resources and ample funds to support their families.

ISKP Activities in Central Asia

The ISKP has carried out rocket attacks against Uzbekistan in April 2022 and Tajikistan in May 2022 showing their hostile Central Asia directed actions. The ISKP has increased its activities in the Central Asian States of Tajikistan, Uzbekistan and Kyrgyz Republic since the Taliban takeover of Kabul in August 2019. It has started disseminating propaganda literature in Central Asian languages, namely, in Tajik and Uzbek. Al-AzaimTajiki has been started, a new Tajik language wing of its official propaganda apparatus. Another group, Khorasan Ovozi, produces Uzbek language propaganda literature. It has a dedicated cell which has been working on recruiting Central Asians to join the ISKP. It has been showing the Taliban and ruling regimes of the Central Asian States on the same page and thereby galvanizing sympathies from locals. It also does not recognize the current geographical boundaries of the Central Asian States and wants to create an Islamic State of Transoxiana. An IMU faction led by Usman Ghazi pledged allegiance to the then Caliph of ISIL, Abu Bakr al-Baghdadi in 2015.

Fergana Valley spanning Tajikistan, Kyrgyz Republic and Uzbekistan has been a fertile ground for the spread of religious extremism and terrorism in Central Asia due to myriad border conflicts, lack of political pluralism and economic stagnation. The IMU, Hizb-e-Tahrir, Jamot, and Islamic Movement of Turkestan have been active in the said Valley and carried out several deadly attacks. The governments in Tajikistan, Kyrgyz Republic and Uzbekistan need to address ethnic fragmentation and economic divisions in the Fergana Valley to arrest the growth of the ISKP.

ISKP Activities in Afghanistan

ISKP mouthpiece Al-Azaim published its eleventh issue of its Pashto magazine *Khorasan Ghag*. Over 54 pages, it covers topics including the recent Taliban and Central Intelligence Agency (CIA) meeting as well as high-level meetings between military and defence officials of Pakistan and the USA. The Salafi Ulema in Afghanistan complains that Taliban security forces continue to threaten the arrest of and kill Salafi Afghans in the country. Most recently, the Taliban have arrested Sheikh Mirajuddin Kushki, a Salafi scholar from Herat in Kabul, who had even made some pro-Taliban preaching. Other articles in *Ghag* include a dedicated write-up on the Transgender Bill passed by Pakistan's Parliament, commenting that the

Islamic Emirate of Afghanistan (IEA) will soon follow in enacting a similar law.

In August 2015, the ISKP formed its National Council (Markaz-e-Shura) in Nuristan province. Maulvi Hussein Ahmed was appointed Provincial Governor and Maulvi Ismatullah was nominated special representative of the province in the National Council. On 05 August 2015, Engineer Sadullah Painda, Provincial Council Chief of Nuristan province, Government of Afghanistan, claimed that the ISKP had begun constructing a military base in Mandawal district, Nuristan province. More than 500 fighters under the leadership of Maulvi Ismatullah (former Taliban governor for Nuristan) and Maulvi Hussein Ahmed joined the ISKP in Nuristan province in 2015. Maulvi Hussein Ahmed, Maulvi Ismatullah and Maulvi Zahir came in touch with the ISKP in Awlagal area of Barg-e-Matal district in Nurestan province along with four Arab entities in 2014. The ISKP in Afghanistan has established its primary power base in the volatile border districts of Nangarhar province. Its fighters bombed a group of blindfolded Taliban supporters of the Shinwari tribe in Shinwari district of Nangarhar province on 10 August 2015. ISKP flags were first raised in Surobi district of Kabul province on 19 January 2015. It had been targeting religious processions and gatherings of the Shia community in Kabul city during the month of Muharram. Hindu temples in Afghanistan have been on the hit list of the ISKP. Terrorists from the Islamic Movement of Uzbekistan (IMU), particularly in Zabul and Faryab provinces, have been operating under the ISKP banner. In November 2015, provincial security officials had claimed that Khak-e-Afghan district had become a Daesh (ISKP) stronghold and Uzbek, Chechen and Arab terrorists were fighting in the area with the support of entities based in Pakistan.

ISKP commander Jehadmal has been active in western Ghor province along with a group of terrorists and was found involved in terror activities against Afghans. The ISKP claims to have a presence in northern Jowzjan and Faryab provinces. Terrorists previously associated with the Taliban have joined the ISKP here. The son of a slain Uzbek commander, Tahir Yuldash Abdulhalilovich (co-founder and former leader of the Islamic Movement of Uzbekistan), has reportedly been luring Uzbek men in northern provinces to join the ISKP.

As part of its campaign, the ISKP carried out an attack against a Sikh gurdwara in Kabul. There have been number of clashes between Taliban and ISKP fighters in various provinces of Afghanistan. The Taliban are punishing Salafists in Afghanistan for their links to the ISKP group. A group of imams (prayer leaders) has been arrested for spreading Salafi Wahhabism and carrying out teaching work, by conducting classes/lessons of monotheism and Sunnah and rejection of heresies and innovations in Islam.

ISKP in India and Implications for National Security

The ISKP is using the internet and social media platforms to incite hatred on religious lines and radicalize its audience in India. Theme of the contents for radicalization revolves around preaching of distorted versions of religious teachings, glorifying slain terrorists, alleged atrocities against Muslims and giving a hue to contemporary emotive issues. Efforts are made to spread a sense of insecurity amidst Muslims and provoke them to indulge in violent activities. The ISKP has a dedicated publication group namely 'Al-Azaim Foundation for Media Production' which publishes its online propaganda magazines '*Voice of Hind*' and '*Voice of Khurasan*'. The Islamic State through the magazines claims itself to be on the right Islamic path and tries to justify its jihad on the religious texts (Quran and Hadith). It also attaches its fight against India as part of the 'Ghazwa-e-Hind' whose outcome it claims would be victory over India. The content of the magazines disapproves democracy, nationalism, secularism, etc., and identifies them with '*shirk*' (polytheism) and '*kufr*' (infidelity). They iterate that the only hope of Muslims is the establishment of an Islamic State under Shari'a laws, wherein the payment of 'Jizya' would be obligatory upon non-Muslims. It interprets the religious concepts and terminologies (*jihad, khilafat*, *sharia*, martyrdom) to justify its ideology and activities. In the light of these terms, it projects other groups such as the Taliban and Al-Qaeda as deviants and places them outside the fold of Islam. It also disregards the Shias. It glorifies its slain members as role models and tries to motivate youths towards its ideology. Through its publications, the ISKP tries to arouse the sentiments of Muslims by exploiting local issues such as Babri Masjid, Gujarat riots, Delhi riots, abrogation of Article 370 and 35A in Jammu and Kashmir, hijab, alleged bulldozer movement, blasphemy, etc. The success of the ISKP cadre will boost the morale of militants/terrorists in Jammu and Kashmir and other places in India to join the terror group and thus pose challenges to national security.

ISKP Links with Pakistan-based Entities

Links of Maulvi Ismatullah, Representative of Nuristan Province in the ISKP's Markaz-e-Shura formed in August 2015, with Pak coordinator Abu Ahmed was traced in 2014. That time Maulvi Ismatullah was Taliban's shadow governor for Nuristan Province and Abu Ahmed has been coordinating terror activities there. Ismatullah visited Pakistan's tribal areas several times. The ISKP in-charge for Alingar district of Laghman province, Jawed, was found recruiting fighters with the help of a Pak national. They had planned to expand the ISKP's area of influence by distributing text books and other literature through seminaries located in the areas. Pak nationals along with Arab nationals are responsible for promoting ISKP ideology in Paktia province of Afghanistan. The then spokesman for Nangarhar Governor Ataullah Khogyani said that ISKP loyalists are mostly Pak nationals.

ISKP's Modus Operandi and Operations in Central Asia and Afghanistan

ISKP fighters have conducted beheadings, public executions and kidnappings. They have engaged in extortion, collection of taxes and smuggled timber into Pakistan to fund their operations. Their modus operandi is coordinated suicide bombing and vehicle-borne improvised explosive device (VBIED) attacks.

Countering ISKP Propaganda

Governments in Central Asian countries and Afghanistan need to evolve a coordinated and cogent approach to counter the ISKP's propaganda both in print and digital media by overcoming geo-political considerations. Law enforcement agencies in these countries need to conduct workshops and training sessions to equip both State and non-governmental organisations (NGOs) to check violent extremism programs. Such initiatives would enable local communities to identify harmful online rhetoric and prevent them from disseminating among the general population. At the same time innovative approaches are required on the part of the governments to develop and disseminate counter-propaganda campaigns among the people who are most vulnerable to fall prey to ISKP propaganda. Multilateral approaches are the need of the hour to counter ISKP actions and the implications arising out of them. Joint working groups (JEGs) and shared database of digital tools in combating terrorism among the countries of Central Asia and Afghanistan would bolster counterterrorism programs and build trust across national boundaries. This initiative would not only counter the ISKP's print and digital propaganda but also weaken its tactics.

Conclusion

The ISKP in Central Asia and Afghanistan is supported by disaffected terrorists from TTP, Afghan Taliban and local cross-border drug smugglers and criminals. Pakistan-based entities are helping the ISKP terrorists active in eastern and southern parts of Afghanistan. Salafism ideology in Nangarhar province of Afghanistan and Fergana Valley of Central Asia is providing a fertile ground for the ISKP to grow. The ISKP is capable of carrying out low-level but deadly attacks within Central Asian countries and Afghanistan. It will continue to sustain its activities in Central Asia and Afghanistan as it has been receiving funds both externally (West Asia) and internally. Disaffected terrorists from TTP, IMU and Afghan Taliban will continue to fight for the ISKP as they can be easily bought. Lack of political pluralism, deteriorating economic conditions, and fertile ground for growth of Salafism would also provide conducive conditions for its spread in the region. ISKP operational capability in Central Asia and Afghanistan, however, remains limited. Its initial gains and territorial claims have waned significantly. Lack of effective control by security forces in Central Asia and Afghanistan will provide space for the ISKP. It cannot function in Central Asia and Afghanistan without the support of entities based in Pakistan and West Asia. Hence, restrictive policies against it need to be continued. Coordinated counterterrorism endeavours among countries of the region and political understanding at the top level would create a more comprehensive strategy capable of defeating the ISKP.

REFERENCE

1. https//www.ng.ru-cis-2022-05-12/5_S434-tajikistan.htm (accessed 31 May 2022)

6

Strategic Partnership and India's Evolving Relations with Kyrgyzstan:

Examining New Security Realities and Security Governance in the Background of Transforming Geopolitics of the Region

Dr. Anita Sengupta

ABSTRACT

India and Kyrgyzstan raised their bilateral relationship to 'strategic partnership' and signed a number of agreements including a bilateral investment treaty on the sidelines of the SCO Heads of Government meeting in Bishkek in June 2019. In the course of bilateral talks during the Summit, it was stated that elevating the bilateral relationship to that of strategic partnership would enable long-term cooperation in a number of fields with special emphasis on defence cooperation on which a decision had been made to set up a joint working group. Among the agreements signed was a MoU for cooperation between the National Security Council Secretariat of India and the Office of the Security Council of the Kyrgyz Republic. Strategic partnerships indicate a new stage of mature relationship that recognizes equality, mutual advantage, and each other's national security interests. In view of the persistence and promise of strategic partnerships in international affairs, this strategic partnership between India and Kyrgyzstan assumes relevance, particularly in the context of the changed geopolitical realities in the Eurasian region and transformation of India's own security perceptions. It also assumes relevance in the context of larger regional arrangements of which India and Kyrgyzstan are now a part. Against this background, this article examines the essential components of India's engagement with the region in general and with Kyrgyzstan in particular, given its proximity to areas of conflict and instability and convergence of interests as far as security governance is concerned.

Introduction

There is, today, the emergence of a pattern of international relationships in which states enter into partnerships with other states based on complementarities of interests in specific but critical areas. These partnerships, unlike the Cold War associations, do not bind them to support each other on all strategic issues under all circumstances but only where mutual help and collaboration can be of long-term benefit to both the states. Generally bilateral in nature, they are not presumed to be aimed against other states or groupings. They are considered strategic in nature because of the importance of the issues involved and the long-term nature of cooperation that is envisaged. India has entered into strategic partnerships with a number of states in core areas of national interest like supply of defence equipment and technology, military exercises, cooperation in the field of nuclear energy, trade and investments, diplomatic support on critical issues, cooperation in science and technology, education, agriculture, information and communications technology, and banking and insurance. Each partnership has a specific character focusing on certain issues. Some of the partnerships are more comprehensive depending on the number of areas in which the two states can actively engage as also the scope and depth of their relations.

Strategic partnerships need to be evaluated in terms of how substantial the co-operation has been, how sustained, and the potential that the partnership holds in the future.[1] According to Foundation for National Security Research experts, India evaluates the extent of diplomatic support that a partner state provides on the basis of three major issues on which India expects diplomatic support (1) India's policy with regard to Pakistan, Afghanistan, Kashmir, and Terrorism; (2) India's Nuclear Policy; and (3) India's Bid for a Permanent Seat in the UN Security Council.[2] Similarly, self-reliance in defence is an important pre-requisite and India has attempted to enhance its defence capability under the rubric of 'modernization'.[3] Economic cooperation is the third important aspect and here it is equally important to evaluate whether the existing relationship is substantial, sustained and has potential for growth.[4] The FNSR argues that based on these three factors, strategic partnerships should be evaluated and bestowed.[5]

Strategic partnerships today, however, are best understood as part of a new 'security practice' signalling the emergence of new forms of security governance in Asia.[6] There is today a broadening of the notion of security from states to societies leading to an increasing differentiation of security arrangements. It has been proposed that this transformation can be conceptualized as *security governance*, characterized by a fragmentation of initiatives among a diverse group of actors.[7] Envall and Hall note that "security governance" implies:

> Emerging sets of practices concerning the management of security by the involvement of non-state as well as state actors, informal as well as formal institutionalization; the regulation of behaviour by informal norms and understandings as well as legal instruments and the uses of new techniques like 'transgovernmental' connections and networks, linking state bureaucracies with similar functions without the intercession of formal diplomatic processes and public-private partnerships or contracting out to private providers to achieve objectives historically pursued by state bureaucracies.[8]

The new structures that have emerged in response to this need for security governance are regional and sub-regional institutions through which an increasing range of activities are carried out. Membership of and relations among them are varied and overlapping as are their functions and obligations. These new institutions were created to address specific security needs of particular regions and most of these were based on values of peace and collaboration, non-expansive behaviour, and the wish to reduce the cost of security. Many of these dealt with localized or non-traditional threats to security and were more fluid and flexible than security regimes or communities. They often emerged from unique interests and resources of a set of actors in solving a particular regional security problem. In the Eurasian region, the regional structure that is emerging as the most significant is the Shanghai Cooperation Organization and any analysis of a strategic partnership and security governance in the region would have to take note of this regional reality in the course of an examination of the evolving bilateral relationship. It would also have to take note of the interest of regional powers, Russia and China, as also the long-term, though unsubstantiated interest that the USA shows in the region.

It is against this background that this article examines the transformation of India's relations with Kyrgyzstan into a strategic dimension in June 2019 when, on the sidelines of the Shanghai Cooperation Organization Summit in Bishkek, a total of fifteen documents were exchanged (in addition to a strategic partnership agreement) in significant areas like avoidance of double taxation. Documents of cooperation were also exchanged between strategic and financial organizations like a Memorandum of Understanding between the National Defence Academy of India and the Kyrgyz Military Institute of the Kyrgyz Republic and a Memorandum of Cooperation between the Export Import Bank of India and the Investment Promotion and Protection Agency of the Kyrgyz Republic.[9] Kyrgyzstan supports India's bid for a permanent UNSC seat, supports non-proliferation of nuclear arms, supports its position on Kashmir and its fight against terrorism; as such, the transformation of the relation into a strategic partnership seems logical. However, the future of the partnership would be dependent on a number of regional and global developments and it is an understanding of these developments that would lead to a correct understanding of the relationship.

A Background to India's Engagement with Kyrgyzstan

From the Indian point of view, the last decade of the 20th century presented a major strategic challenge as far the Central Asian region was concerned. With the collapse of the former USSR and the subsequent Russian retreat from the region, the regional balance was altered and India's favoured position in a region that was identified by its strategic thinkers as "India's extended strategic neighbourhood" was reduced.[10] The emergence of a number of regional players and the potential for local conflicts also significantly changed the strategic environment for India. Along with this was the fact that many of the Central Asian borders are fluid, having been demarcated out of political considerations rather than any ethnic contiguity. The possibilities of demographic changes and the proliferation of non-state actors was also a distinct possibility. The fact that Afghanistan and parts of the Central Asian region were emerging as significant opium producers also made India vulnerable to the opium trade. The consequent proliferation of small arms was another destabilizing factor. For India, therefore, a number of factors, including proximity to Afghanistan, possibilities of export of terrorism, and illicit drug trade enhanced the importance of collaboration on issues of crucial significance.[11]

It has been suggested that Indian economic and security goals dictate that its Central Asian policy look at a larger regional complex that includes other regional powers like Russia, China, and Iran. A 'cooperative framework of inclusive engagement' would be the optimal solution.[12] It suggests that India's geopolitical interests should be defined in broader Eurasian terms. Unfortunately, while an inclusive cooperative framework remains the optimal solution, in reality bilateral engagements often restrict their effectiveness. On the other hand, it is difficult to ignore these larger conceptualizations since they often influence economic prioritization. An effective solution seems to lie in keeping these conceptualizations in mind while negotiating for options that would serve Indian interests. Yet, one needs to take note of the fact that often these conceptualizations themselves prove to be ephemeral in terms of reflecting long-term priorities.

Afghanistan's proximity to Central Asia is another factor of crucial significance and this has meant that security or perceptions of insecurity dominate the strategic discourse in and about the region. Issues that stand out include the challenges that the Central Asian states face in terms of stability, ethnic tensions, radicalization of youth, destabilization of commodity flows, and energy security, and the impact that these could have on Central Asian society. However, security today needs to be defined in 'cosmopolitan' terms through an array of issues like movements across borders, radicalism within states, sharing of water, and various multilateral attempts at combating insecurity. Multilateral engagement on various fronts is thus an effective means of reconnecting with the region. Here, the identification of common developmental frameworks and the legacy of connectivity on various levels are useful. In any case, Indian engagement with the Eurasian region extends beyond recent conceptualizations to periods when connectivity was defined not just in strategic terms but also cultural terms. The people of the region have an ancient tradition of close and friendly relations, which resulted in the development of cultural and economic cooperation. This relation strengthened further due to common heritage and commitment to ideals of tolerance, democracy, secularism, and the desire for peace.

It is here that the story of India's natural connect with its immediate neighbourhood in South and Central Asia comes into focus. Complicated by policy decisions and what C Raja Mohan refers to as "inward economic orientation of socialist India and the neglect of connectivity and commerce at and across frontiers"[13] it remains the first of the concentric circle to which

India would need to reconnect. Raja Mohan goes on to argue that Modi's India has made an attempt to compensate but the scope of its initiative is no match to Chinese efforts to reconfigure the economic geography of the continent. The inclusion of both Sri Lanka and Nepal as dialogue partners in the SCO is a recent political expression of Chinese efforts at inclusion of the sub-continent and the China-Pakistan Economic Corridor a classic geopolitical statement. While a change in mindset about visualizing its neighbourhood as a 'backyard' is a necessity, there also remains the need to rethink its strategy of political involvement, learn to compete with other powers when its interests in the neighbourhood is challenged, and collaborate where necessary before India can hope to regain its leverage.[14]

India shared bilateral ties with the Kyrgyz Republic (Kyrgyzstan) since 1991 with the emergence of the independent Republic. India was one of the first countries to establish diplomatic relations with Kyrgyzstan in 1992. This was followed by the signing of a number of framework agreements on culture, trade, economic cooperation, civil aviation, investment promotion, and avoidance of double taxation and joint training exercises like 'Khanjar' since 2011 to fight against regional and global terrorism. India-Kyrgyz Republic bilateral trade during 2018-2019 was US$ 32.60 million. India's exports to the Kyrgyz Republic was US$ 30.02 million, while Kyrgyz exports to India was US$ 2.59 million. Indian exports have registered a growth of 8.75 per cent on a year-to-year basis. There is opportunity for Indian businessmen in the fields of textiles, railway, hydropower, and mining and mineral explorations. Connectivity would play an important part in the ease of trade between the two countries and there have been efforts to fast track the construction, operationalization, simplification, and streamlining of procedures for transport through the International North South Transport Corridor and the Chabahar sea port.

The transformation of India's relations with the Kyrgyz Republic came in the wake of ties that were cemented through diplomatic visits and exchanges. Kyrgyzstan's first President, Askar Akayev, visited India four times during his term of office. Former Kyrgyz President Almazbek Atambayev made a four-day state visit in December 2016. Former President Jeevbekov was invited to the swearing in of the NDA 2 government by the Indian Prime Minister. Former Indian Prime Minister Narasimha Rao visited Kyrgyzstan in 2005 and Prime Minister Narendra Modi in 2015, and once again in June 2019 for the SCO Summit in the course of which the strategic partnership agreements were signed. As argued earlier, the extent to which this partnership would be substantial would depend on not just the advancement of the bilateral relationship but also regional and global developments as also the Kyrgyz Republic's strategic engagements.

Kyrgyzstan's Strategic Engagements

In the aftermath of 9/11, Kyrgyzstan had indicated complete support for the "war against terrorism". The September 11 terrorist attacks were, in Kyrgyz President Askar Akaev's words, a turning point for the international perceptions of political and security developments in the region. He immediately expressed his condolences to the American people and his full support for the US action against international terrorism and extremism.[15] He also offered Kyrgyz airspace for the American action in Afghanistan.[16] The US government, in turn, indicated that it valued Kyrgyzstan's support and that it would extend economic and military assistance to the Republic. In December 2001, the USA established a permanent military base near Bishkek airport. The establishment of a US base in Kyrgyzstan was, in many ways, an unprecedented step since it was projected to mean, among other things, a radical reorientation of security arrangements from Russia to the USA. Some political groups and the Russian military were highly critical of the US bases and this meant that Kyrgyzstan had to search for a delicate balance between the interests of the two major powers prompting analysts to note of it.

Bishkek's foreign policy makers therefore had to find a balance between the long-standing security arrangements with Russia and the newly-established regime of anti-terrorist cooperation with the USA which brought a US military presence to the outskirts of Kyrgyzstan's capital. In November 2001, US personnel began hastily building the Republic's first American military base, just a few miles away from a Russian-sponsored CIS anti-terrorist centre. Moreover, the visitors were talking about extended cooperation with the independent Kyrgyz defence forces, outraging Russia's generals and political hawks.[17] However, within a year, this situation changed. Towards the end of 2002, it was reported that Russian military units were returning to Kyrgyzstan after having left in mid-1999 in the name of fighting terrorism and maintaining regional stability.[18] Russian military jets began landing at Kant airport, about 20 kilometres from the capital, Bishkek. The Kyrgyz Defence Minister, Esen Topoev pointed out that the Russian air base was being set up in accordance with the *Collective Security Treaty* of the Commonwealth of Independent States.

While Russia's role in central Eurasia remains ambiguous, political analyst Ahmed Rashid notes that a number of factors are now actually leading Russia to regain its influence over the region, not the least of which is the US administration's inability to come up with a coherent aid programme for the region.[19] In addition to the Kant airbase, Kyrgyzstan is now home to other Russian military facilities: a navy base on Lake Issyk-Kul, a seismology centre in the southern town of Mailuu-Suu, and a communications centre in the town of Chaldybar, near the Kyrgyz-Kazakh border. In 2012, all four facilities were united in one single entity called the Russian Joint Military Base.[20] There have also been, in recent times, references in the media about a second Russian base in Kyrgyzstan.

Despite regime changes, Kyrgyzstan continued to remain closely allied with Russia and is part of the Collective Security Treaty and the Eurasian Economic Union. However, Kyrgyzstan's October 2020 parliamentary elections and the protests that followed, leading to the annulment of the results and resignation of the leadership, has led to a pause in the relationship with Moscow expressing dissatisfaction with the ensuing chaos. Russia though remains crucial for the Kyrgyz Republic, its top trading partner and significant aid provider. Kyrgyzstan's relations with China has been growing in economic terms though there remain certain areas of stress including claims made by China on Kyrgyz territory and the treatment of ethnic Kyrgyz in China. There is also concern about the fact that China remains the Kyrgyz Republic's largest creditor and a strategic partnership was established in 2013. The Kyrgyz Republic is a part of the Shanghai Cooperation Organization led by Russia and China where India is now a permanent member. The Shanghai Agreement itself was conceived as part a 'constructive strategic partnership' that would enhance regional security and economic and other objectives as part of the security governance in the region. In fact, the term and practice of forming strategic partnerships first emerged in the region in the mid-1990s with the agreement of a partnership between Russia and China. It is therefore important to take note of the Shanghai Cooperation Organization and its present status in the determination of the future of India's strategic partnership with Kyrgyzstan.

"Constructive Strategic Partnership"

In 1996, Russia announced the establishment of a strategic cooperation partnership with China. The rationale for evolving such a mechanism of cooperation was based on a number of factors. The Moscow-Beijing bipartisan consensus was in favour of evolving a multilateral strategy to combat threats to regional security.[21] The process of the formation of the SCO was deeply connected with this creation of the "strategic partnership" between Russia and China. The signing of the Shanghai Agreement in 1996 came just after the declaration of a Sino-Russian "strategic partnership" in Moscow. In the Russian foreign policy context, the idea of a "partnership" had first been used *vis-a-vis* NATO as the "partnership for peace" in 1994. This phrase, proposed by the Clinton administration, was meant to denote a "peaceful buffer" between Russia and the NATO.[22] As Russian foreign policy shifted in the mid-1990's, President Yeltsin first talked about a "constructive partnership" and then a "strategic partnership" with Zhang Zemin in 1996. The two parties declared their partnership as non-union and non-bloc.[23] The SCO, whose core is based on Russo-Chinese partnership, turned into a multilateral partnership coping with a new threat in the SCO border areas. In 1996, Russian diplomacy had appealed for this "strategic partnership" as a model, which in the 21st century could overcome the historic antagonism between countries with a long, shared border and suggested its desire for the enlargement of the partnership between China and India, which share a long border.[24] China, however, was more cautious about the use of the term "partnership" and expansion of the Shanghai organization. Chinese strategic writings identified the constructive strategic partnership between China, Russia and the Central Asian Republics as a stabilizing multilateral institution that would help define stability and cooperation in the region.[25]

It has been pointed out that the SCO is among perspective organizations, which combine general efforts for security and stabilization along with development of the macro region; as such, it combined aspects of the strategic partnerships with security governance. One of the first suggestions took note of the SCO region being one of the biggest producers and consumers of energy. It was suggested that Russia, China, India, Iran, Uzbekistan, Turkmenistan, Tajikistan, Kazakhstan, Azerbaijan, and Turkey could form a common energy area of producers and consumers of energy sources combining the interests of their development. The formation of an "energy club" would aim at coordinating and harmonizing energy strategies in order to gain common interests of development. It has been noted that this would prove to be among the vital bases for transparency and confidence-building in the macro-region.[26] The so called "SCO Energy

Club" envisaged coordination of member states' efforts in forming the common energy diplomacy, elaborating of mutually acceptable and beneficial approaches for cooperation in the sphere of fuel and energy complex, developing energy dialogue among the states, and ensuring the regional energy security.[27] The recent willingness of member-SCO states to create a Development Bank and Development Fund and support China's proposal to create a Silk Road Economic Belt across the SCO member-states is also reflective of this. In fact, for China, the SCO as a geo-political platform is no longer crucial as the question of disputed borders has either been resolved or is no longer significant as they have become shared Special Economic Zones or can be easily navigated by Chinese trucks carrying products to Central Asian markets. It is the One Belt One Road, an infrastructural project with its own funding agency, the AIIB, that has assumed importance and SCO meetings reiterate commitment to both as an integral part of the organization. It is the need for combined material and political commitment in infrastructural development that seems to be the motivating factor for the acceptance of the expanded membership among the states.

In fact, connectivity played a large part in the Indian decision to apply for membership to the SCO with the general agreement that for India, joining the SCO was about "raising its stakes in Central Asia", of greater connectivity to a wider resource-rich region and an opportunity to work on common issues of concern. This, in conjunction with Iran's membership would ensure that India would be able to move towards developing a platform for trade and transit through Bandar Abbas and Chabahar eventually linking with the North South Corridor. There also remained the possibility of the SCO acting as guarantor for projects like TAPI and the IPI, which have been in the pipeline for a number of years. This would also provide a useful interface for interaction with Afghanistan and its neighbourhood. However, there is also the counter-argument that SCO engagement need not be over-emphasized as bilateral engagements with Central Asian states work just as well as illustrated by the uranium supply deal with Kazakhstan during Prime Minister Modi's visit. The Indian alternative through 'Connect Central Asia' that was projected as the policy initiative on the west would complement its Look/Act East Policy with emphasis on the four "Cs"—commerce, connectivity, consular and culture. It is significant that the policy was unveiled at the first India-Central Asia Dialogue, a Track II Initiative at Bishkek in 2012.

Conclusion

The rise of strategic partnerships in Asia is the result of dissatisfaction with the conceptual and practical status quo in regional security. In response, some Asian states have evolved new policy approaches and practices through new partnerships. Envall and Hall argue that these partnerships have evolved beyond traditional security agreements and encompass political dialogues, trade and investment deals, track-II mechanisms, public diplomacy initiatives, cultural and educational exchanges, and attempts to articulate shared public policy positions or the processes by which to establish or implement them.[28] These partnerships represent moves to find alternative forms of security practice better suited to the perceptions of an Asian regional security environment. An Asian form of security governance is thus emerging with the adoption of new practices like strategic partnerships, and the strategic partnership agreement between India and the Kyrgyz Republic is an example as it identifies areas of common concern and interest and strives to engage with them within the broader parameters of concerns faced by the two states.

REFERENCES

1. Satish Kumar, S. D. Pradhan, Kanwal Sibal, Rahul Bedi and Bidisha Ganguli, "India's Strategic Partners: A Comparative Assessment", Foundation for National Security Research, New Delhi, 2011, http://www.fnsr.org/files/Indias_Strategic.pdf, p. 1.
2. Satish Kumar, etc., Ibid., p. 2
3. Satish Kumar, etc., Ibid., p. 7
4. Satish Kumar, etc., Ibid., p. 11.
5. Satish Kumar, etc., Ibid., p. 13.
6. H.D.P. Envall and Ian Hall, "Asian Strategic Partnerships: New Practices and Regional Security Governance", *Asian Politics and Policy*, Vol 8, No 1, 2016, pp. 87-105.
7. See Elke Krahmann, "Conceptualizing Security Governance", *Cooperation and Conflict*, Vol. 38(1), 2003, for definitions of security regimes, security community, and security governance.
8. Envall and Ian Hall, Ibid., p. 89.
9. Kunal Gaurav, "India and Kyrgyzstan Now Strategic Partners. Here's the Full List of Documents Exchanged in Bishkek", *India.com*, 14 June 2019, https://www.india.com/news/india/india-and-kyrgyzstan-now-strategic-partners-heres-full-list-of-documents-exchanged-in-bishkek-3689432/
10. Julie A. MacDonald and S. Enders Wimbush, "India's Energy Security", *Strategic Analysis*, Vol. 23, No. 5, August 1999.
11. Irina Komissina, "India: Cooperation with the Central Asian Countries in Regional Security", *Central Asia and the Caucasus*, No. 6(24), 2003.
12. Ajay Patnaik, "India-Central Asia: The Quadrilateral Framework", in P.L. Dash (ed.)

Emerging Asia in Focus: Issues and Problems, New Delhi: Academic Publishers, 2007.

13. C. Raja Mohan, "Raja Mandala: Regional India, Global South Asia", *The Indian Express*, 31 May 2016, accessed 13 August 2016.
14. C. Raja Mohan *Reconnecting the Subcontinent: India and the New Silk Roads*, public lecture organised by the Calcutta Research Group in collaboration with Rosa Luxemburg Shiftung on 24 July 2016. See recording at https://www.youtube.com/watch?v=yv0prS2BuuE
15. *Slovo Kyrgyzstana*, 13 September 2001.
16. *Slovo Kyrgyzstana*, 27 September 2001.
17. Rafis Abazov,"Kyrgyzstan's Dilemmas", *Analysis of Current Events*, Vol. 14, No. 2, May 2002.
18. Zamira Eshanova, "Central Asia: Diplomatic Visits Highlight US-Russian Competition", *RFL/RE Report*, 3 December, 2002.
19. Nikola Krastev, "Central Asia: "Taliban" Author Says Russia to Regain Influence in Unstable Region," *RFL/RE Report*, 22 March 2002.
20. "Bishkek, Moscow Agree to Expand Russian Base in Kyrgyzstan",Radio Free Europe, Radio Liberty, 28 March 2019, https://www.rferl.org/a/russian-military-base-in-kyrgyzstan-under-focus-at-putin-jeenbekov-talks/29847265.html
21. Stephen Blank, "Which Way for Sino-Russian Relations?",*Orbis*, Summer 1998.
22. This however did not work since the USA changed its cautious policy towards the NATO and Poland, the Czech Republic, and Hungary became a part of it. For details, see V. Zhurkin, "Russia and the Enlargement of NATO", in T. Hayashi (ed.) *The Emerging New Regional Order in Central and Eastern Europe*, Sapporo: Slavic Research Centre, 1997.
23. See the text of the Russo-Chinese Joint Declaration in *Sbornik: Rossiisko-Kitaiskikh Dogovorov*, 1999 cited from Akihiro Iwashita, "The Shanghai Cooperation Organization and Its Implications for Eurasian Security: A New Dimension of "Partnership" After the Post Cold War Period", in S. Tabata and A. Iwashita (eds.) *Slavic Eurasia's Integration into the World Economy and Community*, Sapporo: Slavic Research Centre, 2004.
24. *Krasnaia Zvezda*, 30 April 1996, cited from Iwashita, "The Shanghai Cooperation Organization and Its Implications for Eurasian Security".
25. Pan Guang, "China-Central Asia-Russia Relations and the Role of the SCO in the War Against Terrorism", *SIIS Journal*, Vol. 9, No. 2, May 2002.
26. Kahramon Asronov, "Energy Factor in Bilateral and Multilateral Cooperation", unpublished paper presented at the IDSA-ISRS Bilateral Seminar on *Emerging Geopolitical Dynamics in Central Asia: India-Uzbekistan Relations*, New Delhi, April 11-12, 2007.
27. Rustam Makhmudov, "Central Asia in the System of Global Energy Market", unpublished paper presented at the IDSA-ISRS Bilateral Seminar on *Emerging Geopolitical Dynamics in Central Asia: India-Uzbekistan Relations*, New Delhi, April 11-12, 2007.
28. Envall and Ian Hall, Ibid.

7

Russia, USA and China in Central Asia: Cooperation or Competition?

Prof. Ainur Eshimbekovna Jorobekov
and
Aigerim Turgunbayeva

Introduction

Central Asia comprises the union republics that became independent countries after the collapse of the USSR. The formation of new states in the region is associated with both internal challenges and the influence of external extra-regional forces. The countries of Central Asia during their independent existence perceived power differently than the triangle of USA-Russia-China, which was a prerequisite for the formation of their multi-vector foreign policy. In the face of the COVID-19 pandemic, the Central Asian countries—Kazakhstan, Uzbekistan, Turkmenistan, Tajikistan, and Kyrgyzstan—faced a particularly difficult test for their governments, health systems, and fledgling economies that rely heavily on commodity exports to global economic engines such as China. Unlike many other developing countries isolated by the pandemic, they had a choice of great power supporters as China, Russia, and the USA competing to provide aid. After the recent rollout of its Central Asian Strategy, the USA has resolved to play against other great powers in the new Great Game. The balance of interests and the presence of Russia, the USA and China in the region is vital for the Central Asian countries, as it provides an independent foreign policy course and the development of Kyrgyzstan, Kazakhstan, Uzbekistan, Turkmenistan and Tajikistan, contributing to a stable situation in the region.

Central Asia is more than just one such front; strategically, the region matters. In relation to its population and economy, no other region is involved in as many acute geopolitical problems as energy, trade, religious extremism, conflict in Afghanistan, hostile Iran, nuclear rivalry in South Asia, international opium trade, Russian aggression in its "near abroad",[1] instability in China's Xinjiang province, and China's "Belt and Road" Initiative.

Russian political and security interests are increasingly converging with those of China, as each of them seeks to assert itself: Russia—to preserve its sphere of influence and buffer against extremism, and China—to stabilize its western flank from unrest associated with the persecution of the Muslim and Turkic peoples. India also sees an opportunity, in its case, to open a second strategic front against its rival, Pakistan, gaining influence on economic and security issues, especially in Tajikistan. And Iran has developed closer economic and cultural ties with both Tajikistan and its neighbour, Turkmenistan.[2] So far, the political uncertainty surrounding the changing of the guard from Soviet-era dictators to new leaders, some with their own autocratic ambitions, has prompted deeper engagement on all sides except the USA.

Critics of US involvement in Central Asia may prefer to let China and Russia compete alone at no cost to the USA. But to the extent that it has ever been possible with the decline of Russian power, COVID-19 has changed the dynamics. Russia's ability to exert influence in Central Asia is eroding as its overwhelmed and inadequately prepared health care system is under siege at home and its treasury is underfunded amid low oil prices. Rather than competing directly with China, Russia is increasingly seeking partnerships with it—in missile defence, military exercises, energy deals, and cooperation against the USA in Syria and the Korean Peninsula. While a history of Sino-Russian mistrust is likely to always burden and constrain this relationship, Russia is likely to partner with China as it is less than ever able to reap the benefits of COVID-19 by ramping up competing influence efforts in Central Asia.[3]

US Interests in Central Asia

The USA focused attention on Central Asia since the formation of the newly-independent states following the collapse of the USSR. Throughout the 1990s, the foremost goal of the USA in Central Asia was to prevent the proliferation of weapons of mass destruction. Trying to fulfil the function of the world policeman, it tried to prevent an increase in the number of nuclear powers, especially with unsettled political systems and national security problems, as well as to suppress the expansion of the influence of radical Islamists, which could later become the reason for the falling of weapons of mass destruction (hereinafter, WMD) into the hands of terrorists and countries trying to create such weapons, including Iran.

It is almost impossible to separate the interests of NATO and the USA from each other, since "Washington not only determines the practical activities of the Alliance, but also uses it to advance its interests in the first place".[4] This can be seen especially well in the second stage of the US policy in Central Asia, which began after the events of 11 September 2001. The need for logistical support of the US military operations in Afghanistan required the participation of the Central Asian countries in the military operation, which provided the opportunity to deploy supply and military bases. The USA later "intended to have a long-term security relationship with the Central Asian countries, which could include access to bases if required",[5] but the ideological interests of the USA, namely the demand for democratization of existing regimes, negatively affected its presence and perception in the region. With Barack Obama's announced limitation of the tasks of the International Security Assistance Force in 2013, a new stage of American interests in the region began. The cooling of relations, the closure of bases on the territory of the Central Asian countries, a decrease in military personnel and military operations led to a reduction in cooperation with the Central Asian countries. Despite the new Operation Resolute Support, which began in 2014, there has been no increased focus on the region. The chief American specialist in Central Asia, F. Starr, criticized the US plans to withdraw from Afghanistan, which would negatively affect the USA's influence in the region and the project for the economic integration of Central and South Asia.[6]

Speaking about American economic interests, it must be said that Central Asia is undoubtedly on the periphery of their interests, which is explained by such factors as the small aggregate GDP of the countries, the lack of access to the sea, a high level of corruption in state systems, and the region's inaccessibility and remoteness from the USA. Nevertheless, it tried to economically gain a foothold in this region, pursuing geopolitical interests. After the collapse of the USSR, American companies quickly began to develop the region's oil and gas resources. To reduce the influence of Russia, and later China, and consolidate in the energy segment used: international development assistance[7] (official assistance to developing countries), foreign direct investment, as well as projects such as TAPI (gas pipeline from Turkmenistan to Afghanistan, Pakistan and India), CASA-1000 (project to transfer electricity from Kyrgyzstan and Tajikistan to Pakistan and Afghanistan), Ñ5+1 (a negotiating platform uniting five Central Asian countries and the USA), the New Silk Road (the US plan for integrating Central and South Asia into a single macro region), the Trans-Caspian pipeline (a gas pipeline from Turkmenistan and Kazakhstan to the Caucasus and beyond to Europe) and others.

Following the recent rollout of its Central Asian strategy, the United States' resolve to play against other great powers in a new Great Game is facing its first major challenge in COVID-19. While the USA may never wield as much influence in Central Asia as its immediate neighbours, engaging the region is essential if it is to avoid transferring power and influence to China, especially in the aftermath of COVID-19. And to participate, the USA must offer alternatives to China and Russia that will help Central Asian governments defeat COVID-19, resist dominance, maintain stability, and continue reforms.

In line with its strategy, the first political goal of the USA is to help the Central Asian states maintain their sovereignty and resist the dominance of other great powers. Competition between great powers is, in particular, competition for strategic influence over valuable resources. To compete with Russia and China on a global scale, the USA must force them to devote more attention and resources to Central Asia, a region that has long been politically dominated by Russia but increasingly dependent on China economically.

The Trump Administration had suffered severe setbacks in its attempts to build a global coalition against the projects of the Chinese government and Chinese companies. Britain has said it will not ban the technology created by Chinese telecommunications giant Huawei from its high-speed 5G wireless network, despite strong pressure from US officials. Mr. Pompeo made his first stop in London during his six-day trip to Europe and Central Asia, and said that the Chinese Communist Party is "the central threat of our time".[8]

At the present stage, the USA is trying to strengthen its presence in the region, which is confirmed by the new US Strategy for Central Asia 2019–2025.[9] The main continuing interest of the USA in the region is countering the growing influence of Russia and China.

China's Interests in Central Asia

The collapse of the Soviet Union could not leave aside China, which has a long border with the newly-independent states. China's policy in the 1990s was mainly aimed at forming friendly relations with new countries, and ensuring a reliable rear, which determined China's further policy in the region.

Initially, China was faced with the task of settling border issues with Kyrgyzstan, Kazakhstan, Tajikistan, and Russia. The establishment of good-neighbourly relations with all participants in the border settlement created the basis for the formation of the Shanghai Five, which was later institutionalized in the SCO in 2001. It should be noted that the SCO was created against the background of the Chechen war in Russia, the exacerbation of religious extremism in the Central Asian countries, the separatist escalation of the XUAR in China and the start of the US-NATO operations in Afghanistan. The emerging international and domestic situation, "the understanding by the states of the region of the impossibility of confronting such global challenges and threats alone served as the basis for the integration processes and the pooling of efforts, expressed in the formation of the SCO".[10]

China is interested in a friendly and stable CAR;[11] this will ensure China's national security and the fulfilment of its geopolitical and geo-economic plans. It was able to reach a compromise on the border issue with its western neighbours and deepen security cooperation. The countries of the region and China are interested in further cooperation in the fight against radical Islamic terrorism, Uyghur separatism and organized crime. This policy was formalized within the SCO.

With regard to economic cooperation, at the moment, China is the main economic partner for the Central Asian countries. Impressive economic growth, trade expansion, huge demographic potential and significant expansion of foreign direct investment led to the strengthening of China's economic and political influence in Central Asia.

In the Nineties, economic interaction between China and the Central Asian countries was not impressive in scale and was concentrated in the oil sector. The growing demand of China for hydrocarbons forced to increase "the presence in the oil and gas sector of new participants in the global energy market, including...the post-Soviet space".[12] Since the 2000s the process of intensive construction of infrastructure for the transportation of oil and gas continued. During the same period, there was a strengthening of Chinese TNCs in the Kazakh, Uzbek and Turkmen energy markets, which contributed to the increase in Chinese consumption of resources from these countries.[13] With the dependence of the Central Asian countries on Russian infrastructure and Western investments, "it was China that made the goal of...diversifying markets a reality".[14]

Since the announcement of the "One Belt and One Road" Initiative in 2013, the importance of the CA countries to China has significantly increased. To satisfy China's interests in transit through the Central Asian countries, the expansion of investments in infrastructure projects and the transport system was used. Another important factor is the financing of projects through lending, a feature of which is "the use of Chinese materials, equipment, technologies or labour in the implementation of projects".[15] The increase in mutual trade and foreign direct investment, and the strengthening of China's political influence were accompanied by the gradual withdrawal of the USA from the region.[16]

Trade between China and Central Asia is actively growing: for example, on railway routes alone, the volume of goods transported in the first seven months of 2020 increased by more than 1.5 times compared to 2019, and this despite the coronavirus crisis. The latter left its imprint on the interaction of the parties: providing assistance to the region, whose economy and health care were hit by the painful blow of the pandemic, came to the fore. On 16 July, the first ministerial meeting of the Central Asia + China format took place, during which these issues were raised. In China, commenting on the first meeting in the C + C5 format, they emphasized that the emergence of the new format is due to the shift of the global economic centre towards Asia and the increasing importance of the Central Asian region in world politics.

The strengthening of cooperation between China and the countries of Central Asia is especially noticeable in the trade and economic sphere. In the years 2001 to 2019, the trade turnover of the parties increased from US$ 1.5 billion to US$ 46.5 billion.[17] The increasing economic influence of China in Central Asia creates both new prospects and new challenges. Thus, mistrust and Sinophobe are growing among the population, caused by both China's economic expansion and historical prejudices. To overcome these problems, China is actively using soft power technology with interaction in the field of external communication, education and science with the Central Asian countries. But the difficulties in promoting China's soft power suggest that China's soft power does not meet the requirements of economic and social interactions between countries.

Russia's Interests in Central Asia

At the moment, Russia's interests in the CARs have significantly transformed. In the Nineties, the priority of Central Asia in Russian policy had decreased for a number of reasons. Russia was unable to send the necessary forces to Central Asia due to internal problems: a deep economic recession, which lasted until 2000, and a weakening of the army. A separate issue is the surge of national identity in the newly-independent states, which affected the attitude towards Russia. Considering also the unsuccessful attempts at economic integration, it can be said that the main instruments of presence in the region were lost for Russia.

A new impetus for the consolidation of the Central Asian direction of foreign policy was given by the US anti-terrorist operation. Russia provided significant assistance in the operation, pursuing its own interests: levelling the security threat in Central Asia, as well as depriving Chechen militants of aid. However, the strengthening of the US position in Central Asia was naturally not viewed by the Kremlin as desirable, which led to the institutionalization of the Collective Security Treaty in 2002.

The strengthening of Russia's political and economic presence in the region proceeded through military-technical cooperation and the deployment of military bases and, to a greater extent, due to the failure of the policy democratization of the USA in Central Asia, which aroused greater interest in cooperation of the countries of the region with Russia.

From the point of view of security, today the main interest of Russia is to ensure stability and prevent radicalization of the countries of the region, and to strengthen the political systems of the Central Asian countries. Central Asia plays a special role as a security buffer between Russia and radical Afghanistan and Pakistan. Another equally sensitive problem for Russia is drug smuggling through Central Asia from Afghanistan.

Presently, economic interests in Central Asia are strategic for Russia. The region is a market for Russian goods and investments, is of particular importance for the energy strategy and provides the necessary labour resources. In almost all countries, Russia is among the top three exporters and importers of CA countries, which indicates interdependent trade. However, its nature is described by the growth of Russia's positive balance, "the reason for this lies in the structure of imports from Central Asian countries",[18] which consists mainly of natural resources and agricultural products. The progressive development of the countries of the region is the Foreign Policy Concept of the Russian Federation: the decree of the President of the Russian Federation of 12 July 2008 No. 1440[19] is the most important point for the policy of Russia. The role of the external factor should also be taken into account; Russia is not interested in strengthening China's economic influence, despite the general cooperation in the region, which will mean the outgoing position of Russia.

Russia's soft power is one of the most important parameters of its presence in the region. The Russian language, Russian culture and the Russian-language information space can be viewed as comparable economic or military-political instruments. Their protection is the most important interest of Russia, since otherwise the ties with the region and the position of Russia may be lost.

Thus, Russia has strategic geopolitical and geo-economic interests in the region. Deep interconnection with the countries of Central Asia and a long border suggest the need for a presence in the region. Ensuring stability and preventing radicalization in the region is one of the most important tasks of Russia's foreign policy. Economic interests are also justified, but the extent to which they are realized is controversial.

Conclusion

The increasing interests of powers in the region led to efforts at developing associations aimed at integration. The countries took into account each other's projects in building an integration model. At the initial stage, Russia wanted the largest possible number of participants, the USA planned to integrate the Central Asian countries to South Asia within the framework of the Greater Central Asia and the New Silk Road project, and China sought to integrate them within the SCO. All projects, one way or the other, sought to reduce the influence of other parties.

The existing "agreement" between China and Russia in Central Asia is based on the countries' relations with the USA and the situation in other regions. The conjunction of the EAEU and the Silk Road Economic Belt (hereinafter referred to as the SREB) is an indicator of the cooperation and common interests of China and Russia,[20] but later it turned out that Russia does not seek to actively promote the SREB project, since "an equivalent trade balance between the EAEU and China is a distant prospect",[21] while China prefers to resolve economic issues with the EAEU countries through bilateral formats. In addition, an important Russian interest is the prevention of uncontrolled economic penetration of China into both Russia and the Central African Republic, which will lead to uncompromising competition with Chinese goods. With the further layering of opposing interests, "China may decide to abandon its current policy of self-restraint in Central Asia".[22] However, despite the increasing economic weight of China in Central Asia, Beijing understands the need to act in Central Asia through Moscow, which has more political tools in the region. Russia "has retained a" special relationship "with the countries of Central Asia", while the only significant factor in China's presence (economic) is not supported by the broad masses in the Central Asian countries. Nevertheless, Russia and China have more points of contact of interests and are able to build their relations in a win-win format. Thus, Russia and China pursue their own interests, but act in the context of "collective cooperation" in relations between themselves, while relations within the USA-Russia-China triangle in the CAR fit into the terminology "balance of power".[23] In the context of the triangle of interests of the Russian Federation-the USA-China, the perception of the interests of the powers by the Central Asian countries is of great importance.[24] The preference by the CA countries of the USA at the initial stages is explained by the need to balance the Russian monopoly presence. And Western countries were seen as more important as a source of investment and assistance in regional problems.

The leaders of the five Central Asian states are used to walking the regional tightrope. The area was contested during the so-called Great Game of the 19th century, when the British and Russian empires vied for influence and control.[24]

Now there a new game is going on. And officials in Central Asia, like many of their colleagues around the world, hedge their bets when it comes to negotiating with Washington, Moscow, or Beijing.

REFERENCES

1. Toropygin, A.V. and Mendagaziev, A.E. Interdependence and perception of the interests of the United States, China and Russia in Central Asia. *Eurasian Integration: Economics, Law, Politics*, no. 3, pp. 88–98.
2. https://foreignpolicy.com/2020/08/03/covid-19-china-new-great-game-central-asia/
3. https://foreignpolicy.com/2020/08/03/covid-19-china-new-great-game-central-asia/
4. Beloborov, Y. What is NATO looking for in a distant land?, RIAC-2018 [Electronic resource]. URL: https://russiancouncil.ru/analytics-and-comments/ columns / asian-kaleidoscope / chto-ishchet-nato-v-krayu-dalekom /? Sphrase_id = 32043063 (accessed 15.08.2020).
5. The Brookings Institution: United States Foreign Policy in the States of Central Asia, 2002. [Electronic resource]. URL: https://www.brookings.edu/ events / united-states-foreign-policy-in-the-states-of-central-asia / (accessed 15.08.2020).
6. SafranchukI. The New Silk Road Concept and the US Policy in Greater Central Asia, *International Life*, no. 7, 2013, pp.. 14–53.
7. Baranovskiy, V. *Assistance to international development as an instrument of foreign policy: foreign experience*, (eds.) V. Baranovsky, Y. Kvashin and N. Toganova, IMEMO. - RAS. - M., 2018, p. 53.
8. https://www.nytimes.com/2020/02/13/world/asia/china-great-game-central-asia-trump.html
9. United States Strategy for Central Asia 2019–2025: Advancing Sovereignty and Economic Prosperity: Report of the Bureau of South and Central Asian Affairs, U.S. Department of State, 2020, p. 2.
10. A. Grozin, Russia in Central Asia: Cooperation and Prospects for Energy Partnership with the Countries of the Region, *Eastern Analytics*, 2019, p. 18.
11. Azmukhanova, A. M.; Dzhumadilova, G. M.; and Amzenova, J. J. China's interests in Central Asia (analysis technical reference), *Society and Security Insights*. no. 1, 2018, pp. 186-194.
12. Zhukov, S. and Reznikov, O. Central Asia and China: economic interaction in the context of globalization, IMEMO.- RAS.- M., 2009, p. 86.
13. Fan, S. US strategy to spread influence in the Central Asian region as a common threat to Russia and China, *International Relationships*, no. 3, 2018, p. 15.
14. Babayan, D. China's policy in Central Asia, the Caucasus and the Northern Caspian region at the end of XX - early XXI centuries: dis. Doctor of Historical Sciences, Institute of Oriental Studies RAS.- 2016.
15. Kashin V. and Korolev, A. China's assistance to the countries of Central Asia, *World Economy and International Relations*, T. 62. no. 3. 2018, p. 82.
16. Toropygin, A.V. and Mendagaziev, A.E. Interdependence and perception of the interests of the USA, China and Russia in Central Asia, *Eurasian integration: economics, law, politics*.- 2020, no. 3, pp. 88–98.

17. https://www.intracen.org/.
18. Nikitenko V. Eurasian vectors of cooperation of the member states of the Shanghai Cooperation Organization in ensuring international and regional security, *International cooperation of Eurasian states: politics, economics, law*, no. 1, 2018, p. 165.
19. [Electronic resource]. URL: http://kremlin.ru/acts/news/785 (date accessed: 15.08.2020).
20. Glazyev S. Yu, Arkhipova V. V., Ageev AI [et al.]. Issues and state of the processes of conjugation of the Eurasian Economic Union and the "One Belt-One Road" Initiative in the views of China and Russia. *Eurasian integration: economics, law, politics*, no. 3, 2019, p. 16.
21. Shamakhov, V. A. and Sluchevsky, V. V. Some aspects of conjugation of EAEU projects "One Belt-One Road". *Eurasian integration: economics, law, politics*, no. 1, 2019, p. 33.
22. Azmukhanova, A. M., Dzhumadilova, G. M. and Amzenova, J. Zh. China's interests in Central Asia (analysis technical information), *Society and Security Insights*, no. 1, 2018, pp. 186-194.
23. Toropygin, A.V. and Mendagaziev, A.E. Interdependence and perception of the interests of the USA, China and Russia in Central Asia, *Eurasian integration: economics, law, politics*, 2020, no. 3, pp. 88–98.
24. https://www.worldpoliticsreview.com/articles/28936/as-u-s-power-wanes-russia-and-china-consolidate-their-influence-in-central-asia
25. https://foreignpolicy.com/2020/08/03/covid-19-china-new-great-game-central-asia/

Books

1. Azmukhanova, A.M.; Dzhumadilova, G.M. and Amzenova J. Zh. China's interests in Central Asia (analytical reference). *Society and Security Insights* no. 1, 2018, pp. 186-194.
2. Babayan D. China's policy in Central Asia, the Caucasus and the Northern Caspian in the late XX - early XXI centuries. dis. Doctor of Historical Sciences, Institute of Oriental Studies RAS.-2016.—S. 429.
3. Baranovsky, V. *Assistance to international development as an instrument of foreign policy: foreign experience*, (eds.).V. Baranovsky, Y. Kvashin, N. and Toganova. IMEMO RAN. - M., 2018.—248 p.
4. Glazyev, S. Yu.: Arkhipova, V. V, Ageev AI [et al.] Issues and state of the processes of conjugation of the Eurasian Economic Union and the initiative "One Belt - One Road" in the views of China and Russia, *Eurasian integration: economics, law, politics*, no. 3, 2019, pp. 13–30.
5. Grozin, A. Russia in Central Asia: cooperation and prospects of energy partnership with the countries of the region, *Eastern analytics*, 2019, S. 23–34.
6. Zhukov, S. and Reznikov, O. Central Asia and China: economic interaction in the context of globalization, IMEMO RAN. -M., 2009.—180 p.
7. Kashin, V. and Korolev, A. China's assistance to the countries of Central Asia, *World Economy and International Relations*, T. 62, no. 3, 2018, pp. 78–85.
8. Kuzmina, E. Economic cooperation of Russia with the states of Central Asia, Russia and Central Asia: new perspectives: materials of the international scientific Conf., dedicated to the 25th anniversary of the establishment of diplomatic. relations

between Ros. The Federation and the states of Central Asia.-MGIMO, 2018, pp. 164–184.

9. Nikitenko, V. Eurasian vectors of cooperation of the member states of the Shanghai Cooperation Organization to ensure international and regional security, *International cooperation of Eurasian states: politics, economics, law*, no. 1, 2018, pp. 25–33.
10. Safranchuk, I. The concept of the "New Silk Road" and the US policy in the "Greater Central Asia". *International Life*, no. 7, 2013, pp. 43–53.
11. Toropygin, A. V. and Mendagaziev, A. E. Interdependence and perception of the interests of the United States, China and Russia in Central Asia, *Eurasian integration: economics, law, politics*, 2020, no. 3, pp. 88–98.
12. Fan, S. US strategy to spread influence in the Central Asian region as a common threat to Russia and China, *International relationships*, no. 3, 2018, pp. 55–64.
13. Shamakhov, V. A. and Sluchevsky, V. V. Some aspects of conjugation of EAEU projects "One Belt - One Road", *Eurasian integration: economics, law, politics*, no. 1, 2019, pp. 28–33.
14. United States Strategy for Central Asia 2019–2025: Advancing Sovereignty and Economic Prosperity: Report of the Bureau of South and Central Asian Affairs, U. S. Department of State. 2020.

Electronic Resources

1. COVID-19 Heats Up the New Great Game in Central Asia. https://foreignpolicy.com/2020/08/03/covid-19-china-new-great-game-central-asia/
2. U.S. Faces Tough 'Great Game' Against China in Central Asia and Beyond. https://www.nytimes.com/2020/02/13/world/asia/china-great-game-central-asia-trump.html.
3. 5 + 1: The Math of Geopolitics in Central Asia. https://cabar.asia/en/5-1-the-math-of-geopolitics-in-central-asia.
4. The Coming US-China Competition in Central Asia. https://thediplomat.com/2020/02/the-coming-us-china-competition-in-central-asia/.
5. As U.S. Power Wanes, Russia and China Consolidate Their Influence in Central Asia. https://www.worldpoliticsreview.com/articles/28936/as-u-s-power-wanes-russia-and-china-consolidate-their-influence-in-central-asia
6. The Dynamics of Sino-Russian Relations in Central Asia. https://www.e-ir.info/2020/10/25/the-dynamics-of-sino-russian-relations-in-central-asia/.

8

International Terrorism as External Threats to the Regional Security of the Central Asian Countries

Prof. Dzhorobekova A.E. and Dr. Abalova N.Zh.

Introduction

The total area of the Central Asian Region (CAR) is 4 million square metres with a population of more than 55 million people. The ethnic mosaic of the region is made up of over 130 different peoples and ethnic groups. CAR borders on Afghanistan (2,087 km), Iran (992 km), China (2,805 km), Russia (6,846 km). International terrorism, religious extremism and ethno-national separatism, organized crime, illegal drug and weapon trafficking, and illegal migration have found fertile ground in the territory of the "Eurasian Balkans".[1]

The states of the Central Asian region are characterized by rather high risks, primarily from the point of view of new security threats, especially terrorism and religious extremism. The peak of the manifestation of these two security threats was the civil war in Tajikistan in 1992-1997, and a two-time invasion of the territory of Kyrgyz Republic and Uzbekistan in 1999-2000 and armed formations of militants of the Islamic Movement of Uzbekistan (IMU).

The intensification of these threats is also associated with neighbouring Afghanistan. Known unresolved regional problems remain acute: drug trafficking, according to experts from the UN Office on Drugs and Crime (UNODC), about 15-20 per cent of Afghan heroin is transported through Central Asia to Russia and Europe. It is worth about US$ 350-400 million,[2] illegal migration, and joint use of water and energy resources. In connection with the expansion of military activity in Syria and the pressure on the illegal armed forces by the international coalition in Syrian territory, the countries of the region are faced with the need to strengthen border security in countering cross-border threats.

Manifestations of Terrorism and Extremism in the Central Asian Region

In recent years, in almost all countries of the Central Asian Region, there have been separate manifestations of terrorism and extremism in such forms as political, religious, and criminal. This is facilitated by both internal and external factors associated with the development of the states of the region:

Internal factors: The political climate in almost all states of the region is characterized by many experts as unstable. The high level of violation of the rights and freedoms of citizens by the authorities, the growth of poverty and unemployment among a large part of the population, the marginalization of the consciousness and behaviour of a significant part of the population—all this contributes to the development of a protest mood among citizens in relation to the official policy of the state and inevitably leads to a radicalization of the views of the population. According to experts, this is the reason that terrorist and other criminal organizations and groups are active in the territories of the states of the region. In this regard, extremism finds fertile soil in the region and a rich potential, which cannot but lead to the activation of terrorist forces in the region.

External factors: Due to the geopolitical position of the Central Asian region, since the countries of the region found themselves surrounded by such zones of political instability and conflicts as the Transcaucasia, the Caucasus, Xinjiang Uygur Autonomous Region of China, Afghanistan, the Middle and the Near East.

One of the external factors posing a threat to the security of the region is separatism in the Xinjiang Uygur Autonomous Region (XUAR) of China, caused by a protracted conflict between the active parts of the indigenous population of this region, the Uyghurs, with the Chinese authorities. The radical part of the Uyghur movement is seeking the separation of the XUAR from China and the creation of an independent state, Uygurstan or East Turkestan. In the future, they plan to include the Chilik district of the Alma-Ata region of Kazakhstan. The armed path of the struggle for independence was chosen by the Uyghur separatists on the basis of the decisions of the World Uyghur Kurultai, which took place in Istanbul at the end of 1996.[3]

The plans of the Uyghur separatists are linked to the seizure of power by Islamists in the Central Asian states, since without a reliable foothold, their struggle is doomed to failure. As a result, according to the intelligence services of CIS countries, the contacts of Xinjiang extremists with the Islamic Movement of Uzbekistan (IMU) and the United Tajik Opposition (UTO) are expanding. At the same time, the leaders of the ETIM are trying to rely on the large (up to 400 thousand) Uyghur Diaspora living in Kazakhstan (about 250 thousand people), Kyrgyzstan (about 50 thousand), in the Andijan region of Uzbekistan (14 thousand people), as well as in some other regions.

Until now, Afghanistan has played and continues to play the greatest threat to the security of Central Asia. Before the anti-terrorist operation in Afghanistan, the latter was a transnational base of international terrorism. Now we can say with a certain degree of certainty that the nest of terrorism has been destroyed; however, it is too early to say that the terrorist threat has been eliminated. The Taliban regime, as the centre of radical forces, fell, but the terrorist forces were not destroyed, only their regrouping took place: many of the terrorists left Afghanistan and found refuge in other states such as Pakistan, the Gulf countries, Tajikistan, Uzbekistan, etc. The territorial proximity of Afghanistan to Central Asia largely determines the state of security in the region.

It should be emphasized that in Central Asia there are four types of causes of terrorism as a socio-political phenomenon, such as socio-economic, ideological, geopolitical, and globalization.[4]

B.A. Mylnikov, head of the CIS Anti-Terrorist Centre (2000-2006), identified the following factors as factors determining the dangerous dynamics of trends in the post-Soviet space, in particular on the territory of the CAR states.[5]

- economic and social crisis, unemployment and impoverishment

of a significant part of the population;
- growth of sentiments of nationalism, ethnic intolerance, religious extremism and separatist sentiments;
- heightened sense of social disorder and insecurity among a significant part of the population;
- loss of ideological and spiritual life guidelines by many people, destruction of moral values of traditional Islam and growth of aggressiveness;
- an increase in crime, a decline in the authority of the government, the law, and faith in its ability to ensure the safety of citizens;
- intensification of illegal drug and arms trafficking;
- ineffectiveness of the executive authorities.

All these factors explain the concern of both the leaderships of the states of the region and the entire world community over the conflict potential of the region, which has acquired a long-term nature.

In recent years, almost all Central Asian countries have observed completely new, in comparison with previous years, tendencies in the manifestation of terrorism and extremism, characterized by the following main factors:

- events took place that contributed to a sharp exacerbation of the internal political situation (the Andijan events in Uzbekistan in May 2005, the assassination of opposition leader Altynbek Sarsenbayuly in February 2006 in Kazakhstan, "revolutions" in Kyrgyzstan);
- the level of criminalization has significantly increased in the process of political struggle in the countries of the region;
- there were practically no traditional manifestations of terrorism and extremism in the form of terrorist acts and armed attacks on state facilities by representatives of relevant organizations and groups such as the Islamic Movement of Uzbekistan (IMU), with the exception of some cases;
- Central Asian governments quite often resorted to adopting new anti-extremist measures, in most cases restricting civil rights;
- an increase in the number of various mass protests, some of which resulted in open confrontation of citizens against government officials.

International terrorist organizations or their subdivisions, radical Islamic fundamentalists and extremist groups operate in the Central Asian region, which causes concern for both the states of the region and the entire world community.

Many radical forces aim to create an Islamic state on the territory of Central Asia with a core in the Fergana Valley, which, according to the plan, should become part of the World Islamic Caliphate.

Among the main terrorist forces in the region, the following should be noted:

- "Islamic Movement of Uzbekistan", an organization of Islamists created in 1996 by the religious leader, T. Yuldashev, who fled Uzbekistan in 1993. IMU militants took part in the civil war in Tajikistan on the side of the United Tajik Opposition, in the Batken events in Kyrgyzstan, in the war in Afghanistan, and fought with the Taliban against the Pakistani army. In 2014, the IMU joined another international terrorist organization, the Islamic State.
- Hizbut-Tahrir al-Islami, an Islamist and neo-fundamentalist organization calling itself a party, was founded in 1953 in East Jerusalem controlled at that time by Trans-Jordan. The founder of this organization is considered the Palestinian politician, lawyer, and theologian Takyuddin Muhammad ibn Ibrahim al-Nabhani. As a pan-Islamist radical movement, the Hizbut-Tahrir preaches the unity of all Muslims and rejects the need for national Islamic states, democracy, and secular forms of government.
- "Muslim Brotherhood", which was founded in 1928 and was initially purely religious in nature and engaged in missionary activities, opposed the "Westernization of the country", defending the ideas of pan-Islamism, the Islamic path of development and Islamic democracy. However, over the years, this structure became politicized; its activists were the first to resort to acts of terror and violence as a means of putting pressure on the state. On 25 December 2013, the Egyptian government officially declared the Muslim Brotherhood a terrorist organization.

The main goal of these organizations is to promote separatism and radical fundamentalism. It is especially important that the terrorist activities of many organizations are closely related to the international drug business and smuggling of weapons from Afghanistan to Tajikistan, Kyrgyzstan, Uzbekistan and further to the CIS countries and Europe.[6]

There is no doubt that the events in the south of Kyrgyzstan, in the North Caucasian part of Russia, the military confrontation in Afghanistan, and acts of terror in Tajikistan and Uzbekistan are all links of the same chain, linked in time and place, and financed and coordinated from one or several centres of international terrorist and extremist organizations.

Islamic Movement of Uzbekistan

Among the modern terrorist organizations operating in Central Asia, the Islamic Movement of Uzbekistan (IMU) should be named, first of all.[7] In August 1996, on the territory of Afghanistan, members of extremist religious groups who fled from Uzbekistan created the Islamic Movement of Uzbekistan, the main goal of which was to create a Muslim theocratic state of the Caliphate on the territories of those countries where Muslims live. The backbone of the IMU was made up of members of the societies, "Adolat" and "Islam Lyashkarlari", as well as parties of T. Yuldashev and J. Namangani. The IMU first announced itself in 1997.[8]

Despite its youth, the IMU is the largest terrorist group in the Central Asian region. As the name suggests, the organization is Islamist. The goals of the IMU proclaimed the fight against the political regime of I. Karimov, suggesting the creation of a territory comprising all the five Central Asian states, as well as China, populated by Uighurs, an Islamic state. The centre will be the Fergana Valley, in particular the so-called FANO, the territory running along the Namangan-Andijan-Osh-Fergana line. It is extremely difficult to pinpoint the locations of the terrorist organizations; nevertheless, the analytical discourse contains statements about the movements of the IMU on the territory of Tajikistan and Afghanistan. The organization has close ties with the Taliban and Chechen fighters.

In August 1999, members of the armed Islamic group (IMU) invaded southern Kyrgyzstan. During this period, armed clashes took place between militants and government forces. A year later, in August, IMU fighters again invaded Kyrgyzstan, and hostilities continued for exactly a month. Among the IMU fighters were representatives of various nationalities. They were well equipped with maps, night vision devices, and high-precision sniper weapons. The invading militants were international terrorists using the banner of Islam. They pursued the goal of destabilizing the situation in the Central Asian region by increasing the amount of drugs being transferred.[9]

In many countries around the world, the IMU is banned as a terrorist organization. Members of this banned organization operate legally in many European countries. Especially in those countries where double standards are applied towards religious extremists and militants fighting under the banner of the national liberation struggle.

Takhir Yuldashev, leader of the IMU, died on 27 August 2009 as a result of a missile strike by an American reconnaissance aircraft.[10] Several of his supporters were killed with him, in particular, the head of the Pakistani branch of the Taliban, Baitullah Mehsud.

Eleven years later, in November 2020, during an operation by the national security forces of Afghanistan, the leader of the international terrorist organization, "Islamic Movement of Uzbekistan" (IMU), 30-year-old Aziz Yuldash, was killed. It is assumed that he is the son of the founder of the movement, Takhir Yuldashev.[11] According to the Ministry of Defence, Aziz Yuldash was involved in terrorist attacks and the massacre of Afghans in the northern provinces and recruited militants to ISIS in north-western Afghanistan in 2017.

Hizbut-Tahrir al-Islami

The Hizb-ut-Tahrir, created in 1953 by Baitul-Maksid (Syria) (according to sources in Jerusalem) from members of the Palestinian branch of another well-known religious and political party, the "al-Ikhwan al-Muslimin" ("Brothers-Muslims"),[12] is one of the most active terrorist organizations in Central Asia. The initiator of the secession from the religious-political party "al-Ikhwan al-Muslimin" ("Muslim Brothers") was the first leader of the party, Taki ad-din Nabhani al Falastini (1909-1979).[13] Party branches exist in Lebanon, Jordan, Egypt and other Arab countries, in Turkey, as well as in some European countries. On the territory of Central Asia and in Russia, the organization did not pass legalization and was banned as a terrorist one. It started its activities in Central Asia in 1995. In Kazakhstan, for the first time, the activities of the Hizb-ut-Tahrir manifested themselves in the South Kazakhstan region, in 1998. It was then that the illegal distribution of leaflets and brochures signed by the Hizb-ut-Tahrir party was recorded in South Kazakhstan for the first time, containing, in fact, calls for a change in the constitutional order in the republic. The main goal of the organization is the return of the Muslim ummah to Dar al-Islam, the establishment of the rule of Sharia law and the creation of the Caliphate. Achievement of this goal is supposed to be carried out in three stages:

1. The first stage provides for educational work among the faithful.
2. In the second stage, the party's supporters will begin to spread the ideas of the Caliphate among their compatriots.
3. The third stage will be characterized by the fall of secular regimes, the creation of the Caliphate itself and the establishment of the power of the Caliph. At the same time, the organization completely rejects violent actions, recalling that the Prophet Muhammad built the first state, despite boycott and persecution, without using violence, but using only political methods and intellectual abilities.

In Kyrgyzstan, the activities of the "Hizbut-Tahrir al-Islami" are prohibited on the territory of the Kyrgyz Republic by the decision of the Judicial Collegium for Civil Cases of the Supreme Court of the Kyrgyz Republic dated 20 August 2003 on the decision of the Pervomaisky District Court of Bishkek dated 14 May 2003 on the proposal of the Prosecutor General of the Kyrgyz Republic.

Recently, a terrorist organization, Akromiya, which was created in the mid-1990s, has been increasingly mentioned led by a former member of the Islamist organization Hizb-ut-Tahrir, Akrom Yuldashev. According to his ideas, if Muslims live in a "land of infidels", then they are allowed temporary marriage, smoking cigarettes and drinking alcoholic beverages. Due to these convictions, A. Yuldashev and his associates were expelled from the ranks of the Hizbut-Tahrir.

Since the beginning of the Nineties, among the Uzbek part of the population, the influence of Wahhabism is increasing through the Hizb-ut-Tahrir al-Islamiya, the Adolat movement, Islam Lashkarlari and other religious movements of extremist persuasions. Particularly active is the Hizb-ut-Tahrir party, which based its program on propaganda activities. Supporters of this party distributed leaflets, brochures, and books in Uzbek, Kyrgyz, Russian. The activities of the party members were very conspiratorial. The members of the groups were relatives who created small enterprises, and paid 20 per cent of their earnings to their party.[14] The activities of Akramia members were noticed in the south of Kyrgyzstan, in the city of Osh.

According to experts from the CIS[2] Anti-Terrorist Centre, there are extremist organizations: 32 in Russia, 23 in Kazakhstan, 18 in Tajikistan, 22 in Uzbekistan and 20 in Kyrgyzstan.[15] Extremist and terrorist organizations operate on the territory of the countries of the Central Asian region: the

Islamic Party of Turkestan, the Islamic Movement of Uzbekistan, the Organization for the Liberation of Turkestan, Hizb-ut-Tahrir and others.[16]

With the deterioration of the situation in neighbouring Afghanistan, the creation and spread of the terrorist alliance—"Islamic State" (IS, the Islamic State of Iraq and the Levant, the Islamic State of Iraq and Sham, the Islamic State of Iraq and Syria)—the region is turning into a zone of increased terrorist threat. Meanwhile, due to its geographic location, Central Asia is an important link in ensuring global security.

Most experts agree that at present the real threat to the countries of Central Asia does not come from the Taliban, but from the IS, which is gaining influence in the northern provinces of Afghanistan. The ranks of this terrorist association are growing at the expense of immigrants from Central Asia, whose number, at the beginning of 2017, was estimated at more than 5 thousand people, while, according to estimates, about 500 people returned to their homeland from the conflict zones.[17] According to A. Kazantsev, director of the MGIMO Analytical Centre, "the classical Taliban, being Pashtun nationalists, of course, will not go to Central Asia—this is a myth, but the invasion of the region by groups of various ethnic extremists associated with both the al-Qaeda and the IS, is not only likely, but generally expected in the light of the situation that has developed in Afghanistan, Central Asia and the Middle East."[18]

Thus, the emergence of modern terrorism in Central Asia is linked to the renaissance of the pan-Islamist ideology. Motivationally, the organizations articulate the struggle against the secular authorities in Uzbekistan. At a deeper level, there is a rejection of nationalism, since the ultimate goal is to build an Islamic Caliphate as a global religious and political system. Methods for achieving goals can be both violent and propaganda.[19]

Kyrgyzstan: Countering the Spread of Terrorism

Terrorism in Central Asia plays with the ethnic feelings of the population. For example, the Islamic Movement of East Turkestan (IDTV), which advocates the separation of the XUAR from China, hopes for the solidarity and support of the Uyghur diasporas in the Central Asian countries.[20] In the summer of 2014, members of ETIM entered the territory of Kyrgyzstan in the Issyk-Kul region, and were killed during a shootout. They found materials of terrorist content, money, and weapons. Also, according to media reports,[21] on the territory of the Kyrgyz Republic, especially in the south, not only the IDTV, but also the IMU, IS, Hizbut-Tahrir and others are also active. "Of the 2,500 mosques operating in Kyrgyzstan, most were built at the expense of foreign sponsors. In general, fundamentalist Muslim sentiments are strong among the Uighurs and Uzbeks in the south of Kyrgyzstan, and any provocation can blow up the situation here."

"According to various unofficial Arab, Turkish, and Western expert assessments, from 170 to 300 citizens of Kyrgyzstan are fighting in Syria and Iraq. There are also citizens of Kazakhstan, Uzbekistan, and Tajikistan. Perhaps the numbers are either overestimated or underestimated. But it is not important to count them—not how many people are already there, but how quickly the process of takfirism can spread. The mechanism of the sect is network marketing: it works both in depth and in strength."[22] There is recruitment from the population, due to financial and moral support in difficult moments that these organizations can offer people, and which the state does not offer.

The population of the country, which has been experiencing difficulties since independence in 1991, is easy to deceive and use for their own purposes. There are often cases when a family has a sick child, and the state cannot cure him for free due to various factors (for example, the lack of a city registration, as a result of internal migration), religious institutions come to the rescue. In similar ways, the population lends itself to the recruitment of terrorists.

According to Yusuf Khanov,[23] some terrorist organizations can unite their efforts "because the IMU is weakened by losses at the top of the organization and unstable funding in recent years. Joining the IS will undoubtedly strengthen its position." The unifying goal of all terrorist organizations is the creation of a caliphate; if all groups unite, this will become the highest threat.

The government of the Kyrgyz Republic is aware that terrorism or religious extremism poses a threat to national security. This is evidenced by the Concept of State Policy of the Kyrgyz Republic in the Religious Sphere, adopted on 14 November 2014, which states that "The goal of state policy in the religious sphere is to create an optimal model of state-confessional cooperation based on the secular nature of the state through effective state regulation of the activities of religious and public institutions to ensure the security of citizens and the state, strengthening interfaith harmony and religious tolerance, countering religious radicalism and extremism based on the principles of human rights and freedom of religion". In order to achieve this goal, there is a need to "improve the legislative framework in the field of regulation of relations between state authorities and local self-government bodies". At the end of 2014, a state religious policy and a set of preventive measures were developed to ensure the secular nature of the state and prevent possible religious offences by a special commission.

The concept says that in order to achieve this goal, it is necessary to improve legal regulation, interaction at the national level, interaction at the local level, information policy, and policy in the field of education.

Organizations, information on the recognition of which is terrorist or extremist in accordance with the procedure established by the national legislation of the CIS member-states, is available in the CIS ATC (copies or dates of court decisions).

1. "Al-Qaeda" is an organization recognized as terrorist, extremist, and its activities were prohibited on the territory of the Kyrgyz Republic by the decision of the Pervomayskiy District Court of Bishkek, Kyrgyz Republic, dated 15 September 2006, at the request of the Prosecutor General of the Kyrgyz Republic.
2. "East Turkestan Islamic Party" ("Sharki Turkestan Islam Partiyasy") is an organization recognized as terrorist, and its activities are prohibited on the territory of the Kyrgyz Republic by the decision of the Judicial Collegium for Civil Cases of the Supreme Court of the Kyrgyz Republic dated 20 August 2003 against the decision of the Pervomaisky District Court of Bishkek dated 14 May 2003 on the proposal of the Prosecutor General of the Kyrgyz Republic.
3. "Jihad Group" (Jamaat al Jihad", "Islamic Jihad Group", "Islamic Jihad Union", "Islamic Jihad - Jamaat of the Mujahideen", and Jamaat of the Mujahideen of Central Asia") are international organizations recognized as terrorist, and its activities are prohibited on the territory of the Kyrgyz Republic by the decision of the Pervomaisky District Court of Bishkek of the Kyrgyz Republic dated June 11, 2008 at the request of the Prosecutor General of the Kyrgyz Republic.

4. "Taliban Movement" is an organization recognized as terrorist, extremist, and its activities were prohibited on the territory of the Kyrgyz Republic by the decision of the Pervomayskiy District Court of Bishkek, Kyrgyz Republic, dated 15 September 2006, at the request of the Prosecutor General of the Kyrgyz Republic.
5. "The Islamic Party of Turkestan" (formerly "IMU") is an organization recognized as terrorist, and its activities are prohibited on the territory of the Kyrgyz Republic by the decision of the Judicial Collegium for Civil Cases of the Supreme Court of the Kyrgyz Republic of 20 August 2003 on the decision of the Pervomaisky District Court of Bishkek dated 14 May 2003 on the proposal of the Prosecutor General of the Kyrgyz Republic.
6. "Islamic State" is an organization recognized as terrorist and extremist, and its activities are prohibited on the territory of the Kyrgyz Republic by the decision of the Oktyabrsky District Court of Bishkek of the Kyrgyz Republic dated 13 February 2015 on the claim of the General Prosecutor's Office of the Kyrgyz Republic.
7. "People's Congress of Kurdistan" ("Kurdish People's Congress", "Workers 'Party of Kurdistan", "Kurdish Workers' Party", "Kondra-Gel") is an international organization recognized as terrorist, and its activities are prohibited on the territory of the Kyrgyz Republic by the decision of the Pervomaisky District court of the city of Bishkek of the Kyrgyz Republic dated 11 June 2008 at the request of the Prosecutor General of the Kyrgyz Republic.
8. "Organization for the Liberation of Turkestan" ("Sharki Azat Turkestan") is an organization recognized as terrorist, and its activities are prohibited on the territory of the Kyrgyz Republic by the decision of the Judicial Collegium for Civil Cases of the Supreme Court of the Kyrgyz Republic dated 20 August 2003 on the decision of the Pervomaisky District Court of Bishkek dated 14 May 2003 on the proposal of the Prosecutor General of the Kyrgyz Republic.
9. "Hizbut-Tahrir al Islami" is an organization recognized as extremist, and its activities are prohibited on the territory of the Kyrgyz Republic by the decision of the Judicial Collegium for Civil Cases of the Supreme Court of the Kyrgyz Republic dated 20 August 2003 against the decision of the Pervomaisky District Court of Bishkek dated 14 May 2003 on the proposal of the Prosecutor General of the Kyrgyz Republic.

10. The "Takfirist-Jihadist movement of Salafist orientation" (Salafism) is a religious association recognized as terrorist and extremist, and its activities were banned in the territory of the Kyrgyz Republic by the decision of the Pervomaisky District Court of Bishkek on 24 October 2012 on the proposal of the General Prosecutor of the Kyrgyz Republic.
11. "Zhaish ul Mahdi" is an organization of a takfirist-jihadist Salafi movement, recognized as terrorist and extremist, and its activities were prohibited in the territory of the Kyrgyz Republic by the decision of the Pervomaisky District Court of Bishkek on 24 October 2012 on the proposal of the Prosecutor General of the Kyrgyz Republic.
12. "Jund-al-Khalifat" (Jund-ul Khalifat) is an organization of the takfirist-jihadist movement of Salafi orientation, recognized as terrorist and extremist, and its activities were prohibited in the territory of the Kyrgyz Republic by the decision of the Pervomaisky District Court of Bishkek dated 24 October 2012 on the claim of the Prosecutor General of the Kyrgyz Republic.
13. "Ansarulloh" (Ansarull Allah) is an organization of the takfirist-jihadist movement of the Salafi orientation, recognized as terrorist and extremist, and its activities were prohibited on the territory of the Kyrgyz Republic by the decision of the Pervomaisky District Court of Bishkek on 24 October 2012 on the proposal of the Prosecutor General of the Kyrgyz Republic.
14. "At-Takfir Wal-Hijra" (At-Takfir Wa-l-Hijra) is an organization of the takfiri-jihadist movement of Salafi orientation, recognized as terrorist and extremist, and its activities were prohibited on the territory of the Kyrgyz Republic by the decision of the Pervomaisky District Court of Bishkek from 24 October 2012 on the proposal of the Prosecutor General of the Kyrgyz Republic.
15. "Akromiya" is a religious movement recognized as extremist, and its activities were banned in the territory of the Kyrgyz Republic by the decision of the Pervomaisky District Court of Bishkek dated 14 March 2014 on the proposal of the General Prosecutor's Office of the Kyrgyz Republic.
16. "Front al-Nusra" ("Jabhat-al-Nusra") is an organization recognized as terrorist and extremist, whose activity is prohibited on the territory of the Kyrgyz Republic by the decision of the Osh city

court of Osh city dated 13 May 2015 at the request of the prosecutor's office of the Osh region.

17. "Zhannat Oshiklari" is an organization recognized as terrorist and extremist, whose activities are prohibited on the territory of the Kyrgyz Republic by the decision of the Osh city court of Osh city dated 13 May 2015 at the request of the prosecutor's office of the Osh region.
18. "Katib al Imam al Bukhari" is an organization recognized as terrorist and extremist, whose activities are prohibited on the territory of the Kyrgyz Republic by the decision of the Osh City Court of Osh on 13 May 2015 at the request of the Osh Oblast Prosecutor's Office.
19. "Jamaat Tauhidva-Jihad" is an organization recognized as terrorist and extremist, whose activities are prohibited on the territory of the Kyrgyz Republic by the decision of the Osh City Court of Osh on 17 March 2016 at the request of the Osh Oblast Prosecutor's Office.
20. "Yakyn Inkar" is a religious movement recognized as extremist, whose activities are prohibited on the territory of the Kyrgyz Republic by the decision of the Oktyabrskiy District Court of Bishkek dated 15 June 2017 on the claim of the General Prosecutor's Office of the Kyrgyz Republic.

Of course, in the six-million-strong Kyrgyzstan, where the share of young people is about a third of the population, which also has a protest potential, there are various alarming tendencies. This is all the more relevant, taking into account the assessments of sociologists that the threshold of young people capable of changing the state structure is only 15-20 per cent. It was young people who, by the way, were the main driving force behind the two violent overthrows of power in Kyrgyzstan in 2005 and 2010.

As in other parts of Central Asia, the most lively debate is caused by the problem of ensuring national security against the background of the growing activity of Islamist groups professing extreme views.

Experts from Kyrgyzstan believe that the most dangerous phenomenon is the takfirist-jihadist movement. In Kyrgyzstan, several organizations are classified as such, including the Islamic State, which was banned by a court ruling in March 2015. The number of women travelling to the Middle East has increased. According to the data of law enforcement agencies, 863

Kyrgyz citizens joined the hostilities in Syria on the side of the ISIS from 2010 to June 2016, of which 188 were women.[24]

A number of factors can be used to call Kyrgyzstanis into the ranks of IS and similar terrorist structures:

- campaigning through social networks, popular communications platforms on the Internet, through personal invitations from jihadists who have already left abroad;
- financial incentives for newly minted militants;
- corruption, which allows foreign agitators to legalize themselves in the Kyrgyz Republic;
- vague control on the part of government agencies when obtaining passports and visas;
- transparency of borders within the CIS and foreign partners of the Commonwealth, which makes it possible to enter the states of the Arab East through third countries, etc.

Among the threatening prospects, we also note the outward attractiveness of the ideas of "social justice and equality" within the framework of a quasi-Islamic state, the false understanding by individual believers of the concept of confessional solidarity, and hence the desire to help brothers in faith in various parts of the planet by any means, the mythologization of jihad and the romanticization of becoming shahid in mass media, etc.

In July 2015, during a special operation in Bishkek, a local cell of young IS supporters, including citizens of Kazakhstan, was liquidated. As a result of which four criminals were killed and seven were arrested. They were preparing for a series of terrorist attacks, including the detonation of an IED on the day of Orozo-Aita on the Old Square in Bishkek, where a traditional prayer service is held, and at the Kant airbase (a military facility of the Russian Defence Ministry 30 km from Bishkek, part of the CSTO structure).

In November 2015, several young radicals made an attempt on the life of the famous theologian and expert Kadyr Malikov, who exposed the extremists. Two of the attackers were detained near the Turkish-Syrian border, where they sought to get across, but were extradited and convicted in Kyrgyzstan.

After the first facts of migration of Kyrgyzstanis to the IS zone emerged, President A. Atambaev in 2014 signed a decree "On the Concept of State

Policy of the Kyrgyz Republic in the Religious Sphere for 2014-2020". The concept is aimed at protecting human rights, freedom of conscience and religion, further strengthening the rule of law and public security, as well as taking measures to preserve the culture, language, and spiritual values of the people of Kyrgyzstan to ensure the country's identity.

What is being done to minimize risks? We list just some of the activities:

1. To raise awareness among the population, the Ministry of Internal Affairs of the Kyrgyz Republic issued about 50 thousand booklets "Islam against extremism".
2. The 10th Department of the Ministry of Internal Affairs of the Kyrgyz Republic has created an online patrol project and removes videos with manifestations of radicalism; employees constantly monitor Internet forums and track recruiters who create special profiles on social networks and are engaged in prevention.
3. The Ministry of Internal Affairs, together with the Spiritual Directorate of Muslims of Kyrgyzstan, is conducting the campaign "We are against terrorism and extremism", which includes a series of seminars.
4. In the regions of Kyrgyzstan, training is regular with the involvement of the population, local government bodies, special services, and the bureaucratic apparatus. There are frequent meetings and round tables with the participation of experts, official clergy, and NGO activists.
5. Employees of the Anti-Terrorism Centre of the State Committee for National Security of the Kyrgyz Republic, together with the Anti-Terrorism Centre of the member-states of the Commonwealth of Independent States (ATC CIS), conduct cycles of explanatory and preventive meetings within the walls of universities, where the main topics are the emerging military-political situation and the recruitment of youth as militants into the ranks of the "Islamic State". They are of great interest to the teaching staff and student youth.
6. The subject of foundations of religious culture has been introduced into the curriculum of general educational institutions. The work on certification and standardization of religious institutions is intensifying. In September 2015, the Theological College began to operate so that there was no separation of young people studying

there from the secular life of the country. In addition, in 2016, the educational institution "The Institute for Training (Retraining) of Leading Personnel of the Spiritual Directorate of Muslims of Kyrgyzstan" began its activity.

7. Note that due to the measures taken, there is already progress. For example, according to the 2017 Global Terrorism Index, Kyrgyzstan was in the 112th place in the 2014 ranking, but in 2015 it climbed to 86th place, and in 2017 to 79th place.[25]
8. By the decision of the courts of the Kyrgyz Republic in 2019, 97 websites and 300 accounts on social networks were banned and blocked, and the information materials published there were recognized as extremist and terrorist.[26]

The government of Kyrgyzstan has approved a plan to counter extremism and terrorism for 2017-2022, which includes activities such as the creation of a specialized centre for the analysis and prevention of cyber threats and the organization of control over foreign missionaries.

Conclusion

Based on the study of international terrorism in the system of external threats to the regional security of the Central Asian countries, a number of conclusions can be formulated (Refer On approval of the Program of the Government of the Kyrgyz Republic on countering extremism and terrorism for 2017-2022. Resolution of the Government of the Kyrgyz Republic No. 394 dated 21 June 2017) :

- The danger of international terrorism is that it has an organizational structure, goals, means, ideology, and social base.
- Modern international terrorism is used as a tool of international state policy; however, it has a fundamentally new political and economic content: the subjects using terrorism have changed, as well as the forms of carrying out terrorist acts.
- With regard to the regional level in relation to Central Asia, the following should be noted: the existing mechanisms within the framework of which the cooperation of regional states in the fight against terrorism takes place (mainly, the ATCs of the CIS, CSTO, and SCO can be distinguished). There is no doubt that these organizations have great potential and fairly good chances to jointly build a regional security system adequate to modern international

political trends and realities, which would be one of the pillars of the emerging global security system, an intermediate link between the global and sub-regional levels.

- Threats and challenges of international terrorism are caused by the presence of both internal and external factors. Afghanistan's proximity to Central Asia, which until now is a theatre of military operations, on the territory of which a number of extremist and international terrorist organizations are based, in the context of globalization can negatively affect the situation in the region along the outer perimeter.
- The leadership of Kyrgyzstan does not hide that it is concerned about attempts to Arabize the republic, the threat of losing its national identity, the imposition of alien values, the import of a different culture and rituals that contradict the freedom-loving mentality of the local community, which has never had excessive fanaticism and dogmatism in history. It is the joint work of state bodies, civil society and religious organizations in a democracy, an open discussion of topical issues and the search for joint solutions in order to preserve the unique spiritual specifics and harmony in Kyrgyzstan that are the best alternative to radicalism.

NOTES AND REFERENCES

1. Eight new national states of Central Asia and the Caucasus (Kazakhstan, Uzbekistan, Turkmenistan, Tajikistan, Kyrgyzstan, Georgia, Armenia and Azerbaijan) formed the territorial core of the "Eurasian Balkans". Z. Brzezinski proposed to classify certain parts of the territories of five more states located along the perimeter of the Caucasian-Central Asian geopolitical region as the "Eurasian Balkans": They were Russia, Turkey, Iran, Afghanistan and China // Brzezinski Zbigniew. The Grand Chessboard. American Primacy and Its Geostrategic Imperatives. N.Y., 1997. p. 123.
2. The Anti-Terrorism Centre of the Commonwealth of Independent States (ATC CIS), created by the Decision of the Council of CIS Heads of State of 21 June 2000, is a permanent specialized sectoral body of the Commonwealth of Independent States and is designed to ensure coordination of interaction between the competent authorities of the CIS member-states in the field of combating with international terrorism and other manifestations of extremism. There is a lot of controversy about violent methods, since the official point of view on the involvement of the IMU, Akromiyya and Hizb-ut-Tahrir in the terrorist attacks in Central Asia, and the point of view of the terrorists may differ. For example, despite the fact that the Uzbek authorities blamed the Hizbut-Tahrir for the attacks, the organization refused to take responsibility for the 16 February 1999 bombings in Tashkent.
3. "Concept of state policy of the Kyrgyz Republic in the religious sphere for 2014-2020", 2014, p. 5.

REFERENCES

1. Bondarets L. M. Foreign policy factor in the conflict situation in Central Asia. Materials of the international conference "The future of the Central Asian states: together or ...". 26-28 June 2001 Bishkek, p. 64.
2. Central Asia 2027: a changing strategic landscape. Possible scenarios for 10 years ahead. Shaimergenov, T. T., Abisheva, M. A., Rakhimzhanova, A. Zh. and others, Astana: Publishing House of the Library of the First President of the Republic of Kazakhstan, Elbasy, 2017, p. 27.
3. Policy of indirect actions. 09 April 2020 17: 56 // http://army.ric.mil.ru/Stati/item/253489/
4. Asanbekov, M. K. International terrorism in Central Asian countries // Sociological research, 2005, No. 9, p. 129.
5. Theses of the speech of the Head of the ATC of the CIS, B. À. Mylnikov, at the international scientific-practical conference "Russia and Central Asia - issues of cooperation and security" // http://www.atcsng.ru/print.cgi?id=48
6. Specificity of manifestations of terrorism and extremism in Central Asia: main trends and results of 2005-2006: Analytical report // Centre for Anti-Terrorist Programs (CAP) http://vvww.antiteiTor.kz/?submenu=monitor
7. Falkov M. Islamic Movement of Uzbekistan (IMU) // Nezavisimaya Gazeta, 2000, 24 August.
8. Mamayusupov, O. Sh. Questions (problems) of religion in the transition period, B. 2003, p. 17.
9. Alimova, K. T. Religious extremism in Kyrgyzstan in the transition period // Actual problems of social sciences: sociology, political science, philosophy, history: collection of articles. Art. by mater. LVII int. scientific-practical conf. No. 1 (53), Novosibirsk: SibAK, 2016, p.14.
10. The Islamic Movement of Uzbekistan has admitted the death of its leader https://online.zakon.kz/Document/?doc_id=30801607
11. The Ministry of Defence of Afghanistan has reported on the murder of the leader of the Islamic Movement of Uzbekistan, https://mediazona.ca/news/2020/11/12/yldash
12. K. Malikov. A short guide to Islam. Bishkek. 2013, p. 111.
13. B. Babadjanov. On the activities of "Hizb at-Tahrir al-Islami" in Uzbekistan // Islam in the post-Soviet space: a look from the inside, M. 2001, S. 156.
14. Babadjanov, B. Fergana Valley: Source or Victim of Islamic Fundamentalism? // Central Asia and the Caucasus, 1999, No. 4 (5), p. 129.
15. Terrorist and extremist organizations https://WWW.CISATC.ORG/1289/134/160
16. Balakina, I. Voice from the underground // Russian newspaper, 8.12.2005.
17. Barrett, R. 2017. Beyond the Ñaliphate: Foreign Fighters and the Threat of Returnees. URL: http://thesoufancenter.org/wpcontent/uploads/2017/10/Beyond-the-Caliphate-Foreign-Fighters-and-the-Threatof-Returnees-TSC-Report-October-2017.pdf
18. [Electronic resource], ccess mode: http://www.ng.ru/cis/2015-10-08/1_ashabad.html
19. Karataeva, L. R. Formation of the system of countering terrorism in Central Asia / Abstract of the dissertation for the degree of Doctor of Historical Sciences, Almaty, 2010, p. 24.

20. Asamudinov, B. "Terrorism and its impact on the security of Central Asia", 2013, p. 3.
21. http: //www.azattyk.kg/, http://www.akipress.org/
22. Malikov, K. "About Syria, which is being prepared for Kyrgyzstan", 2014, http://www.ww.eng.24.kg/politic/187244-kadyr-malikov-o-sirii-kotoruyu-gotovyat-dlya.html
23. Official website of the Anti-Terrorist Centre of the Member States of the Commonwealth of Independent States (ATC CIS) // http://www.cisatc.org/134/160/207
24. Radicalization of women on religious grounds in Kyrgyzstan, 09.03.2019, https://cabar.asia/ru/radikalizatsiya-zhenshhin-na-religioznoj-pochve-v-kyrgyzstane/#_edn1
25. https://gtmarket.ru/ratings/global-terrorism-index/info Global Terrorism Index
26. https://barometr.kg/v-kyrgyzstane-v-2019-godu-zablokirovali-97-sajtov-i-300-akkauntov-za-propagandu-ekstremizma

9

Non-Traditional Security Issues in Kyrgyzstan:
Concerns and Cooperation

Dr. Kamala Kumari

ABSTRACT

With the changing dynamics of security, geo-strategy, and international politics, it is necessary to look at an individual state's overall development and progress from time to time. Kyrgyzstan is an example best suited, as it completes three decade of democracy and development. This paper will try to highlight the non-traditional security issues, particularly, the rise of the drug-narcotics business and trafficking apart from looking at major concerns and responses and the potential prospects of cooperation particularly, with India.

Kyrgyzstan is one of the five 'Stans' amongst the former Soviet Central Asian Republics, with Bishkek as its capital. As neighbours, it has Kazakhstan on the northwest and north, China on the east and south, and Tajikistan and Uzbekistan on the south and west. Kyrgyzstan's border runs mostly along mountain crests. Although geographically surrounded by highly mountainous terrain, Kyrgyzstan has been at the crossroads of several great civilizations as part of the Silk Road and other commercial routes. Kyrgyzstan's history spans a variety of cultures and empires, inhabited by a succession of tribes and clans. In modern times, Kyrgyzstan was one of the first to declare independence on 31 August 1991 from the

USSR and establish a democratic government. Nirmala Joshi has highlighted its difference and outlook, which she feels is linked to its 'ingrained sense of equality' very well depicted in the flag of Kyrgyzstan.[1] Kyrgyzstan began its transformation and developmental process immediately after its independence; however, the result has not been as anticipated.

Kyrgyzstan, being a mountainous country, is source of rivers and streams with two important rivers, the Naryn Darya and the Kara Darya, which together further down make the mighty Syr Darya. Kyrgyzstan being an upper riparian country has immense hydropower potential, apart from fertile plains (Fergana Valley), due to the sediment that the rivers bring down from the mountains. However, Kyrgyzstan has so far not been able to utilise the resources to its advantage. Instead, the country in the last three decades has suffered ethnic and political conflict apart from economic troubles. Kyrgyzstan has fared average in terms of development, be it political, economic, or social. However, it has been treading the path of development slowly but steadily.

The slow and steady progress may not be an issue as of now; but the fast pace at which the world is changing around it does pose a challenge. Amidst this dynamism, Kyrgyzstan cannot keep itself isolated from the developments in the region. Keeping the unconventional security environment in mind, that is something to worry about as Kyrgyzstan falls right in the centre of the drug trafficking route.

Security

The traditional security that has been largely considered to be a politico-military concept and traditionally under the military domain is about the threats against the essential values of the state, like the ability to maintain its territorial integrity and political sovereignty, from weapons, armaments systems, military, and diplomatic issues like pacts and alliances aimed at building special relations between states for security purposes. The essence of traditional security, which was best left to the military strategists earlier, has been constantly changing in contemporary times under the impact of technological innovation, new ideas, and political evolution. With the increasing influence of globalisation, and more so with the end of the Cold War, the concept of security has undergone a transformation and, in the process, several changes and inclusions have happened.

At the same time, the attention of policy makers and the strategist community also shifted towards issues and problems associated with migration, transnational crime, environment, human rights, and drug trafficking and are now increasingly being viewed as aspects of non-military or non-traditional security issues; basically, those challenges and issues that pose a threat to the survival and wellbeing of people and states and arise primarily out of non-military sources, more contagious, and challenging the overall security system.

The changing approach towards security stems from the fact that several such issues like migration, drugs and arms trafficking, organised crime, terrorism, etc., have in some way or the other started to regulate the dynamics of national security and also international relations. At times, due to complex security situations, the elements of traditional security are sometimes factors in making certain issues a non-traditional security threat.

Speaking specifically about Kyrgyzstan, traditional security is not much of an issue considering the fact that it is basically being managed by Russia. Though the country's military assets is the lowest amongst the five Republics, the National Security Concept (NSC), which was signed on 12 June 2012, forms the basis for all security documents[2] and needs special mention as Kyrgyzstan's neighbours, Kazakhstan and Uzbekistan, do not publish all their security documents. The Russian Air Force, in 2002, deployed planes at Kant air base in Kyrgyzstan, forming a joint Russian-Kyrgyz air base under the auspices of the Collective Security Treaty.[3] Later, an agreement was signed to transform the Russian military facilities, including "the Kant air base, the Issyk-Kul naval training centre, and the seismic centre in southern Kyrgyzstan, into one united base. It is expected to stay for 15 years", with a possible extension for five years.[4] However, it is the non-traditional security that is a matter of concern, be it ethic conflict, migration, drugs trade and trafficking and other organised crimes. All these create or accelerate the possibility of internal instability, which is the most serious threat that Kyrgyzstan is likely to face.[5] Corruption makes things worse as the issue of corruption is not just a domestic problem, but also a weakness that could be exploited by an adversary, leading to the government and security apparatus becoming vulnerable targets.

It is an acknowledged fact that corruption has been going on for quite some time, and has "always posed a threat to the rule of law and stood in the way of protecting basic civil and economic rights". With the new trends of transformation, corruption has turned into an instrument of national strategy. Albeit, "the growing threat from strategic corruption has gone largely unnoticed or under-appreciated", and the perceived notion is that in recent years, a number of countries, have been using it to their advantage. What was previously a mere feature of their political systems and on a lesser scale is today being transformed into a weapon on the global stage.[6] Keeping in mind the internal political and social dynamics of Kyrgyzstan, it is vulnerable.

With reports highlighting that "the processing of opium into heroin is now being carried out in laboratories located inside Afghanistan and as the chemical precursors primarily, acetic anhydride, required for the process are provided by Russia via Central Asia as it not available in the country", the negative aspect of this provides stimulus to corruption.[7]

Since Kyrgyzstan is right in the middle of all these, it important to look at its non-traditional security environment.

Non-military or Non-traditional Security Environment

The non-traditional security environment in general in Kyrgyzstan is supposedly very complex; from local to regional to transnational, as ill-defined and porous borders allow for the relatively free movement of people and illicit goods, making it vulnerable to transnational threats. The issues are varied; from illegal migration, border issues, corruption, border crimes, arms and drug-narcotics trafficking, smuggling, water, and ethnic and religious conflicts to armed paramilitary groupings, separatism, extremism, terrorism, and cyber-attacks. Also, armed conflicts related to Afghanistan, as Afghanistan shares a porous border with Uzbekistan and Tajikistan and Kyrgyzstan has a porous border with both of them.

Potentially precarious, these criminal activities like organized crime and narco-trafficking are widespread in the south, particularly in Batken and Osh provinces. According to a report by a Russian-American work group, the longest border of Afghanistan—the Afghan-Tajik border—stretching over 1,206 km has only one guard deployed for over 50 km, and the mountainous landscape further complicates the issue and worsens the situation,[8] making it easy for smugglers to cross the Afghan-Tajik border, which serves as the main route for terrorists and drug traffickers into Kyrgyzstan.

Despite legal provisions to prevent illegal border crossings, inter-state border checkpoints remain highly corrupt and often facilitate influx of a large number of illegal migrants. People can "cross the border for a US$ 50-bribe at the Kordai transit post, one of the busiest connections between Kazakhstan and Kyrgyzstan. The Tajik-Uzbek border also has notoriously corrupt transit points. In emergency cases, one needs to bribe both customs officers and taxi drivers in order to cross borders. The bribe ranges between US$ 50 and US$ 200 each way". Thus, transnational crimes are facilitated by exploiting the region's porous frontiers and corrupt border services.[9]

Intertwined with this are unsettled borders, mainly in the Fergana Valley, adding to the larger concern that exists. Ambiguous borders, particularly around six enclaves in the Batken can give rise to skirmishes over water and grazing rights. Some of these skirmishes can turn violent as well. It has been reported that "along the Batken border, around 16 border conflicts took place, 13 of them took place on the Kyrgyz-Tajik border; 2 on the Kyrgyz-Uzbek, and 1 on the Kyrgyz-Kazakh border; some cases of illegal border crossings also occurred in just 10 months in 2019".[10] The rugged terrain and lack of resources make it difficult for the authorities to control the borders adequately.

Though it is difficult to pinpoint the real causes of ethnic conflict, however, the drug link is very much clear, though "the 'cause and effect' characteristics are ambiguous while the role of the drug industry and transnational or local crime is hard to measure. Sometimes, the shadow economy looms large due to money laundering, giving rise to various drug and crime-related issues". Moreover, a relatively weak state and the corruption factor in Kyrgyzstan during the first decade of this century "post-Tulip Revolution in 2005, made drug trafficking and criminal activities easier, indicating the murky link between drugs, crime, and the state".[11]

Even though the important factors in most of the conflicts are seen as being driven by external factors, such as "Islamic radicals exploiting socio-economic grievances and the extreme politicisation of ethnicity and identity, the role of organised crime in the outbreak of ethnic conflict" cannot be ignored. Actually, there exists interplay between external and domestic factors as well as the "link between local/regional organised crime and the corruption in politics".[12]

Radicalisation in Kyrgyzstan is another complex phenomenon, driven by a combination of factors. Survey-based research on "youth has observed that the risk of radicalisation is higher among certain religious groups as well as in certain geographic parts of the country". "Sympathisers of Salafi groups are more vulnerable to radicalisation than those sympathising with modern Turkish groups, such as Hizmet and Nurcu". Also, the youth from the southern regions of the Batken and Osh are more vulnerable. These regions have a recent history of inter-ethnic conflict. Youth in the northern Kyrgyzstan like "in Naryn, Issyk-Kul and Chui provinces are more resilient to radical religious ideas".[13]

Also, though rare, "terrorist-related activities, for example the 2016 Chinese Embassy suicide bombing incident in Bishkek and continued reports of terrorism-related arrests in 2019" and "reports of returning ISIS fighters, even as the government claims that these individuals are captured upon their arrival in Kyrgyzstan", underscore the potential threat, terrorism poses.[14] The porous, mountainous borders, particularly in the south, make Kyrgyzstan a potential transit route for terrorists as well. Besides, as Anna Matveeva mentions, "...in Kyrgyzstan the Muslim minority finds jihadi ideas attractive...jihadis regard the state as their enemy and a legitimate target"; however, this does not apply to wider society "whose hearts and mind they seek to conquer". Also, the rise of the Islamic State (IS) brought terrorism back to the political agenda. Since the "end of 2016, the government had registered 863 citizens from Kyrgyzstan who had travelled to foreign fighting zones, most of them to join the IS and other jihadist groups in Syria". According to government figures, "most recruits (more than three-quarters) hailed from southern Kyrgyzstan, with an over-representation of ethnic minorities".[15]

Smuggling is another issue that has been an increasing problem in Kyrgyzstan in the post-Soviet period. Situated on the ancient Silk Road, Kyrgyzstan is a "natural transit point for various legal and illegal goods". Illicit trade has already grown to a point where it "threatens national security, since it destroys the internal market for legal goods, promotes bribery, strengthens organised crime groups and various political criminals and encourages money laundering". In general, "corruption, the presence of organised crime and a high level of collusion on the one hand and illicit trade on the other are mutually reinforcing".[16] It would not be wrong to say that drugs is a pressing issue and has always been so, due to the fact that at times it is also used "as a political tool, and illicit narcotics play a major role directly and indirectly in the emergence of insecurity and instability".[17]

Thus, most of the above-mentioned issues are mostly by-products of a drug economy or facilitate and accelerate the illicit drug trade. In other words, Kyrgyzstan is at the epicentre of the global narcotics trade and the drugs issue is the biggest challenge and the real perceived threat to its national security.

Drugs

As mentioned earlier, the drugs situation in Kyrgyzstan is influenced by both internal as well as external factors. The internal factors include poverty, unemployment, porous borders, illegal migration, corruption, "existence of domestic raw material base for drugs production and insufficient funding and technical equipping of the state anti-drug agencies". The external factors are proximity to Afghanistan as a main source of drug production, "international drug mafia activities in the region, absence of unified approach to regional drug security, and permeability of the state borders".[18]

Narco-trafficking and its ill-effects have affected the entire region as it is "inextricably linked with the rise of the Taliban and, along with it, the increase in the production of opium and its trafficking to Russia and Europe through Central Asia". The narco-traffic originating in Afghanistan has "pumped a lot of money into the hands of drug smugglers" in the region, posing a severe challenge for all the CARs,[19] particularly Kyrgyzstan, as it is located on one of the major drug-trafficking routes from Afghanistan to Russia and Europe.

Drugs, mostly heroin, are brought from Afghan labs to Tajikistan and then into Osh in the southern part of Kyrgyzstan as it shares a long, poorly controlled border with Tajikistan, which mostly runs through mountainous terrain. From Osh, it is sent to Bishkek and, from there, across the border to Kazakhstan, and on to Russia.[20] All these factors deeply impact the dynamics of the opium business in the region, in particular, Kyrgyzstan, as Osh is the capital of narco-traffic activity and a major cause of domestic tensions. Osh, which is in the Ferghana Valley, is known as the 'capital of the South' or 'drug capital'. Several factors contribute to Osh being a major hub for Afghan heroin or the regional drug capital; one, is its geographical location. According to Rayhan Demytrie, who has been investigating the impact of drug trafficking, "a quarter of the world's heroin is believed to travel through Central Asia on its way to Russia and Europe". "Osh is a key hub along the route. Lack of jobs, craze for hip hop lifestyle, etc., and youngsters feel it is cool to sniff and take a few puffs once or twice...then, they get hooked to it".[21]

Narco money has seeped into the political process. "The role that drug money plays in making and breaking governments in this region is certainly known to exist, as long as the drug trade from Afghanistan continues almost uncurbed". It is well known, that profits from narco-trafficking have been one of the major sources of sustenance for the Taliban. According to the United Nations Office on Drugs and Crime (UNODC), Afghanistan continues to be the number one producer and cultivator of opium.[22] The threat has been growing as is evidenced by the fact that "poppy cultivation in Afghanistan jumped by 87 per cent to a record level of 9,000 metric tons in 2017. The area under poppy cultivation increased to 328,000 hectares, up to 63 per cent compared to 201,000 hectares in 2016".[23]

The "drug money is so indispensable in the region, that should narcotics production be sharply curtailed in Afghanistan, it might reappear in Kyrgyzstan, even in Tajikistan and Uzbekistan, due to the right climate-soil conditions for cultivation". In fact, during the Soviet period, Kyrgyzstan produced some of the highest grade opium in the world, though, as believed, it was grown for medicinal purposes.[24] There are also extensive thickets of wild cannabis and ephedra in the country, which "contribute to the production of narcotic drugs such as hashish, marijuana, methcathinone, and ephedron". These drugs of the cannabis group had mostly been seized "from 1974 to 1993; however, the volume of illicit trafficking of Afghan origin opioids increased dramatically since 1993, leading to growth of their usage and involvement of certain parts of the population in the criminal drug business". As a result, the share of diacetylmorphine (heroin) use grew by 1999. Also, because of its proximity to Afghanistan where more than "90 per cent of the world's illicit opioids are produced", Kyrgyzstan faces all the "consequences of transit through its territory".[25]

The nature of limited resources and the weakness of the forces to deal successfully with armed groups engaged in narcotics trafficking[26] is another challenge. An "increased production would only serve to reinforce Kyrgyzstan's role in the drug transit and this could lead to more intense battles between illicit networks for control of transit and revenues leading to manifestations of other problems". The network among "drugs and arms smugglers and human trafficking rackets is very well coordinated and strong", as criminals take advantage of the long porous borders to carry out their activities thus, "accelerating the potential threat of organised crimes".[27]

The production and illegal trafficking of narco-drugs, as assumed, would be a highly contentious issue for the region in the near future. Another interconnected issue is the on-going insurgency and the Taliban facilitating the proliferation of arms in the region. In the process, drug cartels and criminal groups have sprung up operating near the border. These groups ensure the safe passage of narcotics from Afghanistan across to Kyrgyzstan through Tajikistan. The proliferation of drugs is a blight on the economic and social environment and a threat to the traditional system of values. Drug addiction "damages the physical, psychological, and emotional health of the whole society, wreaking particular havoc on the younger generation". Society has been at risk from drugs in a number of different ways as the "flourishing drug trade enables separatist, radical, religious, and terrorist movements to spring up and become financially self-sufficient..[28]

The situation becomes very challenging for the government, due to the negative fallout of trafficking, which is the growing number of addicts each day. Even as early as in 2012, according to data from the regional centre in Osh, "there were 530 registered drug addicts in the Osh region and 1,400 in the city." According to the Centre's chief, Abdul Sadieva, "the real figure could be even higher". "Despite awareness about the negative impact of trafficking and addiction, 'trafficking has been facilitated by the ineffectiveness of border control...lack of training and equipping of border guards'. Besides, mistrust and border disputes also facilitate trafficking".[29]

In the recently held 63rd session of the Commission on Narcotic Drugs held in Vienna, Austria, from 2 to 6 March 2020, the Head of the delegation of the Kyrgyz Republic, Oleg Zapolsky, Head of the Counter-Narcotic Service (CNS) under the Kyrgyz Ministry of Interior, expressed his concern that

> "due to the rapid spread of narcotic substances, increased advertising in the internet and expressed readiness to further the active work to eliminate this phenomenon in the country, with broader involvement of youth to drug use prevention measures", the situation was alarming.
>
> According to the Report, "The emergence of so-called "new psychoactive substances", widespread advertising and distribution

> of controlled substances through online technologies, the active use of electronic payment systems and the contactless method of selling drugs, and much more, indicates a new phase in the history of drug control system where we are now", said Mr. Zapolsky. "New challenges and threats have become an objective reality and need to be understood to adopt adequate counter-measures. In this case, the importance of drug prevention as a universal way to improve the impact on the drug-related situation is growing significantly and the main focus in this work should be on young people. With their support, we must build an effective system to counter new challenges and threats".[30]

According to Andrey Seleznev, Head of the United Nations Drugs and Crime Programme Office in the Kyrgyz Republic, "Drug abuse is a serious threat to human health, safety and well-being". He highlighted that "work is aimed at providing comprehensive assistance to the Government of the Kyrgyz Republic in strengthening the capacity of state authorities in combating the illegal spread of narcotic substances, building comprehensive, international and interagency cooperation in eradicating this global threat". Kyrgyzstan, in turn, is actively working to improve national legislation. This includes, first of all, the new version of the Law on Drugs, the new Counter-Narcotics Programme of the Government and the Plan for its implementation, new bylaws and regulatory acts.[31]

It is evident that the drug menace is one of the real issues that make the other non-traditional issues more challenging.

Concerns

Concerns regarding non-military or non-traditional security issues, which are plenty, are genuine and with enormous repercussions on developmental policies, apart from social implications like emergence of a drug culture amongst youth, which makes them vulnerable to human trafficking and drug-related crimes. The situation is complex as most of these issues are interconnected and until and unless they are solved, the concerns will remain.

The non-traditional security threat is not a recent phenomenon; it has been there for a long time. In recent times, though, debates and discussions around security has broadened. They have not really succeeded in cohesively including transnational organised crime and drug trafficking as a security issue.

As a result, weak states in developing and post-Communist regions are experiencing an increasingly negative effect of these phenomena on security in the military, political, economic, and societal sense. These issues are a prominent example of the links between drug trafficking and military threats to security. The Islamic Movement of Uzbekistan (IMU) has been a major actor in the drug trade from Afghanistan to Central Asia and the most violent non-state actor in the region. Even the Kyrgyz government, at one point, had assessed that the "IMU was responsible for about 70 per cent of the drug crime in the region". It has also been suggested that it was more than just a "criminal organisation using terrorist activities and military campaigns as devices to obscure or protect its drug business".[32] The link between the drug trade and armed conflict is of fundamental importance for understanding the challenges to security, particularly in this region.[33] Also, with trends in violent conflicts pointing to increasing connections between organised crime, actors of conflicts and terrorists, and to the 'nexus' which is unlikely to abate in the near future, makes the situation more complex and challenging.[34] Kyrgyzstan is very likely already facing such a situation.

The menace of drugs has always been an issue in Kyrgyzstan. In earlier times, "from 1916 to 1974, the country held a leading position in the world" with regard to industrial production of medicinal opium. It was estimated to have reached "80 per cent of the USSR production of medicinal opium and was equal to 16 per cent of the global legal opium production". However, the Presidium of the Supreme Soviet of the USSR in 1974 decided to terminate legal cultivation of opium poppy in the Kyrgyz SSR, as it seemed "one tenth of produced opium leaked into illicit traffic, causing drug addiction of the population".[35]

The drug trafficking phenomenon even today has been posing serious threats of a societal, economic, and political nature. There has been a "dramatic increase in drug addiction (gradually changing from the abuse of opium to its highly addictive derivative, heroin), the explosion of HIV/AIDS among intravenous drug users, a noticeable increase in drug-related crimes, and the increasing involvement of the population in drug-related activities leading to a drug culture, especially among youth". The economic threats include the "growing corruption of state officials, border guards, law enforcement and customs officers. The political threats include the challenges posed by transnational criminal groups to weaken state institutions by corrupting and infiltrating them".[36]

Drug trafficking undermines the social structures and political systems and the government's inability to deal with the devastating effects of the drug trade makes way for interference by external powers, making the situation even more complex and challenging. The top leaders have from time to time highlighted the underlying threat as "Kyrgyzstan serves as a transit for narcotics carriers and if not restrained decisively", and timely, the drug mafia's role in making and breaking governments might turn out to be true.[37]

The linkages between crime and terrorism are too complex to be explained through the framework of a 'crime–terror nexus'. The locally embedded militant networks actively seek to control both the moral order and the political economy of their localities, though international terrorist actors have limited linkages to organised crime. However, "the most productive relationship for criminal networks is with the state and this 'state-crime nexus' has more analytical utility than a framework that links crime to terrorism, though it sidelines other social actors".[38]

Besides, the link between the drug trade and radical ethnic and religious groups complicates the matter further as the connection between religious extremist groups and contraband weapons, terrorist activity and the drug trade exists. Often sighted, the Islamic extremist threat emerged on Kyrgyzstan's political agenda in the late 1990s, as the radical 'foreign' Islamic influences found "fertile ground in Osh, the more religiously conscious southern part of Kyrgyzstan. Also, as the central governmental control was weaker in the south than in the north, Osh had become the 'capital' of Wahhabism".[39] The region is still considered to be as sensitive and vulnerable as before due to economic issues like poverty, unemployment, lack of opportunities for higher education, etc., that have been the main reasons for these problematic issues like drug trafficking, organised crime, ethnic conflicts, militancy, and radicalisation.

The Tajikistan and Afghanistan factors further complicates the matter.

Tajikistan is not only an issue with regard to drug trafficking and organised crime but also a potential threat of border conflict. If small scale incidents that are common in the Batken and Isfra regions are not tackled in time, they could lead to a security threat. "Petty disputes could lead to ethnic polarisation, and the new nationhood ideologies of 'us against them' association, which is a result of fear", become a catalyst for "identity formation in cross-border communities and reinforces the perceptions of collective insecurity", and further fosters the emergence of strong ethnic borderland identities.[40]

Besides, "Kyrgyzstan's border issues have always been considered too complex and sensitive to develop policies and initiatives". However, in March 2020, the Kyrgyz President, Sooronbai Jeenbekov, during his visit to the Batken region, stressed, the "importance of resolving cross-border disputes constructively, through 'wisdom and endurance' requiring negotiations", apart from "considering the local population's views". Development slowed down due to the COVID-19 pandemic, and Kyrgyzstan had to take unprecedented measures to limit border crossings and interaction with regard to cargo transportation and movement of goods.[41] Moreover, the border issue is so intricate that it is equally difficult to implement policy initiatives.

Besides, it is not the porous border alone that escalates conflict in the Batken-Isfara area; rather, it has been the "greater focus on security through the militarisation of borders that has transformed the nature of relations". Strict border regimes often "contribute to instability instead of strengthening the fragile peace by hampering cross-border movement across invisible frontiers that have been long governed by established rules, traditions and history". The involvement of border guards and the use of military hardware are more likely to escalate the conflict to a completely new level.[42]

This phenomenon is very common around the Tajik border exclaves, as trouble sparks periodically and the fragility of the border signifies its potential as a flashpoint. The "increased focus on border security has exacerbated and in some cases generated conflict, as people who were once able to easily move across the invisible frontier, governed by local rules and history are not able to do so. Now the national governments are trying to play a bigger role and not always doing so with sensitivity to local rules". Therefore, the border remains a national-level concern and the fluid borders with a booming drug trade from Afghanistan northward pose a potential security risk.[43]

> There are several instances for example: The only road linking residents of Vorukh, a Tajik enclave in Kyrgyzstan's southernmost province, to the rest of Tajikistan opened on 25 July after a three-day blockade. The road had been blocked unlawfully following a flare-up of violence for two days, which left one person dead, 30 people injured and several hundred villagers evacuated. Sometimes,

intervention by national governments and international actors may disrupt the delicate balance of social and economic life on the border, leading to conflicts. Although, many of the "well-intentioned" initiatives like some infrastructure projects or policies meant to enhance security, actually end up intensifying local tensions. Like, for example, in 2008, "a road was built with World Bank support that bypassed Tajik enclaves to link Kyrgyz villages with the nearest regional capital was supposed to give locals a sense of connectivity; instead, it made Vorukh's Tajik community feel cut off....The nature of government intervention in terms of projects that simultaneously separate and connect, enhance security, and exacerbate threats, extends into citizens' expectations from the state"....There have been some "instances when Ferghana Valley communities have preferred the government to stay out of local affairs". Kyrgyz political scientist Emil Dzhuraev recently argued in the local *'El-Gezit'* that "Bishkek and Dushanbe have erred in consistently ignoring their distant border regions; citizens there are resentful about having been left to fend for themselves. Kyrgyzstan and Tajikistan's recent renewed interest in border delimitation suggests that the governments want to dedicate more attention and resources to the communities living in the Ferghana Valley". However, sometimes, these words and photo-worthy meetings seem to be void and sound hollow.[44]

The security issue and the instability in Afghanistan further complicates the problem due to opium cultivation and drug trafficking. The drug trade will continue to flourish until serious steps are taken to promote greater political and economic stability, as poor economic conditions only promote such menaces.

Regardless of national and regional initiatives, Kyrgyzstan still faces serious hurdles in turning words into action.

These issues and concerns highlight the point that unconventional security challenges like those mentioned above do have the potential to challenge national security and, hence, require more attention.

Response to the Challenge of Non-Traditional Threats

The changes in the approach towards traditional security have also changed the way the non-traditional security issues are being approached, especially with regard to the response to the challenges of non-traditional issues.

Changes in areas like "...weapons and armaments as a means of traditional security are incomparably more advanced today than in past times, a new form of cooperation is gaining momentum at the regional level, complementing and gradually overcoming the tried and tested form of military alliances",[45] that shapes the security programmes of most of the states. With regard to non-traditional security also, several policy changes are taking place so as to complement the national security priorities.

With regard to Kyrgyzstan as well, several steps have been planned to deal with non-traditional issues.

As for narco-drugs, the Parliament of Kyrgyzstan in 1994 decided "to join the Single Convention on Narcotic Drugs of 1961, the Convention on Psychotropic Substances of 1971 and the UN Convention against Illicit Traffic in Narcotic Drugs and Psychotropic Substances of 1988". Since then, Kyrgyzstan has been fulfilling the requirements and norms of international law and follows the guidelines of the International Narcotics Control Board (INCB).[46] Kyrgyzstan has attempted to deal with the threat of drug production and trafficking in several ways, including establishing a National Drug Intelligence Unit. The government has also worked on "writing anti-trafficking legislation stepping up interdiction activities, and increasing its cooperation with the western states". Kyrgyzstan has also "signed all the major United Nations drug conventions, and is party to several regional initiatives like the Shanghai Summit Declaration" (August 1999). This, 'eleven-point' declaration "pledged cooperation in fighting terrorism, arms and drug trafficking, national separatism, and religious extremism".[47]

Kyrgyzstan continues to step up its efforts in terms of drug prevention, health protection, education, law enforcement, and local government agencies, civil society, parents, and the media, along with coordination with the state authority on drug control, to implement drug prevention measures, primary drug prevention through workshops and educational events, secondary drug prevention in general, and specialized treatment to drug and other psychoactive substances addiction through health care organisations. Though there are not any "fully functional rehabilitation centres under the Ministry of Health of Kyrgyzstan, there are harm reduction programmes targeted at injecting drug users, implemented by medical experts, social workers, and law enforcement and local government bodies, which are part of the tertiary prevention". Also, comprehending the significance of international cooperation drug combating, Kyrgyzstan actively develops international coordination systems.[48]

Kyrgyzstan correspondingly entered the "global system of control over narcotic drugs, psychotropic substances, and precursors". In 2017, by a decision of the Economic and Social Council (ECOSOC), Kyrgyzstan rejoined the "Commission on Narcotic Drugs with the right to vote until 2021".[49]

In addition, the foreign policy concept of Kyrgyzstan prioritises "the full legal designation of the state border, and building and strengthening of confidence-building measures in border areas with neighbouring countries".[50] Kyrgyzstan's National Development Strategy for 2018-2020 reflects the same.[51]

Kyrgyzstan, recognising the UN mandate in the field of crime prevention and criminal justice, consistently respects all its international obligations and actively cooperates at the regional and global levels in order to combat crime.

The international community also, aware of the threat in this region, has developed several limited assistance programs "to help curb the growing problem of narcotics production and trafficking in Kyrgyzstan, and providing technical assistance for anti-drug programs and law-enforcement training". Since 1993, the United Nations Drug Control Program has provided anti-trafficking assistance. The "UNODC has played a leading role in establishing drug control agencies and drug control programmes in spite of bureaucratic impediments and limited resources". The 'Osh Knot' project for cross-border cooperation and coordinating law enforcement bodies in the Ferghana Valley in the late 1990s is one such example, and it made some progress, though it was dismantled later on.[52] There is also the United Nations Development Assistance Framework for 2018-2022 as well.[53]

UNODC's Regional Office for Central Asia (ROCA) Programme in Bishkek focuses on "strengthening capacities to confront threats from transnational organised crime, supporting implementation of a balanced, comprehensive and evidence-based approach to the drug problem that addresses both supply and demand, strengthening crime prevention and building effective criminal justice systems, tackling corruption and its catastrophic impact on societies, and countering terrorism", including implementation of the 19 international legal instruments against terrorism.[54]

UNODC, in co-operation with the OSCE centre in Bishkek, conducted a series of events in Batken, Osh, and Jalal-Abad in the south of Kyrgyzstan from 26 to 28 June 2014 to enhance public confidence in the Kyrgyz police.[55]

The Central Asian Regional Information and Coordination Centre (CARICC) serves as the "information and coordination platform for combating the illicit trafficking of narcotic drugs, psychotropic substances and their precursors". The Border Cooperation Component of the UNODC Programme for Central Asia is designed "to counter the trafficking of Afghan opiates through the northern route by establishing border liaison offices (BLOs) at key border crossing points (BCPs), and is considered as a key element for enhanced cross-border communication and intelligence-sharing" in order to "detect and intercept smuggling, including narcotic drugs, psychotropic substances and precursor chemicals, while facilitating legitimate international trade".[56]

The UNODC Program for Central Asia 2015-2021, which is financially supported by the governments of Japan, the USA, and Russia, through its programme office in Kyrgyzstan, provides "active support to the Counter-Narcotics Service (CNS) under the Ministry of Interior of Kyrgyzstan "within the framework of Sub-program 1: 'Combating transnational organised crime, illicit drug trafficking, and prevention of terrorism' and, thus, UNODC also contributes to enhancing the security of Kyrgyzstan".[57]

According to the UN Office on Drugs and Crime, through its rapid assessment that was conducted recently, the Central Asia Regional office stated that, "COVID-19 has impacted the drug market: production, trafficking and use pattern...The operation regime of 'Trust points' in Kyrgyzstan has also been simplified for its outreach workers; some have started e-portals and the use of phones, social support and detoxification/ rehabilitation services has increased".[58]

According to the UNODC 2019 report, in order to "institutionalise crime prevention work, UNODC's implementing partner 'Foundation for Tolerance International' (FTI) and the 'Management Academy' signed a memorandum of understanding (MoU) to introduce a course on crime prevention in the curriculum of the academy", which is the main training institution for staff of local self-government.[59]

UNODC, recently, on 25-26 November 2020, conducted a two-day webinar, on 'the merits of intelligence-led policing and the use of software' with the objective "to enhance the crime analysis capacity of the agencies in combating illicit drug trafficking and explain the concept of intelligence-led policing for the investigators and operative officers from the law enforcement agencies of Kyrgyzstan". Around twenty-one, mid- to senior-level officers from the Ministry of Internal Affairs and State Border Guards Service of Kyrgyzstan participated. The workshop aimed to "increase the potential of law enforcement agencies on intelligence gathering and information management".[60]

The UNODC and Counter Narcotics Service of the Kyrgyz Ministry of Interior enhanced their cooperation. "One of the initiatives is to combat illegal drug trafficking and also to 'Support to Drug Control' programme, in Kyrgyzstan.[61] As highlighted by Yoshihiro Yamamuro, Ambassador Extraordinary and Plenipotentiary of Japan to Kyrgyzstan, the "spread of drug abuse is still one of the global threats and the successful fight against the drug threat directly depends on the close cooperation of the relevant departments of the countries of the region with international organisations". He opined that "UNODC projects make a significant contribution with a systematic approach and active efforts at all available levels will contribute to combating illicit drug trafficking and have a positive impact on security both in Kyrgyzstan and in the region as a whole". In this regard, UNODC received funds amounting to US$ 2.7 million in March 2018 from the Government of Japan to support drug control efforts in Kyrgyzstan.[62]

The "Support to Drug Control in Kyrgyzstan", initiative, which is funded by the Government of Japan and UNODC "procured all necessary equipment and vehicles and initiated construction of administrative facilities for the Counter-Narcotics Service in Talas, Jalal-Abad, and Karkyra". Likewise, funded by the US State Department Bureau of International Narcotics and Law Enforcement Affairs, the "Drug Law Enforcement Systems for Criminal Intelligence Collection, Analysis and Exchange and Pilot Intelligence-Led Policing initiative (ILP), enhanced the law enforcement officers' skills, increased their knowledge in intelligence gathering and added information management to support on-going investigations by creating and providing sophisticated analytical reports". In 2019, "seven 'Intelligence analysis' and 'Intelligence-led policing' trainings were provided to over 126 law enforcement officers/analysts at different levels". Using the intelligence enables them "to identify hotspots, repeat offenders, threats, and risks. In a way, the ILP initiative complements community policing, which aims to build trust and develop communication between the police and the public".[63]

Also, according to the 2019 report, UNODC, in 2019, "started a new project 'Establishment of Mobile Operational Teams in Kyrgyzstan' funded by the Russian Federation. It brought its best expertise to the search complexes (multi-terrain vehicles, and UAVs), synergy (for example, UAVs to be used in interests of all law-enforcement agencies) and contribute to improvement and development of relevant legal acts, and regulating the use of UAVs". In continuation, the next step is to deliver "special training and procure the equipment". The project's "successful implementation will allow Kyrgyz law-enforcement agencies to save and optimize resources, identify new channels of smuggling drugs, trafficking of human beings, illegal cultivation, better investigation of transnational crimes by identifying and collecting new evidences and provide faster incidence responses". Several seizures were done like "13 kg heroin in Bishkek and averting the smuggling of Afghan opiates and heroin".[64]

In June 2020, the United Nations Office on Drugs and Crime (UNODC) Regional Office for Central Asia, conducted a series of online Coordination Group Meetings in Kyrgyzstan with the Chairperson of the State Customs Service under the Government on 3 June 2020, "under the UNODC-World Customs Organization (WCO) Global Container Control Programme (CCP) with the purpose of holding consultations with CCP beneficiary agencies to review CCP progress" and plan "future cooperative initiatives including distance learning activities for 2020".[65]

Recently, 29 October 2020 marked the opening of a newly-refurbished analytical centre for Kyrgyzstan's Counter Narcotics Service (CNS). As part of a "larger US$ 200,000 initiative funded by the US Department of State and coordinated by the UN Office of Drugs and Crime, the refurbishment project upgraded the physical facility to modern standards and provided a dedicated server, computers, and internally secured network". The US government-funded project also provided "training for analytical officers and a new ArcGIS mapping and i2 intelligence analysis software". The CNS centre's analytical products have already helped "seize large shipments of opiates and psychotropic substances", and destroy narcotics shipments generally smuggled through Kyrgyzstan to markets in Kazakhstan, Russia, and the European Union.[66]

Overall, the response to non-traditional challenges has been forthcoming and there is immense potential for further cooperation. In this regard, it is important to look at the India-Kyrgyzstan partnership.

India and the Kyrgyzstan Way Forward

India, like Kyrgyzstan, has been dealing with several non-traditional security issues for years and over the past few decades, there have been very vocal and persistent flagging of these issues on several international forums.

Keeping the already warm and cordial relations that the two countries share in view, there is immense potential in the bilateral relations, which India elevated to a strategic partnership in 2019.

Ties between India and Kyrgyzstan have traditionally been warm and friendly, thanks to India's historical and civilisational links and its enduring cultural and spiritual connect. After the independence of Kyrgyzstan on 31 August 1991, India was among the first countries to establish diplomatic relations in March 1992. A resident mission of India was set up in May 1994. Prime Minister Narendra Modi visited Kyrgyzstan in 2015, which was the first prime ministerial visit from India to that country after a gap of 20 years.

India has been working hard to do away with all possible hitches with regard to business, trade, and commerce. The Prime Minister during his 2019 (13-14 June) visit to Bishkek announced a line of credit of US$ 200 million for financing development projects in Kyrgyzstan. It is most likely the two countries would work in tandem towards counter-terrorism and drug and narcotics control as India has expertise and experience on these two very common concerns. India is positioned between the two most popular routes of drug trafficking—the 'golden triangle' and the 'golden crescent'—the major opium production regions in the world. Most of the opium fields are controlled by the Pakistani ISI, which later transports opium poppy to Pakistan for processing into heroin and then traffics it all over the world through the two routes.

Recently, a new route has come into play. The governments of Tanzania, Mozambique, and South Africa have seized back-to-back heroin consignments originating from Pakistan. Pakistani nationals have also been arrested in some of these cases. Earlier, the 'Golden Crescent' was the most prominent route used by the ISI to traffic heroin. However, these seizures highlight that a new southern route of drug trafficking has been established, comprising a well-established supply chain. Due to back-to-back seizures of Pakistani drugs in the Indian Ocean Region and along the Line of Control

(LoC) by Indian security agencies, Pakistan is now using this new route to traffic drugs to India,[67] further complicating the situation.

The UNODC Representative of South Asia, Sergey Kapinos, has on several platforms raised the seriousness of the situation regarding drug crimes in the region and called for cooperation with regard to information and intelligence sharing. He had also called upon the Minister of State for Home Affairs, Kiren Rijiju, in New Delhi on 28 December 2016 to apprise him about the global and regional trends in trafficking and other forms of transnational organized crime. Rijiju assured necessary support and cooperation.

The National Academy of Customs, Excise, and Narcotics (NACEN), Financial Intelligence Unit, and Enforcement Directorate of the Government of India, cooperate with UNODC. The importance of UNODC-NACEN cooperation in the area of drug law enforcement and linked capacity-building initiatives, particularly in building on the UNODC's eLearning programme in India[68] could be further extended to Kyrgyzstan as well.

Therefore, emphasis is being given to counter-narcotics measures and it is expected that the two countries will cooperate and coordinate in this regard. India and Kyrgyzstan have together attended several conferences and summits on terrorism, drugs, and crimes so as to have a better understanding of the challenges and mechanism to solve and cooperate with other like-minded partners to work together and make the region safer.[69] The SCO summit 2019 discussed the non-conventional issues such as the fight against drug trafficking and terrorism apart from other issues.[70] It is hoped that both India and Kyrgyzstan would be able to share expertise, information, and intelligence to move forward in this regard. Even the SCO Secretary-General, Vladimir Norov, on several occasions and on several platforms, has highlighted that SCO too has been working on important issue like terrorism, extremism, drugs and crimes.[71] India has been dedicated on this sensitive issue and, earlier this year, organised a two-day conference on 'Combating Drug Trafficking for the Bay of Bengal Initiative for Multi-Sectoral Technical and Economic Cooperation (BIMSTEC) on 14 February 2020.[7]

The potential for cooperation is also in fields like education, agriculture, medicines and pharmaceuticals, and tourism. Common security concerns like threats of terrorism, extremism, and drug-trafficking are an added incentive for an enhanced India and Kyrgyzstan partnership.

At this point, it would be appropriate to say that cooperation between India and Kyrgyzstan is taking shape and indicates a fruitful future.

Conclusion

Non-traditional or non-military security issues in Kyrgyzstan are very complex, ranging from local to regional to transnational. The issues are varied, from illegal migration, border issues, corruption, border crimes, arms and drug-narcotics trafficking, smuggling, water, ethnic and religious conflicts to armed paramilitary groupings, separatism, extremism, terrorism, and cyber-attacks. There also armed conflicts related to Afghanistan. The problem of drugs due to the ever-expanding drug market, drug addicts (largely youth) and the crime-drug-terror nexus, is the most challenging as it is the key link for other issues.

The multiplicity of security challenges like porous borders, ethnic clashes, mass migration, narco-drug trafficking, extremism, terrorism, rising unemployment, the Afghan conundrum and so on are several issues and concerns, apart from the emergence of a drug culture amongst the youth, that makes them vulnerable to human trafficking and drug-crimes. These reasons are sufficient to substantiate the fact that non-traditional security issues are not mere concerns as they do have the potential to challenge national security and hence require more attention.

Keeping these concerns in mind, there seems to be changes in the way non-traditional security issues are being approached these days. Responses to non-traditional challenges have been forthcoming both by the national government and also by other countries like Russia, Japan, and the USA, apart from UNODC and other agencies.

There is immense potential for further cooperation, particularly between India and Kyrgyzstan. Since both India and Kyrgyzstan share some common concerns like drug trafficking and terrorism, they would be able to share their experiences, expertise and intelligence for countering terrorism and drug trafficking and move forward together. India-Kyrgyzstan cooperation has already taken shape and points to a promising future.

REFERENCES

1. Nirmala Joshi, "Kyrgyzstan: The road to stability", 12 September 2011, Gateway House, https://www.gatewayhouse.in/kyrgyzstan-road-stability/
2. For details, refer to https://vesti.kg/component/k2/item/13270-kontseptsiya-natsionalnoy-bezopasnosti-kyirgyizskoy-respubliki.html; http://www.vesti.kg/index.php?option=com_k2&view=item&id=13270&Itemid=117
3. Antoine Blua, Central Asia: India Forging Stronger Regional Military Ties, 19 February 2003, https://www.rferl.org/a/1102280.html
4. Anna Matveeva, "Russia's changing security role in Central Asia", *European Security*, 22April 2013, pp. 478-499, 485, https://www.tandfonline.com/doi/pdf/10.1080/09662839.2013.775121. Accessed on 27 October, 2020
5. https://www.sipri.org/publications/2014/sipri-policy-briefs/external-support-central-asian-military-and-security-forces
6. Philip Zelikow, Eric Edelman, Kristofer Harrison, and Celeste Ward Gventer, "The Rise of Strategic Corruption: How States Weaponize Graft", July/August 2020. https://www.foreignaffairs.com/articles/united-states/2020-06-09/rise-strategic-corruption?utm_medium=newsletters&utm_source=weekend_read&utmcontent=20201121& utm_campaign=FA%20Weekend_112120_The%20Rise%20of%20 Strategic %20Corruption&utm _term=FA%20Weekend%20Read-012320. Accessed on 18 November 2020.
7. Nirmala Joshi and Kamala Kumari, "Understanding Central Asia's Security and Economic Interests", *India Quarterly*, Volume 75, Issue 1, March 2019, pp. 29–42.
8. Aleksandra Bolonina, "Security Dimension Of China's Presence In Central Asia", *Asia Focus* #108, April 2019, https://www.iris-france.org/wp-content/uploads/2019/04/Asia-Focus-108-Eng.pdf
9. Kamala Kumari, "Security Issues and Security and Military Capabilities of Central Asian Republics: An Overview", in *Central Asia Today: Issues and Concern's*, Academic Excellence, Delhi, 2019, pp. 246-289, ISBN No.: 978-93-83246-71-7.
10. December 5, 2019, "How many conflicts were there on the border with Kyrgyzstan in 10 months of 2019?" https://ru.reporter.kg/skolko-konfliktov-proizoshlo-na-granitse-s-kyrgyzstanom-za-10-mesiatsev-2019-go-podrobnosti/. Accessed on 6 November 2020.
11. Erik Leijonmarck and Camilla Asyrankulova, "The Role of Organized Crime and Drug Trafficking in Kyrgyzstan's Ethnic Crisis", *Policy Brief*, No. 39, 13 October 2010, https://isdp.eu/content/uploads/publications/2010_leijonmarck-asyrankulova_the-role-of-organized-crime.pdf
12. Erik Leijonmarck and Camilla Asyrankulova, "The Role of Organized Crime and Drug Trafficking in Kyrgyzstan's Ethnic Crisis", Policy Briefs, 13 October 2010, No. 39.
13. Emil Nasritdinov, Zarina Urmanbetova, Kanatbek Murzakhalilov and Mametbek Myrzabaev, " Vulnerability and Resilience of Young People in Kyrgyzstan to Radicalization, Violence and Extremism: Analysis across Five Domains ", Research Institute for Islamic Studies, Bishkek, Kyrgyzstan, CAP paper, No. 213, January 2019, https://centralasiaprogram.org/wp-content/uploads/2019/02/CAP-paper-213-Emil-Nasritdinov.pdf
14. https://www.state.gov/reports/country-reports-on-terrorism-2019/kyrgyz-republic/

15. Anna Matveeva, "Radicalisation and Violent Extremism in Kyrgyzstan: On the Way to the Caliphate?", *The RUSI Journal* 163(1): 30-46, January 2018, https://rusi.org/publication/rusi-journal/radicalisation-and-violent-extremism-kyrgyzstan-way-caliphate
16. Alexander Kupatadze, Smuggling and Organized Crime in Kyrgyzstan, https://www.files.ethz.ch/isn/46165/Kupat_eng.pdf
17. Tamara Makarenko, "Drugs in Central Asia: Security Implications and Political Manipulations", 2001, https://www.persee.fr/docAsPDF/cemot_0764-9878_2001_num_32_1_1600.pdf
18. Anti-drug program of the Government of the Kyrgyz Republic, Approved by Decree No. 54 of the Government of the Kyrgyz Republic as of 27 January 2014, https://www.unodc.org/documents/centralasia/prodocs/Anti-drug_program_ENG.pdf
19. Martha Brill Olcott, "Russia, Central Asia and Caucasian Threats: A Four Year Assessment", Testimony prepared for the House Committee on Armed Services (HASC), Threat Panel Hearing on Threat In Eurasia, 22 September 2005, https://carnegieendowment.org/files/OlcottTestimony Sept 2005.pdf
20. Central Asia's 'Drug Capital' Fights To Stem Tide Of Narcotics, 4 January 2013, https://www.rferl.org/a/osh-is-awash-in-drugs/24815565.html
21. 22 October 2010. https://www.bbc.com/news/world-asia-pacific-11599977
22. World Drug Report, 2013, https://www.unodc.org/unodc/secured/wdr/wdr2013/World_ Drug _Report_2013.pdf
23. https://news.un.org/en/story/2017/11/636182-afghanistan-opium-production-jumps-87-cent-record-level-un-survey
24. Kamala Kumari, "Security Issues and Security and Military Capabilities of Central Asian Republics: An Overview", in *Central Asia Today: Issues and Concerns*, Academic Excellence, Delhi, 2019, pp. 246-289, ISBN No.: 978-93-83246-71-7.
25. Anti-drug program of the Government of the Kyrgyz Republic, Approved by Decree No. 54 of the Government of the Kyrgyz Republic as of 27 January 2014, https://www.unodc.org/documents/centralasia/prodocs/Anti-drug_program_ENG.pdf
26. Dmitry Gorenburg, "External Support for Central Asian Military and Security Forces", January, 2014, https://www.sipri.org/publications/2014/sipri-policy-briefs/external-support-central-asian-military-and-security-forces
27. Kamala Kumari, "Changing Dynamics in Asia: Implications for Central Asian States", *Contemporary Central Asia*, Vol. xix, No. 3, September-December 2015, pp. 17-31, 0, 22, 23.
28. Martha Brill Olcott and Natalia Udalova, Drug Trafficking on the Great Silk Road: The Security Environment in Central Asia", No.11, March 2000, https://carnegieendowment.org/files/drugs.pdf
29. Nirmala Joshi and Kamala Kumari, "Understanding Central Asia's Security and Economic Interests", *India Quarterly*, Volume 75, Issue 1, March 2019, pp. 29–42, 37.
30. https://www.unodc.org/centralasia/en/news/kyrgyzstan-and-unodc-cooperate-at-countering-drug-trafficking-in-the-country.html.
31. https://www.unodc.org/centralasia/en/news/kyrgyzstan-and-unodc-cooperate-at-countering-drug-trafficking-in-the-country.html. Accessed on 18 November 2020.
32. Phil Williams and Vanda Felbab-Brown, "Drug Trafficking, Violence, And Instability", April 2012, p. 44, https://publications.armywarcollege.edu/pubs/2174.pdf

33. Svante E. Cornell, Narcotics, Radicalism, and Armed Conflict in Central Asia: The Islamic Movement of Uzbekistan, December 2005, *Terrorism and Political Violence* 17(4): 619-639, 619.
34. https://collections.unu.edu/eserv/UNU:3134/unu_cpr_crime_conflict_nexus.pdf
35. Anti-drug program of the Government of the Kyrgyz Republic, Approved by Decree No. 54 of the Government of the Kyrgyz Republic as of 27 January 27, 2014, https://www.unodc.org/documents/centralasia/prodocs/Anti-drug_program_ENG.pdf
36. Maral Madi, Drug trade in Kyrgyzstan: structure, implications and countermeasures, pp. 249-273 | Published online: 21 October 2010, https://www.tandfonline.com/doi/abs/10.1080/0263493042000321362
37. Tamara Makarenko, "Drugs in Central Asia: Security Implications and Political Manipulations", 2001, https://www.persee.fr/docAsPDF/cemot_0764-9878_2001_num_32_1_1600.pdf
38. David Lewis, "Crime, terror and the state in Central Asia", October 2014, Global Crime 15(3-4).
39. Johan Engvall, "Religion and the Secular State in Kyrgyzstan", Central Asia-Caucasus Institute and Silk Road Studies Program, 2020, http://www.silkroadstudies.org/resources/Religion_and_the_Secular_State_in_ Kyrgyzstan_-_Johan_Engvall_-_10.06.20_-_FINAL_wCover.pdf
40. Anna Matveeva, Divided we fall...or rise? Tajikistan–Kyrgyzstan border dilemma, *Cambridge Journal of Eurasian Studies*, Volume 1, 13 February 2017, pp. 1-20.
41. Chyngyz Israyilov, "Tackling Kyrgyzstan's Border Issues: Illusions and Reality", 8 April 2020, https://cabar.asia/en/tackling-kyrgyzstan-s-border-issues-illusions-and-reality
42. Kemel Toktomushev, "Understanding Cross-Border Conflict in Post-Soviet Central Asia: The Case of Kyrgyzstan and Tajikistan", *Connections*, Volume 17, No. 1, 2018, pp. 21-41, https://www.jstor.org/stable/26933983?seq=21#metadata_info_tab_contents
43. Catherine Putz, "Kyrgyzstan and Tajikistan's Unresolved Borders", 23 November 2015, https://thediplomat.com/2015/11/kyrgyzstan-and-tajikistans-unresolved-border/
44. Colleen Wood, The Enduring Difficulty of Settling the Kyrgyzstan-Tajikistan Border, 2 August 2019, https://thediplomat.com/2019/08/the-enduring-difficulty-of-settling-the-kyrgyzstan-tajikistan-border/
45. Fulvio Attinà, " Traditional Security Issues" in *China, the European Union, and the International Politics of Global Governance*, pp. 175-193, https://link.springer.com/book/10.1057/9781137514004
46. Anti-drug program of the Government of the Kyrgyz Republic, Approved by Decree No. 54 of the Government of the Kyrgyz Republic as of 27 January 2014, https://www.unodc.org/documents/centralasia/prodocs/Anti-drug_program_ENG.pdf
47. Tamara Makarenko, "Kyrgyzstan and the Global Narcotics Trade", 8.December 1999, https://eurasianet.org/kyrgyzstan-and-the-global-narcotics-trade
48. Anti-drug program of the Government of the Kyrgyz Republic, Approved by Decree No. 54 of the Government of the Kyrgyz Republic as of 27 January 2014, https://www.unodc.org/documents/centralasia/prodocs/Anti-drug_program_ENG.pdf
49. https://www.unodc.org/centralasia/en/news/kyrgyzstan-and-unodc-cooperate-at-countering-drug-trafficking-in-the-country.html

50. Concept of Foreign Policy of the Kyrgyz Republic adopted by the Decree of the President of the Kyrgyz Republic of 11 March 2019, http://cbd.minjust.gov.kg/act/view/ru-ru/430045
51. National Development Strategy of the Kyrgyz Republic for 2018-2040, Presidential Decree dated 31 October 2018, No. 221, http://www.president.kg/en/sobytiya/12774_ utverghdena_nacionalnaya_strategiya_razvitiya_kirgizskoy_respubliki_na_2018_2040_godi
52. https://issuu.com/gjia/docs/6.1_-_crime_goes_global
53. For details, see https://www.unodc.org/documents/evaluation/indepth-evaluations/2018/Cluster_evaluation_UNODC_law_enforcement_and_border_control_ in_ Central_ Asia_ EVALUATION_ REPORT_Dec_2018.pdf
54. https://www.unodc.org/centralasia/en/unodc-in-central-asia.html
55. https://www.osce.org/bishkek/120492
56. For details, see Annual Report 2019, https://www.unodc.org/documents/centralasia//2020/August/Annual-Report-2019/ROCA-AR-2019-ENG.pdf
57. UNODC contributes to enhancing security of Kyrgyzstan, 13 November 2020, https://www.unodc.org/centralasia/en/news/unodc-contributes-to-enhancing-security-of-kyrgyzstan.html
58. "Brief overview of COVID-19 impact", August 2020, https://www.unodc.org/documents/centralasia//2020/August/3.08/COVID-19_impact_on_drug_ use_ in_Central_Asia_en.pdf
59. Support to Crime Prevention in the Kyrgyz Republic, 2019 https://www.unodc.org/documents/centralasia//2019/4._INL_ Final_ Report_ Crime_ Prevention.pdf
60. https://www.unodc.org/centralasia/en/news/unodc-conducted-a-two-day-webinar-for-officers-of-the-ministry-of-internal-affairs-and-state-border-guards-service-of-the-kyrgyz-republic.html
61. "UNODC and Counter Narcotics Service of the Kyrgyz Ministry of Interior enhance cooperation", https://www.unodc.org/centralasia/en/news/unodc-and-counter-narcotics-service-of-the-kyrgyz-ministry-of-interior-enhance-cooperation.html
62. https://www.unodc.org/centralasia/en/news/unodc-supports-the-kyrgyz-government-in-fight-against-drug-trafficking.html
63. Annual Report 2019, https://www.unodc.org/documents/centralasia//2020/August/Annual-Report-2019/ROCA-AR-2019-ENG.pdf
64. Annual Report 2019, https://www.unodc.org/documents/centralasia//2020/August/Annual-Report-2019/ROCA-AR-2019-ENG.pdf
65. 7 July, 2020, https://www.unodc.org/centralasia/en/news-cj/container-control-programme-sets-up-priorities-in-central-asia-during-covid-19-period.html
66. U.S. Provides the Kyrgyz Republic's Counternarcotics Service New Tools to Fight Drug Trafficking, https://kg.usembassy.gov/u-s-provides-the-kyrgyz-republics-counternarcotics-service-new-tools-to-fight-drug-trafficking/
67. ISI's Drug Nexus Exposed, Tanzanian National Arrested for Trafficking Heroin in India, 4 October 2020, http://www.indiandefensenews.in/2020/10/isis-drug-nexus-exposed-tanzanian.html
68. https://www.unodc.org/southasia//frontpage/2017/Feb/india—unodc-and-government-of-india-discuss-cooperation-of-drugs-and-crime.html
69. UNODC Report 2019, https://www.unodc.org/documents/centralasia//2020/August/Annual-Report-2019/ROCA-AR-2019-ENG.pdf

70. SCO Summit 2019, Bishkek, Kyrgyzstan, http://eng.sectsco.org/
71. Vladimir Norov's Speech, Raisina Dialogue, 14-16 January 2020, New Delhi, India.
72. "India is vulnerable to trafficking of narcotics: Officials", February 2020, https://timesofindia.indiatimes.com/india/india-is-vulnerable-to-trafficking-of-narcotics-officials/articleshow/74149953.cms

10

State Policy of Kyrgyzstan in the Religious Sphere and the Process of Radicalization in the Context of Globalization

Dr. K.K. Malikov

ABSTRACT

This article examines the state policy of the Kyrgyz Republic in the religious sphere and the process of globalization in the context of globalization. The author substantiates the importance of regulating the religious sphere in the republic by forming a new layer of normative legal acts. The classification of those convicted for crimes of terrorism and extremism is presented. The tendencies of the threat of radicalization, which are embodied in the al-Qaeda and ISIS, the concentration of interests of Russia, China, Turkey, India, Iran, KSA, the proximity of Afghanistan, and the Fergana Valley as a centre of religious activity in Central Asia are considered. Further, external labour migration, the Civil War in Syria, the crisis of liberal and democratic reforms in Central Asia, the insufficient level of education of the population, and radical information related to modern technologies have also been considered.

Key words: *Kyrgyzstan, politics, religion, radicalization, globalization, terrorism, extremism, al-Qaeda and ISIS.*

The processes in the religious area of Kyrgyzstan differed in their development, presenting an image of a parallel world, with little interaction with society in general and to socio-political and economic relations in the republic. A clear transformation has been noted since 2008-2009. At that time, there has been a rapid growth of public interest in Islam and religion in general—in society, in the mass media, various issues of streamlining foreign missionary activities, problems of proselytism, interfaith conflicts, extremism, establishing the presence of religious objects, etc.

In 2008, experts prepared a new Law "On Freedom of Religion and Religious Organizations" which was signed on 31 December 2009, by the President of the Kyrgyz Republic.[1] This law limited missionary activity focused on proselytism among ethnic Muslims. In 2014, for the first time in the country's history, a meeting of the Kyrgyz Defence Council was dedicated to the religious situation in the country. This showed that the authorities are giving serious attention to the situation in the religious field. Since 2014, the state has not been just an observer, but an active participant and neutral arbiter in the religious sphere, taking into account new threats and the obligation to regulate and control processes.

In Kyrgyzstan, an attempt is being made to open a model of secularism based on the harmonious development of two value systems in one legal, democratic state. More than 95 per cent of the population of Kyrgyzstan is Muslim, and there is recognition and creation of conditions for the development and support of the Hanafi School of Thought[2] and Akid Maturidia[3] by the state. Within the framework of the current legislative framework, with the support of the state, a public fund for the development of spiritual culture "Yiman"[4] was registered, which aims at developing culture and education. Such support from the state made it possible to create a material and intellectual foundation for the training of our own religious personnel, in order to limit the impact of extremist ideologies and non-traditional trends on the part of the states of the Persian Gulf.

In the currently developed Strategy for Sustainable Development until 2040,[5] a place is also given to religion and spirituality. Today, a new layer of normative legal acts is being formed to regulate the religious sphere. Thus, threats to the national security of the Kyrgyz Republic and the risks of a ban are determined, in order to prevent further radicalization. Also, monitoring is carried out and the causes or sources of the spread of destructive ideologies are identified.

Classification of Convicted for Crimes by Terrorism and Extremism

Level 0 *No radicalization*	*Level 1* *Extremism*	*Level 2* *Violent extremism*	*Level 3* *Terrorism*
Extremist, terrorist organizations			
	Hizbut-ut Tahrir	Taliban Movement, ETIM (Islamic Movement of East Turkestan)	ISIS, Islamic Movement of Uzbekistan
Understanding of basic religious postulates, terms			
	• Moderate political Salafism. Translation of shahada as the idea of monotheism and worship of Allah. • Political doctrine of monotheism (Islam as a political system)	• Salafism is political. Translation of the shahada as tavhidhakamiya (monotheism in subjection to the Shariah). • The political doctrine of monotheism (Islam as a political system).	• Wahhabism in Belief and Political Extreme Salafism. Translation of the shahada as tavhidhakamiya (monotheism in subjection to the Shariah). They call themselves muvakhhidin - monotheists, except for the rest of all Muslims. • Jihadist doctrine of monotheism
Dualistic (dual) ideology "Believers vs. Unbelievers"			
	• Kafirs are considered those who do not believe in Allah (atheists). • Muslims are those who say that they believe in Allah & perform 5-fold prayers, hold Orozo, eat halal. If a Muslim does not perform the rituals, he is considered a sinner (fasiks), but he remains Muslim. • Apostates are considered those who stopped believing in Allah and left Islam (for example, went to Christianity). • Taking takfir is considered possible only by Allah or on the basis of a person's own admission in front of witnesses that there is no god. People are not allowed to endure takfir without strong evidence or reasons.	• Kafirs are considered not only those who do not believe in Allah, but also those who do not perform the rituals (do not read namaz, do not hold Orozo). • They believe that law enforcement and judicial officials are infidels, as they defend the infidel laws of a secular state and democracy. Also, those Muslims who recognize secular laws. For example, convicts are called infidels correctional staff. • It is believed that some Muslims can endure takfir to others, even if Muslims recite five times prayer, but they recognize secular laws. Takfir is also taken out to Sufis, Shiites.	• Kafirs are considered not only those who do not believe in Allah, but also those who even perform rituals (namaz, orozo), but do not accept the ideology of jihad and takfir. • It is believed that law enforcement and judicial officials are apostates (even if they recite namaz), since they defend kafir (secular) laws and the state. Also, those Muslims who recognize secular laws are considered apostates (those who came out of Islam, who can be killed). • Takfir is/are tolerated by other Muslims if they do not accept ideology, or recognize secular laws. Takfir is taken out to Sufis and Shiites.

	Attitude to the ideas of a secular state, democracy, human rights		
	• Disapproving attitude towards the ideas of democracy, a secular state, human rights—as a system of disbelief and delusion. But takfir is not tolerated by Muslims. • There is no call to overthrow the system violently (jihad) • Prohibition of terrorism as a method.	• Non-recognition of democracy, a secular state, human rights—as a kafir system, while takfir is imposed on Muslims who support secular laws. Active support for the ideas of overthrowing the existing state system. • Resolution of terrorism as a method. • Call for Jihad.	• Non-recognition of democracy, a secular state, human rights—as a kafir system, at the same time they endure takfir and call on to physically kill Muslims who support secular laws. Calls for the overthrow of the state system, including using violent methods. • Resolution of terrorism as a method. • Call for Jihad.
Attitude to the construction of an Islamic state (caliphate/emirate), the establishment of Sharia, understanding of jihad			
	• Support and approval of construction of an Islamic state, the establishment of Sharia as a legal system. • Support non-violent methods of promoting an Islamic state. They understand jihad more as a struggle with oneself, with one's own ignorance. • Consider it possible for representatives of other religions to live and live peacefully on the territory of the Islamic state.	• They support and approve of the construction of an Islamic state, the establishment of Sharia as a legal system. • Support violent methods of promoting an Islamic state. Jihad is understood as military action in order to build an Islamic state. They express a desire to take part and leave for Syria, Afghanistan, etc. • They consider it impossible for representatives of other religions to live and live peacefully on the territory of an Islamic state. • View members of other religions as a threat to their religious beliefs, including Muslims with other religious beliefs.	• They travel to countries where jihad is taking place (understand by jihad military actions against infidels and with the aim of establishing an Islamic state)—Syria, Afghanistan, etc. • Supports violent methods in building an Islamic state. I understand jihad as military action in order to build an Islamic state. • They consider it impossible for different religions to live and coexist peacefully. • View representatives of other faiths as a threat, and also other Muslims who do not share their religious beliefs.

Sources of studying religion—books, websites, chats, lectures			
	• Koran • Hadith • Books on political Islam (for HT—authors Taqiya din and Nabhani, Zulum)	• Koran (verses of the sword - about jihad & kufr) • Hadith (about jihad, slavery, etc.) • Books on political Salafi ideology (Muslim Brothers - Said Qutb, Mavdudi)	• Koran (verses of the sword - about jihad and kufra) • Hadith (about jihad, slavery, etc.) • Books on militant Salafi political ideology & Wahhabism (Abu Musab, Makdisi, Misri, etc.).
Availability and dissemination of information, including extremist/terrorist ideas (literature, messages, lectures, nasheeds, etc.)			
Contact both with extremist and terrorist organizations, and with individual extremists/terrorists			
	Have contradictions in ideology with Takfirite groups (although sometimes they have contacts and connections)	Cooperate closely with terrorist groups and support ideology and methods	They closely cooperate with representatives of violent extremism and see them as like-minded people
Relationship with family and immediate environment			
	They do not consider their relatives to be infidels or apostates, even if they are against this ideology.	They consider their relatives to be infidels if they do not share their religious beliefs. For example, they may refuse food prepared by their mother if she reads namaz only once. Divorced (divorced) his wife (husband), who did not share their views.	They consider their relatives to be infidels and renounce them.
Committing and/or planning administrative, criminal offences			
			• Forgery of passports • Illegal possession of phones (not registered) or multiple phones • Possession of counterfeit credit cards • Documents containing the planning of terrorist acts • Availability of materials for making homemade weapons and/or manufacture homemade weapons.

On Threats of Radicalization

Touching upon the threat of terrorism and extremism,[6] it should be recognized that this threat has both an internal and external character. Namely, terrorist organizations have external control and often act as an instrument of some countries. This is not a secret and has been voiced in the mass media by Hillary Clinton in relation to al-Qaeda and Donald Trump in relation to ISIS. In the information space of Kyrgyzstan, reports appear on the arrests, suspects in impending terrorist attacks, and returnees with the aim of continuing terrorist activities.

In the context of aggravated relations between the USA and Russia on the Syrian issue,[7] Central Asia is steadily turning into a platform for postponing confrontation, where the interests of Russia, China, Turkey, India, Iran, and KSA are also present. The division of regional and global forces into opposing blocs—the Russian Federation, Iran and the bloc—the USA, the EU, Qatar, Turkey, and KSA in the Syrian conflict is reflected in the regional security of the Central Asian region.

A special role in ensuring a stable security system in the Central Asian region is played by Afghanistan and the level of preparedness of NATO states led by the USA and the CSTO countries led by the Russian Federation on terrorism and drug trafficking. The Fergana Valley, where Kyrgyzstan, Tajikistan and Uzbekistan meet, remains a vulnerable point within the Central Asian region. In the Fergana Valley, since the days of the USSR, there have been a number of complex problems associated with the delimitation of borders, as well as access to irrigation and drinking water, the problem of drug trafficking from Afghanistan and the drug business, overpopulation and social problems, youth unemployment, radicalization, interethnic problems, etc.

The Fergana Valley has historically been a kind of traditional centre of religious activity in Central Asia. Muslim communities in modern times are experiencing not only a generational conflict, but also the growth of religious intolerance and radicalization in relation to other groups, as well as to state policy, secular institutions of power. In part, this manifests itself on the interpersonal level when assigning labels: "Salafit", "Sufi", "Tabligavets", "Nurzhi" or at Friday prayers. The intense propaganda of Takfirite and jihadist ideologies among young people has the most dangerous consequences.

Since the 2000s, the external labour migration of Tajiks from Tajikistan

Kyrgyz from Kyrgyzstan, and Uzbeks from Uzbekistan to Russia has increased. Labour migrants from Central Asia see Islam as a guarantor of the preservation of their identity. Thus, the process of Islamization occurs among Central Asian labour migrants in Russia.

The civil war in Syria in 2011, and the emergence of the ISIS in 2014, became the basis for the spread of jihad and the departure of young Central Asian citizens to Syria. In this regard, Islam, represented by traditional imams, is experiencing a shortage of educated, professional personnel and so far cannot oppose in any way the trend of radicalization of believers.

The conceptual issue is that the national constitutions of the Central Asian countries do not fully represent the model of secularism, state-confessional relations and the rules of the "game". Meanwhile, the process of Islamization is increasingly asserting itself and, in fact, is irreversible. Given the fact that a significant part of the population of Kazakhstan, Kyrgyzstan and Tajikistan is Muslim, the states pursue a policy of supporting traditional Islam (Sunni direction, Hanafi legal school, Maturidite doctrine) in their countries in opposition to "imported" religious movements from outside.

Field studies conducted by the analytical centre "Religion, Law and Politics" in 2015-2016 show that young citizens of Kyrgyzstan aged 18 to 28 who travel to Syria to join the ISIS do so mainly for ideological reasons. The analysis carried out and the results of interviews among detained militants show that the main reason for radicalization is a deep crisis in the minds of certain "risk groups", i.e., among young people. The most important issue for young people is the issue of social justice, the lack of social benefits, the lack of prospects for self-development, and the lack of opportunities to find a job, leading to an antagonistic position towards the entire system.

There is also a crisis of liberal and democratic reforms in Central Asia[8] and the disillusionment of the population with the ongoing reforms. Western liberal values are losing their relevance. The ideological vacuum is filled with religious values, some of which have a radical feature imported from outside (via the Internet, extremist literature, underground education, contacts).

Today, young people are in search of spiritual, ideological guidelines. Even with regard to questions that have a connection with international politics, young people are beginning to look for answers in political Islam. Here, the issue of value orientations, the ideological or psychological component, acquires significant relevance.

Returning militants and sleeping cells within the Central Asian countries and those organizations that sympathize with the ISIS or al-Qaeda may pose a particular danger. Thus, individual field commanders of the Islamic Movement of Uzbekistan and the Islamic Jihad Union stationed in Afghanistan, part of the Hizb-ut-Tahrir in Central Asia, have already announced their readiness for joint action with the ISIS. The number of those who got acquainted with the ideas of a radical interpretation of Islam in prisons is also growing rapidly. There is a process of merging former criminals with the terrorist ideology of the ISIS, the IMU, etc.

The places of deprivation of liberty in Kazakhstan, Tajikistan and Kyrgyzstan remain a hotbed not only for organized crime, but also for extremists. At the same time, there is an increase in those convicted of extremism. Various phenomena and processes can act as other factors of radicalization. The key factor is the low level of education and awareness of Islam and its various streams.

Primary propaganda information from Internet sites, YouTube, Facebook, Odnoklassniki, WhatsApp, occasionally focus on the introduction of jihad, declaring a secular state hostile. Thus, possession of modern technologies allows international terrorism (ISIS, al-Qaeda) to recruit young people through social networks. For example, in the ISIS system, the special media unit, Al-Furqan, is successfully functioning, which, to the envy of the al-Qaeda and al-Nusra Front, effectively uses all the tools ike the world wide web: publishing ideas and messages; placing scenes of extermination of columns of military equipment of government troops; attacks on military families and executions of civilians.

Thus, in May 2014, "Al-Furqan" posted a documentary film "Clink of Swords"[9] on the Internet. According to CNN cinematographers, the quality of shooting and editing is comparable to the products of American cinema, both in terms of entertainment and realism. The propaganda film "Clink of Swords" and the subsequent film "Flame of War" were released on the Internet and received a record number of views. The traditional clergy are unable to resist the specialized propaganda of terrorist groups, since modern technologies have allowed terrorist organizations to recruit young citizens into their ranks through the Internet.

Summing up, we can say that the analysis of the causes of radicalization among young people in Kazakhstan, Kyrgyzstan, and Tajikistan, shows the presence of a number of internal and external factors for radicalization. At the same time, internal factors represent the defining dynamics of radicalization within countries, and these are social and economic stability, the level of education among young people, their involvement in social processes in society, a timely government policy in the field of countering extremism and its prevention. Therefore, in the coming years, topical issues will be discussions around the politicization of believers, the process of Salafization and the threats of takfirism, state control of religious organizations, as well as understanding and interpretation of the secular state, the boundaries between the rights of believers and the secular part of the population, the role and place of religion, folk customs and traditions and the spiritual foundations of the national ideology.

Unfortunately, in general, in the countries of Central Asia, there are dangerous internal conditions for recruitment with the prospect of constantly replenishing new recruits among young people. In addition, in the Central Asian countries today—Uzbekistan, Kazakhstan and, to a lesser extent, Turkmenistan, and then Tajikistan, there exists a vertical structure of power, a rather powerful repressive apparatus and weakness or absence of political opposition parties. Destabilization in one of these countries for political, social, economic, ethnic or religious reasons, can lead to infiltration from outside by various extremist groups or the activation of sleeping cells.

The Central Asian countries face threats of the return of their citizens from the conflict zones and the penetration of radical persons or small terrorist groups with the aim of carrying out terrorist acts, and participating in the destabilization of the situation in any of the points of Central Asia. Also, the events in Syria and Afghanistan and the ability of the USA and Russia in the fight against extremism and terrorism will continue to affect the security of the region.

REFERENCES

1. Law of the Kyrgyz Republic. No. 282 dated 31 December 2008 on freedom of religion and religious organizations in the Kyrgyz Republic. http://cbd.minjust.gov.kg/act/view/ru-ru/202498.
2. Ali-zadeh, A. A. Hanafi madhhab, Islamic Encyclopaedic Dictionary, M. Ansar, 2007.
3. Maturities and their Features. Https://islam.global/obshchestvo/islamskoe-pravo, maturidity-i-ikh-osobennosti

4. Charter of the public foundation. "Fund for the Development of Spiritual Culture" Yyman". Http://cbd.minjust.gov.kg/act/view/ru-ru/21186
5. National Development Strategy of the Kyrgyz Republic for 2018-2040, http: // mineconom.gov.kg/storage/directs/documents/209/15421950795bec078718fff.pdf
6. Theory and practice of information counteraction to extremist and terrorist activities: Monograph. Sundiev I. Yu. [and others];—M., 2014.
7. Mukhin V. Russia and the United States are entering a new phase of rivalry in Syria. https://www.ng.ru/armies/2021-02-09/1_8078_russia.html
8. Prospects for democratization of Central Asian countries or how to awaken dormant institutions? https://kun.uz/ru/news/2019/05/10/perspektivy-demokratizatsii-stran-tsentralnoy-azii-ili-kak-razbudit-spyashchiye-instituty
9. Abu Sabeel. "The Clash of Swords" is a shocking ISIS film that is striking in its cruelty. https: //golosislama.com/news.php?id=24324

11

An Assessment of the Shanghai Cooperation Organisation:
An Indian Perspective

Prof. Nirmala Joshi

Today, the Shanghai Cooperation Organisation (SCO) is facing extraordinary challenges that are likely to affect its functioning as a regional grouping. One of the prime factors is that Russia, a leading member of the SCO, is heavily involved militarily in Ukraine. This has brought about a fundamental shift in global politics and will have an impact on the SCO. The shape of the SCO will be clear after the coming summit meeting in September 2022. It must be noted that regional groupings are expected to effectively project and promote the interests and concerns of its members as well as of the region. Such groupings help in promoting regional consciousness, which in turn, helps in maintaining peace and stability. The SCO is the only grouping in Eurasia committed to ensure the security and stability of the region. It comprises eight members—Kazakhstan, Kyrgyzstan, Tajikistan, Uzbekistan, India, Pakistan, Russia, and China. Analysts believe that China has the potential to emerge as a global power, while India and Russia do so as regional powers.

At present, the SCO space has assumed tremendous geopolitical significance as the region has acquired centrality in the ongoing reconfiguration of the world order. This is most evident in Asia including Eurasia. The Bishkek Declaration of the June 2019 summit meeting clearly highlighted the shifts that were underway. The Declaration stated, "The modern world continues to change rapidly, the global balance of power is going through a reconfiguration, primarily due to the emergence of new development centres in Asia and the connectivity and interdependence between participants in international relations is deepening. However, the situation in global politics and the economy remains turbulent and tense".[1] One of the prominent trends in the reconfiguration is the change brought about by Russia in Europe leading to a strong European geopolitical entity and the onset of the Cold War, the US-China economic war with the strengthening of the Russia-China Strategic Partnership and intense geopolitical competition. This trend has affected most nations especially in Asia as well as the process of globalisation. Another noticeable trend is the rise in the level of violence among nations to settle issues such as the Nagorno Karabakh, the escalating violent clashes on India's land borders by China, with territorial claims by the latter against the former, or the continuation of violent activities in Afghanistan, Iraq, and Syria. Besides, China's rise as the second largest economy has given its policy a high degree of assertiveness. However, China's ambition to emerge as a global power received a major setback with mounting international criticism of its irresponsible conduct by keeping the outbreak of corona virus a secret. It led to the worldwide spread of COVID-19 that has claimed millions of lives. It has undoubtedly dented China's ambition to emerge as a global power. All countries, including the Central Asian Republics (CARs), have been affected by COVID-19. Probably the international opprobrium it has earned has strengthened China's bellicosity and insensitivity. It was evident when China raised unfounded territorial claims on Kazakhstan, Kyrgyzstan, and Tajikistan and violent clashes erupted on India's boundary. Incidentally, all are members of the SCO. It may be emphasized that the core principles of the SCO as a regional grouping are to adopt a multilateral approach to differences among members in an attempt to resolve them, ensuring regional security and promoting economic development. These core principles seem to have dissipated.

India had always evinced keen interest on acquiring membership of the SCO. Initially, it was to establish its presence in a region that is of vital importance from geopolitical, strategic, economic, historical, and cultural perspectives. Gradually, Indian interest widened; it wanted to be considered as a leading player and not a balancer. Recognised as one of the leading Asian powers, India initiated its first regional Connect Central Asia Policy (CCAP) in 2012. The policy signalled India's desire to play a proactive role in wider Asia. One of the pillars of the CCAP was connectivity, an attempt to reach out to Central Asia and beyond. Given India's growing interests in the region, its attempts to involve itself in the construction of the Chabahar port and its aspirations to join the SCO, reflected India's ambition to establish its presence/influence in the region particularly in Central Asia and beyond. In the words of Prime Minister Narendra Modi, "We see an important place for Central Asia in India's future".[2] In Indian foreign policy priority, the SCO space is of crucial importance in its strategic calculus. In view of the rapidly changing geopolitical situation moving towards tension and turmoil, the question at present is can the SCO fulfil its core objective of maintaining peace and stability in the region? Importantly, can the SCO resolve differences and settle issues among its members? In order to assess the role of the SCO, it is essential to examine its evolution as a regional grouping.

From Shanghai Five to SCO

By the turn of the century, the regional environment was deteriorating. Afghanistan had emerged as the epicentre of religious extremism and terrorism under the Taliban rule. The devastating attack on New York and Washington D.C. on 11 September 2001 led to the 'War on Terror' launched by the North Atlantic Treaty Organisation (NATO). Its troops were led by the International Security Assistance Force (ISAF) of the USA. The war on terror changed the geopolitical landscape of the region as the USA and its allies had established their military presence in the region. In view of the unabated insurgency that led to a worsening security scenario, an acute need was felt to transform the Shanghai Five from a mechanism created to manage peace and stability on the border to a regional grouping and institutionalise it as an international organization. It was perceived that the issues of security were becoming complex; hence, an institutional framework was necessary.

As a consequence, the SCO was established in June 2001 at Beijing with Uzbekistan co-opted as a member. The Declaration of the SCO stated, "The Shanghai Organization declares itself to be a new model of regional cooperation, which aims to produce good neighbourly relations, mutual trust, equality and common development and is neither with, nor antagonistic, to third parties...every member should strictly honour the principles of good neighbourliness, equality, and mutual benefit, friendly cooperation, and development".[2] At the St. Petersburg summit in 2002, the Charter of the SCO was signed. It reflected China's core concern of maintaining peace and stability on its borders with the CARs. "...In security terms, we can look forward to peace and friendly new borders between China and Central Asia. This cooperation on attacking the three forces and transnational crimes became the key components of security cooperation".[3] In 2006, Chinese President Hu Jintao proposed that the basic principles of coordination and unity among members be raised to the stature of treaty relations. Subsequently, a Treaty of Good Neighbourliness, Friendship, and Cooperation was signed. Central to it was China's basic concern of peace and stability on its borders. At the Yekaterinburg summit in Russia in 2009, a Convention on Counter-Terrorism was signed which laid the groundwork for a legal framework among the members for counter-terrorist operations.

Structures of the SCO

In keeping with its institutional framework, the SCO also established its structures. They are: Heads of State, Heads of Government, Council of Ministers of Foreign Affairs, Defence, etc. Among the structures was the Regional Anti-Terrorist Structure. It was tasked to arrange studies of regional terrorist movements and exchange information about counter-terrorist policies. With the objectives of the SCO clearly laid out and structural arrangements initiated, it is important to understand the trajectory of this grouping.

An Assessment

Twenty-one years down the line, the SCO has held regular meetings both at summit and structural levels. At each meeting, commendable declarations, resolutions, and programmes were approved. Some of the milestones in the history of the SCO need to be recounted. At the Astana summit (2005) the SCO gave a forceful call to the USA to announce a timeframe for withdrawal from military base facilities in the region. The Astana Declaration came against the backdrop of the Tulip Revolution, reportedly an attempt by the West to usher in democracy or mere regime change. Nevertheless, it led to escalating violence at the border between Kyrgyzstan and Uzbekistan. It was suspected that the West had incited the violent incidents. At the summit, it was pointed out that ensuring the security and stability of the region was the right and responsibility of the countries themselves. The Astana Declaration implied that Russian, Chinese, and Central Asian interests were compatible and were capable of ensuring regional security. It must be pointed out that the military base facilities were under a bilateral agreement and that the SCO had no role. Later, in November 2005, Uzbekistan asked the USA to vacate its Karshi Khanabad or K 2 base, while Kyrgyzstan did not comply, but much later it asked the Manas air base to be vacated.

Later, in reply to a question on why the SCO had not attempted to resolve the differences between Kyrgyzstan and Uzbekistan, since both are members of the SCO, former Secretary-General Deguang said "...the grouping strictly observes the principles of non-interference in the country's internal affairs. However, it does not mean that we cannot take joint action in the cause of common struggle against terrorism."[4] In reality, the SCO does not have the mechanism by which it could involve itself in the affairs of countries. The SCO does not have either the legal framework for such actions, or the tools to involve itself in violent clashes between its members.

A second major milestone was in 2009 when President Barack Obama announced that the coalition forces would be withdrawn by the end of 2014. The war on terror had led to nowhere, while the Taliban were confident and in a resurgent mood. Undoubtedly, the withdrawal of coalition forces from Afghanistan would usher in a new situation. It would once again impact the geopolitical situation, for the coalition forces had neither destroyed the safe havens, nor the terrorist infrastructure. The SCO was confronted with a huge challenge and it is doubtful if the SCO in its existing format even today (2022) could ensure regional security. The forces of extremism and terrorism are gaining ground after the chaotic withdrawal of US forces from Afghanistan on 9 July 2021.

An outcome of the likely changing Eurasian landscape was the Moscow seminar in 2009. An Afghan-SCO Contact Group was formed with the aim of overseeing regional security. At the St. Petersburg summit in 2009, a Convention on Combating Counter Terrorism was adopted, paving the way for a legal framework for counter-terrorism activity. Although all countries were afflicted with the scourge of terrorism, they could not craft a unified policy towards issues of regional security and combating insurgency in Afghanistan. Possibly, the definition of terrorism varied from country to country. Nevertheless, it was agreed to support the ongoing process of reconstruction in Afghanistan, though as a bilateral effort.

Another landmark development was at the Ufa (Russia) summit in 2015 when India and Pakistan were invited as full members, upgrading their status from 'Observer' countries to full members. India's membership at that juncture was, in the opinion of Dr. Alexander Lukin, a reputed Russian scholar, due to India's political weight and economic attractiveness among developing countries..."as this country can make a significant contribution to the Central Asian countries and help diversify their external economic relations".[4] At the Qingdao summit in China in June 2018, the high point of Prime Minister Narendra Modi's speech was that connectivity with our neighbourhood and in the SCO region is our priority. India welcomes any such (connectivity) project, which includes sustainable, transparent and respects member states' sovereignty and territorial integrity.[5]

In spite of laudable Declarations, Resolutions, and Programmes, the SCO, at the end of twenty-one years, did not emerge as a compact and efficient grouping. Its responses to challenging issues were feeble. For instance, at the recent Moscow summit in November 2020 being held against the backdrop of violent military clashes by China on India's boundary, the SCO did not put forward an appropriate response that sought to resolve the differences or attempt to see that the clashes did not escalate into a full-fledged war, though both India and China are members. The Moscow Declaration of November 2020 merely stated, "The SCO will continue building up its contribution to ensuring peace and security and settling international and regional conflicts solely by the political and diplomatic methods based on the principles of equality, respect for sovereignty, territorial integrity, and non-interference in internal affairs of states and renunciation of the use or threat of force."[6] It merely reiterated its core principles and, meanwhile, the military stand-off between India and China continues until date. There are factors, however, that have impinged on the effectiveness of the SCO as a regional grouping. It is necessary to examine them. The Anti Terrorist Structure (RATS) is yet to evolve as an effective organisation. There has been a trust deficit among the members and they have been reluctant to share information about terrorist movements, etc. Recently, however, RATS is playing an active role. It has organised military drills on counter-terrorism and the last meeting was held in Delhi, May 2022. Whether, RATS emerges as effective arm of the SCO is not clear at the present.

Challenges

For any regional grouping to emerge as an effective one, cohesiveness and compactness are absolutely essential. Today, the SCO space has been caught in the vortex of a 'Cold War'. One of the biggest challenges confronting the region is the continuing Russian military intervention in Ukraine. It has led largely to Russia's isolation in global affairs, international criticism, and sanctions. These developments do not bode well for the region. Intertwined is the steadfast support rendered by China at the diplomatic level; for instance, China has been abstaining from United Nations resolutions criticising Russia. How the will the strong Russian-Chinese strategic partnership impinge on the SCO? Whether it dominates the proceedings or pass mild resolutions will be evident in the coming summit in Tashkent in September 2022. This has created a sense of apprehension among the Central Asian States, as they have been looking to Russia to ensure their security. However, it cannot be discounted that the Russian-Chinese Strategic partnership also contains seeds of competition. Perhaps in the near to medium terms, the partnership will play a cooperative role.

In the emerging scenario, the SCO has become a mute spectator to the unfolding developments. An essential component of a regional grouping is cohesiveness and compactness. What is required is a collective and a multilateral approach to rejuvenate its ideals. One of the shortcomings of the grouping was that it was not formed in an evolutionary manner. It must be remembered that the Shanghai Five was converted into the SCO at the behest of Russia and China, and the CARs concurred with this decision. A grouping formed from top to bottom lacks compactness, for it does not necessarily reflect common interests, values, and the system of governance. For instance, at the St. Petersburg summit in 2002, China was able to get an endorsement of its 'One China Policy' and the principle that Taiwan is an inalienable part of China. According to Jyotsna Bakshi, an expert on Eurasian affairs, "...there exists certain resentment in the Central Asian circles that under Russian and Chinese influence they are called upon to express views on issues that do not directly concern them and which tend to antagonise the West." Another example at the Astana summit (2005) was that China announced a loan of US$ 9 million for infrastructure development but, in the absence of a multilateral mechanism, it was China that decided which project was to be supported. In the process, most of the resolutions remained on paper and were not implemented. The resolutions were adopted by consensus and the voting system was not preferred. The military clashes between India and China are a poor reflection of the SCO's core principle of a 'good neighbourly' attitude.

The Shanghai Five was primarily a Chinese initiative formed after the settlement of its lengthy border and its core objectives were peace, tranquillity, and a good neighbourly attitude on the border. Except for adding regional security as its aim, the SCO did not change its earlier core objective.

Another major impediment is that Russia and China have launched their own integrationist projects in the SCO space in the wake of the impending shifts by the US decision the withdraw forces by the end of 2014. The projects are the Eurasian Economic Union (EEU) in 2011 by Russia. It had earlier initiated the Collective Security Treaty Organization (CSTO) in 2003, a defence integrated project. China initiated its Silk Road Economic Belt (SREB) referred to as the Belt and Road Initiative (BRI). These projects seek to promote not only economic cooperation among the countries but, importantly, have a strong geopolitical content. It is evident that a competitive element between Russia and China over Central Asia could emerge. The EEU has expanded to a broader concept, 'Greater Eurasia', which includes not only countries of the post-Soviet space but also countries located on the rim of Eurasia, such as India, Singapore, South Korea, Japan, China, etc. Incidentally, all the countries mentioned have an opening to the oceans while the SREB aims to revive the ancient trade route, which connected China with Europe via the vast Eurasian land mass. Consequently, the Chinese priority has focused on infrastructure development in the region. For Russia and China, their respective projects are of high priority, for to both of them, Central Asia is of utmost importance and success depends on the cooperation of CARs. Given the focus on integrating Central Asia by both the projects, the issue is what the status of the SCO is. Some Chinese experts believe that the emergence of the SREB is a reaction of its leadership to the slowness and ineffectiveness of the SCO.

Thus, we find the main shortcoming of the SCO is the absence of strong multilateralism for an efficient regional grouping. Will the SCO in its present format be able to overcome this drawback? Foreseeing the emergence of regional grouping projects, they could overshadow the SCO. Lt. Gen. Klimenko of the Institute of Far Eastern Studies of the Russian Academy of Science, made a thought-provoking observation. He said, "The SCO, having an impressive potential, is not a fully fledged regional security institution, but continues to seek its own identity".[7] In the view of well-known expert Martha Brill Olcott "...the SCO should best be viewed as a source of confidence building and possibly, even conflict prevention, but not as a conflict mitigating organization".[8]

India and the Way Forward

In view of the evolving strenuous environment in Eurasia, the significance of the SCO cannot be discounted, though the grouping may have lost its shine. A cooperative effort is required to rejuvenate its principles and ideals so that it could play its desired role. Since, for India, the SCO holds tremendous significance, it should initiate measures in cooperation with other like-minded countries that share common principles, values, and political outlooks to foster and promote a vibrant multilateral regional grouping.

Due to the tense and uncertain global order, multilateralism has weakened considerably. An apt observation was made by External Affairs Minister Dr. Jaishankar when he said at a roundtable of the ASEAN-India Network of Think Tanks, "Multilateralism has failed the test as the world lives through an unprecedented challenge in the wake of the corona virus pandemic, which has thrown up trust as the most valued commodity in international relations today".[9] Regarding the SCO, a multilateral approach will make the grouping broad based and infuse it with equality and build a collective approach. One of the main points of focus of India's strategy is to build an effective multilateral grouping. While speaking at a meeting of defence ministers of SCO countries in November 2019 Defence Minister Rajnath Singh said, "Terrorism continues to disrupt our societies and undermine our developmental endeavours....We need approaches, which are inclusive, transparent, and firmly anchored in multilateralism. Successful multilateralism also needs adherence to the core principle of respect for sovereignty and territorial integrity, non-interference, and mutual cooperation".[10] Further, Singh said India was ready to share its experience in skill development and capacity building. India believed they are valuable assets of maintaining a geopolitical balance between oceans and land. It will have to therefore assiduously focus on common interests and challenges. For India, the SCO offers a valuable geopolitical asset for maintaining a balance between the oceans and the land. If India has to play a meaningful role, it will have to focus assiduously on its interests and challenges. A proactive diplomacy not only to guard its sovereignty and territorial integrity should be initiated, but also build its presence/ influence as well. From that perspective, connectivity to its area of interest is imperative, as this region is landlocked. Connectivity is the key that could lay the foundation for sound economic development.

Initiatives like the International North South Transport Corridor, Chabahar port, and the Ashgabat Agreement clearly emphasize the focus of India on connectivity. Since the region is of vital importance, India will have to focus greater attention not only on the CARs, but on Chabahar port, which is India's best hope for reaching the region not only for trade and transit but to establish a credible presence in the region and promote people-to-people contacts.

Concluding Observation

The world is witnessing the rudiments of two broad groups emerging at the global level. An outcome of the onset of a 'Cold War' is the emergence of a strong geopolitical European entity against Russia. On the other hand, China is faced with tensions in the South China Sea and the formation of QUAD. The SCO space is flanked by two mighty geopolitical blocs. Another significant issue is the rising challenges, both conventional and non-conventional, and threats and therefore a robust and collective multilateral approach is essential to make the SCO an efficient and an effective regional grouping, so as to be able to tackle regional security issues.

At present, the SCO can, at the most, initiate a positive discourse on regional issues; for example, a dialogue among members on Afghanistan. How the challenges posed by the Russian military intervention or the India-China military clashes on the border and the continuing stand-off will impact the SCO is uncertain at this juncture. Undoubtedly, its outcome will not only shape the future of Eurasia, not only that of the SCO, but of Asia as well.

REFERENCES

1. Bishkek Declaration of the Shanghai Cooperation Organization's Heads of State Council, http://eng.sectsco.org/documents.
2. Michael Fredholm, (ed.), *The Shanghai Cooperation Organization and Eurasian Geopolitics* (Denmark, Stockholm International Program for Central Asian Studies, 2013), p. 179.

3. Sun Zhuangzhi, "New and Old Regionalism: The SCO and Sino Central Asian Relations", *The Review of International Affairs*, vol. 3, no. 4, Summer 2004, p. 601.
4. Dr. Alexander Lukin, "Should the SCO be Enlarged?", *Russia in Global Affairs*, April-June 2011, p. 36.
5. http://www.mea.gov.in, Media briefing by Secretary (West) at Qingdao, 10 June 2018.
6. The Moscow Declaration of the Council of Heads of State of the Shanghai Cooperation Organization, 10 November 2020.
7. Shanghai Cooperation Organization Model 2014, no. 26, p. 11.
8. Martha Brill Olcott, http://carnegieendowment.org/2010/10/12/Kyrgyzstan-perspectives-and-implications-for-region-pub. 42385
9. http://www.nbcnews.com/politics/national-security/bounties-or-not-russia-has-worked-expand-its-clout-Afghanistan-in 1232529
10. http://www.news.com/amp.news/india/india-urges-SCO-nations-to work-together-to-defeat-terrorism-combat-climate-change-2371521-htm

12

Implications of the Evolving Afghan Situation on Regional Security with Particular Reference to India and the Kyrgyz Republic

Pankaj Tripathi

Afghanistan has been a country ravaged by near continuous conflict during the past four decades. High levels of violence and fighting have been the norm during this long period. There were a few years between 2001 and 2004 that appeared relatively stable, but then the Taliban started regrouping after receiving shelter and safe haven in neighbouring countries and the levels of violence in the country since then have kept growing until the collapse of the Ashraf Ghani regime and the Taliban takeover in August 2021.

The Taliban takeover of Kabul came about within a year of the start of the intra-Afghan talks between the Ashraf Ghani-led Afghan government and the Taliban that started on 12 September 2020. These talks, in turn, flowed from the US-Taliban deal of 29 February 2020, titled, 'Agreement for Bringing Peace to Afghanistan' outlining a timetable for a full US troop withdrawal from Afghanistan within 14 months.[1] The reasons for the sudden collapse of the Afghan national security forces in 2021, after the withdrawal of the USA and NATO forces, have been widely analysed and speculated upon and need no reiteration here.

Following the February 2020 US-Taliban deal, there appeared to be a broad consensus among security analysts and area experts that the accord would give the Taliban some form of international legitimacy, even though the accord repeatedly emphasised that the 'Islamic Emirate of Afghanistan' was not recognized by the USA as a state. Bill Roggio, Senior Fellow at the Foundation for Defence of Democracies, had said then, "The USA wants out of Afghanistan and it has ceded to all the Taliban demands". The Taliban see the agreement as "an end-of-occupation deal".[2] This succinct assessment has come true.

The Expansion of IS-KP

The security dynamics within Afghanistan in the first year of the Taliban-2 regime, however, continues to remain uncertain and complex, reflected, inter alia, in the growing presence and activity of the Islamic State Khorasan Province (IS-KP). There have been a number of terror attacks in Kabul and Northern Afghanistan that have been mostly claimed by or ascribed to the IS-KP, which has been seeing resurgence after the departure of US troops. According to Michael Kugelman, Deputy Director of the Asia Program at the Wilson Centre, a US Think Tank, the IS-KP had been resilient against US-led airstrikes and has "emerged even stronger" after the Taliban takeover.[3]

A November 2021 UNAMA briefing on Afghanistan states that once limited to a few provinces of Afghanistan and Kabul, the IS-K has expanded to nearly all the provinces and seemed increasingly active with the number of IS-KP attacks, mainly targeting the Shia community, increasing from 60 in 2020 to 334 by mid-November 2021.[4] It may be recalled that the Ashraf Ghani government in Afghanistan, prior to the Taliban takeover, had confirmed that it was holding IS-KP-affiliated militants from Central Asia. A figure of 408 such prisoners, including women and children, was then given. Some of these probably escaped and rejoined the IS-KP when the Taliban freed around 2,000 prisoners when it seized Kabul.

As per claims made in the IS's weekly *al-Naba* newsletter, since 15 August 2021, the IS-KP has claimed five attacks in Kunduz province and four in Takhar province, both bordering Tajikistan.[5]

Map 1

Source: Maps of India.

The increased IS-KP activity has implications for the Central Asian states (CAS), more so for states bordering Afghanistan. Notably, the IS-KP has increasingly started disseminating propaganda directed at Uzbek, Tajik, and Kyrgyz speakers in the region, portraying the Taliban regime as a Pashtun organization rather than an Islamic movement and attempting to exploit fault lines between the Taliban and different ethnic groups that feel marginalized. It seeks to encourage attacks beyond Afghanistan in Uzbekistan, Tajikistan, and Kyrgyzstan.

The IS-KP's media organ, *Al-Azaim,* has begun publishing in Central Asian languages. For example, in 2022, it published two books in the Uzbek language, in the Latin alphabet used in Uzbekistan, and released a number of audio recordings in the Uzbek language. It also uses audio speeches of the Islamic Movement of Uzbekistan (IMU) ideologue, Asadulloh Urgenchiy. In the Tajik Cyrillic used in Tajikistan, *Al-Azaim* released a book, '*Why Jihad is obligatory*', in March 2022. Its Uzbek-language *Xuroson Ovozi* (Voice of Khurasan) group on Telegram has also begun translating and publishing statements of IS-KP operatives. *Xuroson Ovozi* has published a translation of a statement from the *Al-Azaim* media team pledging allegiance to the new IS leader, Abu al-Hassan al-Hashemi al-Quraishi, alongside other IS-linked media groups around the world. In March 2022, *Al-Azaim* published a Tajik version of the statement.[6]

Telegram groups publishing in Tajik Cyrillic include Protectors of the *Ummat*, *Movarounnahr* (land beyond the Amu Darya) and Voice of *Khurasan* and usually include contacts for aspiring jihadis seeking instruction and assistance. Though these channels are taken down by the platforms, they quickly reappear, usually with the same administrators. The IS-KP has also claimed firing rockets into Uzbekistan and Tajikistan.

Resistance against the Taliban

Moreover, the fighting in some pockets of Afghanistan such as some districts of Panjshir and in Andrab district between the National Resistance Front (NRF) under the leadership of Ahmad Masoud and the Taliban has resumed with the advent of spring with the resistance gradually being more organised.[7] There have also been reports of scattered resistance to the Taliban elsewhere too, including in some places by local Pashtuns as also allegations of war crimes and human rights violations by Taliban fighters, especially in Panjshir.[8] Prospects for stability in Afghanistan, therefore, remain uncertain. It is probable that the fighting between the resistance forces and the Taliban continues in the months to come, though there may be a decrease in intensity later during the winter months.

Then there is the issue of public protests against Taliban policies and the suppression of such popular though unorganised protests. Contrary to earlier promises, the Taliban have resumed their earlier severely gender-discriminatory practices from the 1996-2001 period, like imposing a ban on girls attending high school and imposing various restrictions on the free movement of women in public places and at work. This is worrisome and may turn out to be a critical factor in non-recognition of the Taliban regime by the international community and, therefore, a development that is likely to keep the Afghan situation unstable. According to a UNAMA briefing, by November 2021, a "general curtailment of Afghan women and girls' fundamental rights and freedoms" was already visible ranging from "limiting their right to work to the absence of women from major decision-making fora and from senior echelons of the civil service".[9]

Inclusivity, broadly implying political, gendered, and ethnic inclusivity, given Afghanistan's ethnically diverse population with large Tajik, Uzbek, and Hazara populations, has been another international demand on the Taliban regime. The composition of the caretaker cabinet, so called by the Taliban themselves, however, remains entirely male, essentially Pashtun, and almost all Taliban members. According to UNAMA, in both Kabul and at the provincial level, "appointments continue to appear designed more to rewarding fighters than promoting governance and inclusion".[10]

Taliban-AQ ties and presence of foreign militants in Afghanistan

The Taliban pledge, as per the deal, to guarantee Afghanistan is never again used by jihadist movements such as the al-Qaeda (AQ) and the Islamic State (IS/ISKP) group to plot attacks abroad today lies discarded. Knowing the Taliban's long working relationship with the al-Qaeda, this was a promise that they were unlikely to keep.

According to the UN, in 2020, the al-Qaeda was active in 12 Afghan provinces along the country's eastern and southern borders and it estimated the total number of AQ fighters in Afghanistan to be between 400 and 600 (the estimate in 2017 was 200).[11] If one looks at the number of AQ-associated fighters in Afghanistan, it would be in the thousands. The AQ, along with the Haqqani Network (HQN), was reportedly establishing new training camps in Eastern Afghanistan.[12]The AQ and HQN are also known to be bound by ties of marriage among families of key leaders.

Besides history and literature to this effect, and the repeated open endorsement of the Taliban by the AQ leadership, the presence of major AQ camps close to the Af-Pak border, such as in Shorabak district of Kandahar province (spread over a very vast area, destroyed in a joint operation in October 2015 by the US and Afghan forces), in areas either controlled by the Taliban or under significant Taliban influence were tellingly indicative of a continuing operational relationship.

Notably, following the capture of the IS-KP leader, Abdullah Orakzai, a Pakistani national, by the Afghan forces in Kandahar province on 4 April soon after the attack, Pakistan was quick to seek his extradition. Afghanistan had then refused the Pak request saying the two countries did not have an extradition treaty. It would be interesting to know the current whereabouts of Farooqi.

Prior to the Taliban takeover, Afghan officials had been repeatedly asserting that hundreds of foreign combatants were fighting alongside the Taliban in provinces like Badakhshan in the north and Helmand in the south. The then Governor of Badakhshan, Zakaria Sawda, had claimed that more than 400 foreign fighters, mostly from neighbouring Tajikistan and Uzbekistan, had joined the Taliban and were fighting Afghan security forces in the districts of Warduj, Jurm, and Yamgan.[13] The Badakhshan province borders China and Pakistan and is of particular concern to China seeking to contain Uighur militancy. Sawda had claimed that these foreign fighters included combatants from China's Xinjiang region and Russia's North Caucasus region of Chechnya.[14] The head of the Provincial Council then claimed that foreign fighters in the province had also joined IS militants and included IMU fighters, who have professed allegiance to the IS-KP.

A similar claim by Afghan officials regarding foreign fighters supporting the Taliban had been voiced by the then Governor of Helmand, Yasin Khan, who had stated that the Taliban were supported by foreign fighters belonging to the AQ, and anti-India terrorist groups like the JeM and the LeT during the offensive on Lashkargah in October 2020.[15]

Fractured Polity

Another fundamental factor that makes progress on some form of political reconciliation difficult in the country is the existence of differences among the Afghan political elite, divided along ethnic and tribal lines. Pashtuns, the largest ethnic group in Afghanistan, generally support a centralized state that guarantees their control of the government. However, non-Pashtuns support decentralization as it would imply a more inclusive and equitable distribution of power. Then there are divisions among the non-Pashtuns—the Tajiks, Uzbeks, Hazaras and other smaller ethnicities. Further, tribal identities within the Pashtuns and others are strong, creating a complex and shifting web of loyalties and affiliations.

Besides the disparate views on the future of Afghanistan among the various ethnicities and groups of Afghan society, the Taliban are also said to have conflicting views about the Afghan state. Some believe in being more open to accommodation, while others believe in the full restoration of the Islamic Emirate.

The Afghan political system has been modelled on centralisation of power and the supreme role of Islam. Even Afghanistan's 2004 Constitution prescribes that "no law shall contravene the tenets and provisions of the holy religion of Islam".[16] With the Taliban, a conservative and stricter interpretation of Islamic law (Sharia) is already on display. The Taliban's actions are, however, consistent with their longstanding political goal of re-establishing their Islamic Emirate though they belie the promises made to the international community.

The internal divisions within the Taliban over policy and distribution of power were likely to become more evident after they came to power. This appears to be happening. The Taliban in power seem more divided than when they were fighting the previous Afghan government. Issues relating to governance, big and small, seem to be taking their toll. Governance could well turn out to be the biggest predicament confronting the Taliban. The disgruntlement could surface because of various reasons such as intensification of internal rivalry in a changed situation where the Taliban occupies the political centre-stage, particularly in the absence of a widely accepted *Amir-ul-Momineen* like Mullah Omar. For some, this could be a mismatch with their expectations of power.

Then there is the possibility of ethnic fault lines deepening within the Taliban as has been reported recently from some of the Northern provinces. Some Taliban field commanders, who became disgruntled, could shift allegiance along with their supporters, possibly to the IS-KP.

Implications: Domestic and Regional

Domestically, the biggest and most immediate fallout of the Taliban gaining control has been on women and girls—their rights and agency have been adversely affected. During the Taliban-1 regime, the Taliban made people strictly follow Islamic law under which girls were not allowed to attend school, women had limited access to work, and their movements and appearance were carefully controlled. The same situation appears to be repeating itself. Mullah Abdul Ghani Baradar, the founder of the Taliban movement, was once asked by Shahabuddin Yaqoob Quraishi, the former Chief Election Commissioner of India, how the Taliban would treat women if the USA left Afghanistan. "Women would have rights", he said, "but only according to the Taliban's interpretation of Islamic Sharia law".[17]

The second major fallout has been on the general economic condition of Afghanistan and its people with the withdrawal of Western financial support. Without humanitarian aid channelled through the UN and a few countries, including India and the CAS, the hunger situation in Afghanistan would have been catastrophic. Even with this aid, it remains grim. Then, there has been the migration of Afghan businessmen and traders to neighbouring countries, including to the Central Asian region and the

Middle East. Today, one can find such Afghan businessmen/traders in all the five countries of Central Asia, in Iran, and in the Middle East.

Regionally, Pakistan seems to have gained the most with the Taliban takeover though there are already indications of tensions in the relationship. This seems so, at least on the surface. Pakistan started playing an important role as soon as the possibility of US-Taliban negotiations strengthened in late 2018. The earlier quadrilateral initiative comprising Afghanistan, the USA, Pakistan, and China had come to a standstill in 2017 due to the differing positions of the quad members on the way ahead. Through the Taliban regime, it seeks to play the role of an important influencer in Afghanistan's affairs. Its closeness to the Taliban regime also provides Pakistan with an important leverage vis-a-vis the USA, especially at a time when it continues to be under Financial Action Task Force (FATF) pressure and in economic duress.

This is not to say that the Taliban would not try to distance themselves from too close an identification with Pakistan, as among the Afghan people, in general, the country continues to remain associated with cynically perpetuating violence in their homeland.

Implications for the Kyrgyz Republic

Unlike the three Central Asian states of Tajikistan, Uzbekistan, and Turkmenistan that border Afghanistan, the Kyrgyz Republic does not share a border with Afghanistan. However, it has been impacted significantly by the heroin produced in Afghanistan, one of the major drug-trafficking routes—the northern route—from Afghanistan to Russia and Eastern Europe passes through Tajikistan and the Southern Kyrgyz city of Osh in the Ferghana Valley. From Osh, the bulk of the drugs is then transported to the capital, Bishkek, and then northwards to Kazakhstan and Russia. Kyrgyzstan shares a long border with Tajikistan running through mountainous terrain that is difficult to patrol. Kyrgyzstan, falling on a major drug-transit route, has also resulted in rising drug addiction locally.[18]

The Taliban had announced a ban on poppy cultivation in Afghanistan in early April 2022. If properly implemented, it will lessen the flow of drugs through the Central Asian countries, including the Kyrgyz Republic. How effective the ban will be in the medium and long terms, however, remains to be seen. Also, whether it will have sustained political support.[19] There are reasons to be doubtful. Poppy cultivation and heroin production in

Afghanistan had grown as the conflict areas expanded in the years preceding the Taliban takeover. The previous Taliban ban (July 2000 to October 2001) was too brief and its enforcement had begun to weaken before the NATO invasion in October 2001.

In terms of a direct security impact on Kyrgyzstan caused by the activities of a terrorist group that is still active in Afghanistan, one incident looms large, i.e., the Batken conflict of 1999. The Batken conflict in the summer (July-September) of 1999 involved fighters of the Islamic Movement of Uzbekistan (IMU), then led by Juma Namangani and Tohir Yo'ldosh (Yuldashev), and Kyrgyz forces. Russia provided support to the Kyrgyz forces. A number of IMU fighters were killed/injured and retreated into Tajikistan. Later, under international pressure, the IMU was persuaded by the Islamic Renaissance Party of Tajikistan to also leave the Tavildara valley in Tajikistan, where it was based.

A year ago, a similar direct conflict in Kyrgyzstan seemed improbable. However, the rise and expansion of the IS-KP in Afghanistan and its links with the IMU present a different security scenario today that calls for caution and close monitoring. As mentioned above, the IS-KP has increasingly started disseminating propaganda directed at Uzbek, Tajik, and Kyrgyz speakers in the region telling people from these countries to join the IS-KP in Afghanistan and guiding them how to go about it. The Afghan Taliban, and AQ relationship also continues, and after losing its alliance with the IMU, the AQ has improved its ties with a number of other Central Asian groups in Afghanistan, such as Khatiba Imam al-Bukhari, Katibat al Tawhid wal Jihad, and the Islamic Jihad group. These groups are based in Northern Afghanistan.[20]

Implications for India

Given the ground reality that the Taliban freely used safe havens in Pakistan and were dependent on Pak support, their holding centre-stage in Afghan polity, by corollary, amounts to a corresponding increase in Pakistan's influence in Afghanistan. Simply put, with the Taliban regime in Afghanistan, Pakistan would aspire to influence decisions of the Afghan government that it perceives would have a bearing on Pakistan, and make concerted efforts to exclude India from the Afghan political and economic space. To what extent the Taliban regime gives in to Pak pressure on excluding India as it settles down remains to be seen.

On the other hand, the Durand Line as the border between the two countries is bound to be contentious. A notable development has been the mediation by the Afghan Taliban to reach a ceasefire between the Pakistan security establishment and the Tehrik-e-Taliban Pakistan (TTP). This is likely to give significant manoeuvring space to the Afghan Taliban vis-a-vis the Pak security forces in the time to come.

With the Taliban in power, the use of the Af-Pak border region for training by anti-India terrorist groups such as the LeT and the JeM can also be expected to increase. The number of infiltration-attempts by these Pakistan-based groups in Jammu and Kashmir have been on the rise. Another factor to be kept in mind is that both the LeT and the JeM are known to have ties with the AQ and there has been evidence pointing at these terrorist organisations acting as links between the Afghan Taliban and the AQ.

For India, continuing to work closely with the USA, Russia, and the Central Asian countries with respect to the situation in Afghanistan, including cooperation in intelligence matters, offers the best course of action. It has been pursuing this course since the Taliban takeover in August 2021. In doing so, India can draw on the enormous reservoir of goodwill that exists in Afghanistan for India. The Taliban are also aware of the work done by the Indian government and Indian companies such as for the construction of the Salma dam, educational institutions, hospitals, and numerous electric supply stations/sub-stations for the benefit of the country.

In a recent significant development, India sent an official delegation to Kabul on 2 June 2022.[21] This may eventually lead to some form of an Indian diplomatic presence working in a purely functional manner in Afghanistan, such as for issuing visas to Afghans wanting to go to India for medical treatment or for facilitating trade that is currently going on in a limited way only through the Wagah-Attari border after having crossed the US$ 1.5 billion mark in FY 2019-20.[22]

The imperative to strengthen ties with the Central Asian States in such a situation cannot be overstated. Early conclusion of preferential trade and investment agreements and improved air connectivity and surface connectivity through Iran (Bandar Abbas and Chabahar ports) with the CAS countries could have a significant positive impact on building an India-CAS economic relationship.

Map 2

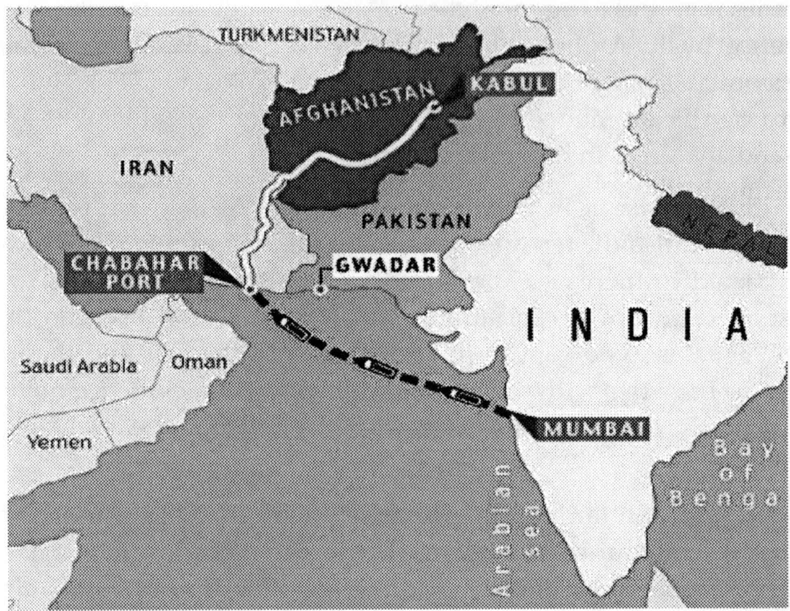

Source: Chabahar: Gateway to Afghanistan and Central Asia, Brahma Chellaney, Hindustan Times, 26 April 2018

Here, consolidating bilateral relations with the Central Asian countries and the countries in the Middle East, in the security and economic domains, would be useful for the government. They are countries that do not aim to dominate Afghan polity and wield undue influence or rule by proxy. The course of developments in Afghanistan will have a bearing not only on the future political orientation of the country, but also on the regional security environment.

An Economic Perspective on Afghanistan-Central Asia Ties

On a number of platforms and discussion forums, representatives of Central Asian countries have been showing a willingness to facilitate efforts at establishing peace in Afghanistan and have underlined the potential value of Afghanistan as a transit hub between the Central Asian region and the world, particularly South Asia.

Notably, the issue of economic growth and infrastructure development could be one positive element in the CAS-Afghanistan relationship even with Afghanistan under strict Taliban rule and the IS-KP becoming more active. It is an area, which is most likely to see a synergy between the CAS governments and the Taliban, especially given Afghanistan's dependence on energy and food supplies from the Central Asian States. Focused discussions on providing humanitarian aid and the development of local infrastructure and entrepreneurship could be useful. In this endeavour, India and the Central Asian countries could play an important role by supporting an inclusive socio-economic development model in Afghanistan in a coordinated manner.

REFERENCES

1. Agreement for Bringing Peace to Afghanistan between the Islamic Emirate of Afghanistan, which is not recognized by the USA as a state and is known as the Taliban by the USA, 29 February 2020.
2. Elise Blanchard, with Thomas Watkins, Afghan Peace Process Risks Collapse as Violence Flares, *AFP News*, 29 April 2020.
3. Christina Goldbaum, With Spate of Attacks, ISIS begins bloody New Chapter in Afghanistan, 1 May 2022, *The New York Times*, accessed 4 June 4, 2022. https://www.nytimes.com/2022/05/01/world/asia/afghanistan-isis-attacks.html
4. SRSG Lyons Briefing to the UNSC on the situation in Afghanistan, 17 November 2021, UNAMA, accessed 4 June 2022. https://unama.unmissions.org/srsg-lyons-briefing-unsc-situation-afghanistan-3
5. Lucas Webber and Riccardo Valle, Islamic State in Afghanistan seeks to recruit Uzbeks, Tajik, Kyrgyz, 17 March 2022, eurasianet, accessed 5 June 2022. https://eurasianet.org/perspectives-islamic-state-in-afghanistan-seeks-to-recruit-uzbeks-tajiks-kyrgyz
6. Ibid.
7. Nirupama Subramanian, Engaging with the Taliban, 3 June 2022, *The Indian Express*.
8. Saikiran Kannan, As Taliban battles Massoud-led resistance in Afghanistan's Panjshir, civilians in the line of fire, 21 May 2022, *India Today*, accessed 6 June 2022. https://www.indiatoday.in/world/story/taliban-battles-massoud-led-resistance-afghanistan-panjshir-civilians-in-line-of-fire-deep-dive-1952448-2022-05-21
9. SRSG Lyons Briefing to the UNSC on the situation in Afghanistan, 17 November 2021, UNAMA, accessed 4 June 2022. https://unama.unmissions.org/srsg-lyons-briefing-unsc-situation-afghanistan-3
10. Ibid.
11. Twenty-sixth Report of the Analytical Support and Sanctions Monitoring Team Submitted Pursuant to Resolution 2368 (2017) Concerning ISIL (Da'esh), Al-Qaeda and Associated Individuals and Entities, New York City: United Nations Security Council, 23 July 2020, https://undocs.org/S/2020/717
12. Ibid.
13. Gulabudin Ghubar, 22 districts in Badakhshan face security threats: Official, 16 October 2020, *Tolo News*.
14. Ibid.
15. Ibid.
16. Article 3, Chapter 1, The Constitution of the Islamic Republic of Afghanistan.

17. Katerina Tiliakou, Will the US-Taliban Agreement lead to real Peace?, 3 March 2020, TRT World.
18. Central Asia's 'Drug Capital' Fights to Stem Tide of Narcotics, 4 January 2013, www.rferl.org.
19. The Taliban's poppy ban redux, 13 April 2022, Global Initiative against Transnational Organized Crime, accessed 7 June 2022. https://globalinitiative.net/analysis/talibans-poppy-ban-afghanistan/
20. Asfandyar Mir, Afghanistan's Terrorism Challenge—The Political Trajectories of Al-Qaeda, the Afghan Taliban, and the Islamic State, October 2020, Middle East Institute, p. 6.
21. Nirupama Subramanian, Engaging with the Taliban, 3 June 2022, *The Indian Express*.
22. India-Afghanistan Commercial Brief, Embassy of India, Kabul website, accessed 7 June 2022.

13

Political Processes in Central Asia:
A Case Study of Kyrgyzstan

Dr. Rashmini Koparkar

Central Asia emerged on the world stage after the disintegration of the Soviet Union in 1991. The birth of the five countries of Kazakhstan, Kyrgyzstan, Tajikistan, Turkmenistan and Uzbekistan became a matter of curiosity as well as concern for the world community. In the beginning, apprehensions were raised about their territorial integrity, political stability and economic viability. The Central Asian Republics (CARs) have faced several political, economic and security challenges in the post-independence period. Nevertheless, they have tackled them to quite some extent, and have eventually strengthened their sovereignty and statehood. In 2021, the CARs will celebrate the completion of thirty years of independence. This is an opportune time to delve into the progress they have made as well as the challenges they face.

In the aftermath of the Soviet disintegration, all the five CARs went through political and economic transformation. They simultaneously initiated the processes of democratization and transition to a market economy. Similarly, they also embarked upon a program of nation-building. These processes were difficult as well as complex. There were geographical, historical, socio-cultural, as well as external factors that influenced the circumstances. While there are certain common elements defining the political processes in all five CARs, each republic has adopted its unique model of transformation and development, and has followed different political trajectories. Therefore, it becomes worthwhile to look into each case independently.

This article focuses exclusively on the political processes in the Kyrgyz Republic. The country has been a part of the larger Central Asian geo-politics, and has experienced similar trends of political transition. It has also met with similar economic and security challenges. Despite this, it stands out as a unique instance in Central Asia. This distinctiveness comes from a variety of reasons. Geographical complexities, economic hardships, North-South dichotomy, and strained ethnic entanglements add to the existing political intricacy.

On the one hand, Kyrgyzstan has been at the forefront of the democratization process compared to other CARs. It has cultivated democratic institutions like a strong legislature, multi-party system, local self-governments, active civil society, and free media. However, on the other hand, it has also gone through a great degree of political instability in the last two decades, including several regime changes, popular protests, and revolutions. Nevertheless, both the aspects of democratization and instability make Kyrgyzstan an interesting case, not only in Central Asia, but also in the larger Eurasian context. The nation's quest for democracy is a finding path through several hurdles and challenges, and this is an ongoing process.

This article focuses on post-Soviet political processes in Central Asia with special reference to Kyrgyzstan. In the beginning, it gives a brief note on the political transition in all the CARs, and tries to find out the underlying common elements. Then, it investigates the case of Kyrgyzstan in detail. It analyzes the influence of various factors like history, geography, demography, culture, and economy. The article gives an in-depth account of post-independence political developments, and gives an assessment of these events with respect to the democratization process.

Political Processes in Central Asia: An Overview

Central Asia has historically been at the crossroads of human civilizations; this unique location has contributed immensely in its evolution as a region. It has witnessed various political campaigns, commercial exchanges, migrations, and cultural give-and-take. These factors continue to impact the contemporary geo-politics of the CARs. Moreover, the region belongs to both sedentary and nomadic peoples who have traditionally inhabited these lands. While Tajiks and Uzbeks represent the sedentary culture, Kyrgyz, Kazakhs, and Turkmens are from the nomadic traditions. Interaction as well as competition between these groups has shaped regional politics.

In the second half of the 19th century, Central Asia was conquered by Tsarist Russia. Following the Bolshevik Revolution (1917) and the Civil War (1917-1920), this region was brought under the Soviet umbrella. As per Lenin's diktat, the Soviet Socialist Republics (SSRs) were created on the basis of the 'nationality' principle.[1] This was for the first time that the CARs were given their current names and specific borders. However, such divisions proved to be difficult because of the linguistic intermix and ethno-cultural spillovers. The Soviets also tried to alter the demographics of the region through forced deportations, economic resettlements, and labour migrations. All these republics were multi-ethnic in their composition, with the titular nationalities forming the majority.[2] However, one has to acknowledge that Soviet rule did bring about a considerable change in the region in the form of infrastructure development, transport and communication networks, literacy, employment, and industrialization.[3]

The Central Asian SSRs did not develop independence movements like their European counterparts, probably because of their overdependence on Moscow. In fact, these republics voted to remain in the Soviet Union in the March 1991 referendum.[4] However, declarations of independence were subsequently passed as the Soviet collapse became inevitable. In the aftermath of the disintegration in December 1991, these newly-independent countries were thrown in the difficult situation, underlined by political uncertainty, economic hardships, and socio-cultural entanglements.

Even after independence, the CARs were ruled by the leadership that had risen from the Soviet ranks. However, the ideology of communism had become defunct, and thus, these leaders had to find a new basis to gain legitimacy. This vacuum was filled by nationalist ideas, and the ruling elites became champions of nationalism.[5] Similarly, the erstwhile Soviet identity was also replaced by the newly emerging national identities. In the case of the CARs, the process of nation-building and construction of national identity remained largely an exercise from above, as the state played an active role in it.[6]

All the five republics adopted their own nationalizing programs, which reflected their dilemma between the civic and ethnic forms of nationalism.[7] The actual end-result was mostly between the two forms, and was significantly different in the case of each of the CARs. Nevertheless, by and large, the national identities were based on historical golden periods, national heroes, ethno-linguistic motifs, and cultural symbols of the titular nationalities. Re-glorification of Timur in Uzbekistan, veneration of Manas in Kyrgyzstan, and re-occurrence of Samanids in Tajikistan were clearly visible. Apart from this, cultural motifs like *Tunduk* in Kyrgyzstan, carpets in Turkmenistan, and blue ceramics in Uzbekistan were also noteworthy. On one hand, the national identities based on ethno-cultural symbols gave people a sense of unity, and led to national consolidation. However, on the other hand, the process of nation-building remained a complex task because of the presence of ethnic minorities, un-delimited borders, and competition over limited natural resources.

The CARs initiated programs of nation-building and state-building almost simultaneously. This made these processes both easy as well as complicated. The major challenge for state-building was the lack of any prior experience or expertise in the field of democratic governance.[8] All these republics adopted democratic constitutions and created institutions like parliaments, elections, multi-party systems, and so on. However, the majority of them have been struggling to accept democracy as the governing principle.[9] This struggle comes mainly from the presence of conflicting ideas among the national discourses, which include resilience of Soviet ideas and institutions, reinvention of historical and cultural traditions of pre-Soviet periods, and the influence of Western liberal ideas and institutions.[10]

Considering Huntington's theory of waves of democratization, the process that underwent in the CARs can fall under the third wave.[11] However, experts like Mcfaul argue that some of these countries are stuck between democracy and authoritarianism. He has also coined the term 'transitional regimes'.[12] Some scholars of democracy have argued that the mere presence of parties, parliaments, and elections cannot make a nation a democracy. In fact, in certain cases, these elements facilitate 'the non-democratic regimes by non-violent means'.[13] Though this view is a little farfetched, it can be said that the CARs have established democratic institutions; however, they still have a long way to go in order to adapt democracy in practice.

All the CARs have shown a tendency of super-powerful presidents. Except Kyrgyzstan, the other four states have had long-serving Presidents, who were repeatedly re-elected with thumping majorities. They have also made necessary changes in the constitutions or have even conducted referendums to extend their term or increase the number of terms. Turkmenistan and Uzbekistan went through a smooth power transfer in 2006 and 2016, respectively, only because of the death of the long-serving first presidents. After coming to power in 2016, Uzbek President Shavkat Mirziyoyev had introduced a number of key reforms in a range of sectors, including towards making the government more inclusive and democratic. Kazakhstan's first president, Nursultan Nazarbayev, who ruled the country for 30 years, stepped down in March 2019, and chose his successor, Kassym-Jomart Tokayev. However, Nazarbayev still holds considerable power and is the chairman of the Security Council.[14] Tajikistan has been ruled by one president, Emomali Rahmon, since 1992.

These long-standing presidencies have been justified by a number of reasons. Firstly, it serves the Central Asian people's quest for stability. It is generally considered in the CARs that strong presidents can maintain stability, ensure security, and tackle internal and external threats. Secondly, it is also the general perception that such regimes deliver better, especially in terms of economic progress, infrastructure development, and rise in living standards. Thirdly, a strong president is also sought after to conduct an independent and balanced foreign policy. Besides, all the CARs, except Kyrgyzstan, seem to have followed an evolutionary transformation, consisting of step-by-step reforms.[15]

Political Process in Kyrgyzstan: Determining Factors

After briefly discussing the political processes in the region, it becomes easy to look at the case of Kyrgyzstan. The country had emerged out of a similar historical context as the other CARs. After becoming independent in 1991, the Kyrgyz Republic, like other neighbours, initiated similar political and economic transitions. It also faced the initial challenges of democratization and economic transformation during the whole of the 1990s. Its pursuit for nation-building was similar to that of any other CAR, and so was its program of promoting ethno-cultural motifs for national consolidation. Despite all this, Kyrgyzstan stands out as a unique case in Central Asia.

In order to understand the distinctiveness of Kyrgyzstan, it is important to study various geographical, historical, socio-cultural, and economic factors. It is a small and landlocked country, bordering China on the east, Tajikistan on the south, Uzbekistan on the west and Kazakhstan on the north. Kyrgyzstan is an overwhelmingly mountainous country. It is divided into northern and southern regions because by the Tien Shan ranges. These two uneven regions signify geographical diversity, as well as socio-economic and cultural differences. The north-south dichotomy has played an important role in the contemporary politics of Kyrgyzstan.

The southern region of Kyrgyzstan is mainly covered by the Fergana Valley, which Kyrgyzstan shares with Uzbekistan and Tajikistan. The Fergana Valley is plain, fertile land, densely populated, and has been the cultural and agricultural epicentre of the region. It has witnessed highly developed urban civilization since ancient times. On the contrary, the mountains are mostly occupied by the traditional Kyrgyz people who take pride in their nomadic lifestyle. These groups of peoples have cohabited for centuries; however, power-sharing equations of the post-independence period have aroused a feeling of competition amongst them.

The population of the Kyrgyz Republic is about 6.5 million,[16] out of which 73 per cent belong to the Kyrgyz ethic group, followed by around 14.7 per cent Uzbeks and six per cent Russians.[17] The Russian minority is mostly concentrated in and around Bishkek, whereas the Uzbeks mainly inhabit the Fergana Valley in the south. Unlike the Russians, who migrated to this region in Tsarist or Soviet times, the Uzbeks have lived in south Kyrgyzstan for centuries. They play an important role in the economy, based on agriculture. The Uzbeks and Kyrgyz groups in the south have clashed twice, in 1989 and then in 2010, which was one of the worst ethnic conflicts in post-Soviet Central Asia. Their competition is not only about distribution of resources, but also about the share in power arrangements.

Various factors like remote location, harsh terrain, and limited resources have led to economic adversity for the people of Kyrgyzstan. In fact, the country is trapped in a vicious circle, where economic hardships lead to political instability, which, in turn, causes a fall in growth. According to the World Bank classification, it is classified as the lower-middle income economy,[18] and 22.4 per cent population lives below the national poverty line (2018).[19] It is heavily dependent on agriculture, gold, and remittances from Russia. All these factors play their part in determining the political processes in Kyrgyzstan.

Post-independence Political Developments

In the aftermath of the Soviet disintegration, Kyrgyzstan had a similar start as any other CAR. Askar Akayev, who had risen from the Soviet ranks and elected to the Presidency in 1990, continued to rule the country. He was re-elected, with a thumping majority, as the President of independent Kyrgyzstan in December 1991. In the initial years, there were some attempts at creating democratic institutions and a pluralist polity. Scholars like John Anderson described the Kyrgyz Republic as 'Central Asia's Island of Democracy', on the premise that its people enjoyed a greater degree of freedom than people in the surrounding countries.[20] However, this description was only in comparison to the other four CARs, who were showing clear authoritarian tendencies.

Kyrgyzstan suffered a heavy blow from the unexpected independence, which was multiplied with the sudden shift to a market economy. At the end of the century, the state was struggling through a high budgetary deficit, and more than half of its population was living under the national poverty line.[21] This era also saw widespread corruption, criminalization, and sharp social differences. The ruling elites had started showing traits of authoritarianism,[22] without much respect to the rule of law. Akayev, who was a northerner, was criticized for marginalizing the southerners and denying them any positions of power.[23] During his presidency, the north-south disparity started widening. He was ousted from power in March 2005 through a popular uprising, which was termed by the West as the 'Tulip Revolution'.

After Akayev's ouster, Kumranbek Bakiyev, a southerner, became the interim president. He was elected to power in July 2005 with an overwhelming majority. During his election campaigns, Bakiyev had promised to eliminate corruption and improve living standards. However, in reality, his term proved to be even more authoritarian and corrupt than that of his predecessor. The regional divide kept widening, and the economy continued to deteriorate. By 2010, about 43 per cent people were living below the poverty line, and the unemployment rate had reached 18 per cent.[24] These factors led to several other problems like drug trafficking, unorganized crime, and ethnic clashes. Despite this, Bakiyev was re-elected in the 2009 presidential election.

Within six months of Bakiyev's re-election, he had to face popular unrest, which led to violent clashes between his supporters and opponents.

In April 2010, his rule was overthrown and an interim government was established under the leadership of Rosa Otunbayeva. However, Bakiyev's rule had created a deep rift between the southern Kyrgyz and the Uzbeks,[25] which ultimately resulted in a devastating ethnic conflict in the Fergana Valley, in the immediate aftermath of the revolution.

During Otunbayeva's interim presidency, a new Constitution was adopted that declared Kyrgyzstan a parliamentary democracy, making it an exceptional case in Central Asia. It also restricted the presidential tenure to a single term of six years and prohibited him/her from re-election. In 2011, Almazbek Atambayev was elected the Kyrgyz president as per the new constitutional law. Nevertheless, in spite of adopting the parliamentary government, the president continued to hold considerable power. Atambayev's tenure of six years gave the country relative stability, but only at the cost of more corruption and concentration of power in the hands of a select few.

As Atambayev's term ended in 2017, and the constitution restricted him from re-election, he stepped down as the President. At the background of long-serving presidents in other CARs who amended constitutions to increase the number of terms, this move was considered as a sign of graciousness and respect for democratic principles. The 2017 presidential election was also significant as it marked the country's first peaceful transition of power from one elected leader to another.[26] In October 2017, former Prime Minister Sooronbai Jeenbekov, whose candidature was supported by Atambayev, was elected the new President. This verdict was seen as the people's urge for stability and democratization.[27]

The euphoria of peaceful transition was short-lived, as Jeenbekov tried to acquire all power for himself. Firstly, he was a southerner, who had received overwhelming support from the Fergana Valley region. After his election, the north-south tensions continued to linger. Secondly, he indulged in a constant political struggle with former president Atambayev over power-sharing. The latter continued to hold influence through his high-level appointees in the government,[28] who were gradually dismissed by the former. Atambayev also became the party chief, and tried to influence the decision-making process. Their power struggle culminated in the revocation of Atambayev's immunity as ex-president and his dramatic arrest. He was sentenced to 11 years' imprisonment on various charges, including corruption and unlawful release of a prisoner.[29]

Kyrgyzstan was once again thrown in political instability in October 2020, following the parliamentary elections, which resulted in only four out of 16 parties clearing the seven per cent threshold. Three of them were considered pro-Jeenbekov.[30] The opposition parties criticized the elections as rigged and started nationwide protests. The protesters also seized the parliament building and the White House. They released several high-profile prisoners, including former President Atambayev, and nationalist leader Sadar Japarov. Eventually, the elections were annulled, and Japarov was made the Prime Minister, and then the interim president after Jeenbekov's resignation.[31] In January 2021, Japarov was elected as Kyrgyzstan's new president. Similarly, in a nation-wide referendum, the parliamentary form of government, introduced by the 2010 constitution, was also changed back to the presidential system.[32]

Assessing the Political Processes: Democratization vis-à-vis Instability

After going through the post-independence political developments in Kyrgyzstan, one can say that the country has been going through periodic shocks of political instability. While the other CARs have seen one or two presidential regimes till date, Kyrgyzstan has had six presidents in last 30 years. The most disturbing fact is that almost all the previous presidents were criticized for concentration of power in the hands of a select few, regional or clan bias in appointments, nepotism, corruption, and an authoritarian style of decision-making. Moreover, on every instance of regime change, the successor criticized the predecessor for all these things, and promised to tackle them and deliver better; but seldom succeeded.

The second worrisome factor is the style of regime change. In words of Mattuo Fumagalli, "'Revolution', best understood in the Kyrgyzstani context as presidential replacement engineered through elite-led popular protests, typically in the wake of disputed elections, is starting to become the country's modal form of leadership change".[33] Similarly, as discussed earlier, politics in Kyrgyzstan is influenced by several other factors, and what appears like regime change is generally a reflection of the struggle between clans and regions, which is based on local power-sharing and business interests.[34] As a matter of fact, post-independence political processes seem to have intensified, rather that lessened, the social cleavages pertaining to region, ethnicity, or clan.

In the last two decades, Kyrgyzstan has seen frequent movements, protests, and uprisings. This is not confined to the capital, Bishkek, but often spread to other cities as well. On the one hand, it can be a disturbing and destabilizing factor. It limits the capacity of the government to carry out day-to-day business. However, on the other hand, it is also a reflection of a democratic way of life. Kyrgyzstan is one such country that respects the people's right to protest, unlike the other CARs in which such protests are ruthlessly crushed. However, there is a need to create a greater awareness among the people for the responsible use of this right.

Even though protests and people's movements are part of the democratic system, true democracy is much more than that. It is about conducting free and fair elections; about empowering the legislatures; about allowing a free press; about creating a vibrant civil society; and about establishing local self-governing bodies. Kyrgyzstan has made considerable progress in all these aspects of democracy. However, consolidation of these democratic institutions should be an urgent priority. Creating a system with separation of power and effective checks and balances is also the need of the hour. The institutional and procedural aspects of democracy should be strengthened through constitutional means, in order to reduce the risk of future violent regime changes.

For a small and economically weak country like Kyrgyzstan, maintaining national unity and political stability is of utmost importance. The nation has already undergone a great degree of upheaval in recent years. The post-parliamentary election standoff coincided with the COVID-19 pandemic, the greatest public health crisis of our times. In such a scenario, it becomes a requisite for the newly-sworn in president to stabilize the situation, and tackle various human security challenges the nation is facing.

REFERENCES

1. E. H. Carr, *The Bolshevik Revolution*, London: Macmillan Press, 1969, p 139.
2. Anita Sengupta, "Beyond Boundaries: Identity, Nationality and Consciousness in Central Asia", *Contemporary Central Asia*, 1998, Vol. 2(1), 33-53, 34.
3. Francis Newton, "Soviet Central Asia: Economic Progress and Problems", *Middle Eastern Studies*, Vol. 12(3), Special Issue on the Middle Eastern Economy, October 1976, 87-104, pp. 87-88.
4. Kathleen Collins, *The Logic of Clan Politics in Central Asia: The Impact on Regime Transformation*, Cambridge: Cambridge University Press, 2006, p. 158.
5. Shahram Akbarzadeh, "Nation-building in Uzbekistan", *Central Asian Survey*, 1996, Vol. 15(1), 23-32, 23.

6. Charles Kurzman, "Uzbekistan: The Invention of Nationalism in an Invented Nation", *Critique*, No. 15, 1999, p.78.
7. Anna Matveeva, "Democratization, Legitimacy and Political Change in Central Asia", *International Affairs* (Royal Institute of International Affairs 1944), Vol. 75(1), January 1999, 23-44.
8. Fatima Kukeyeva and Oxana Shkapyak, "Central Asia's Transition to Democracy", *Procedia - Social and Behavioural Sciences*, No. 81, 2013, 79-83, 80.
9. Ibid.
10. Tulsiram and Ajay Patnaik (eds.), *Eurasian Politics: Ideas, Institutions and External Relations*, 2013, New Delhi: KW Publishers Pvt. Ltd, p. v.
11. Samuel P. Huntington, "Democracy's Third Wave", *Journal of Democracy*, Spring 1991, Vol. 2(2), 12-34.
12. Michael McFaul, "The Fourth Wave of Democracy and Dictatorship: Non-cooperative Transitions in the Post-communist World", *World Politics*, Vol. 54(2), January 2002, 212-244, 212.
13. Oxana Kharitonov, "Post-Soviet Political Regimes and Institutions", in Tulsiram and Ajay Patnaik (eds.), *Eurasian Politics: Ideas, Institutions and External Relations*, 2013, New Delhi: KW Publishers Pvt. Ltd, pp. 43-46.
14. Arkady Subnov, "Kazakhstan: What is Nazarbayev's Transition Plan About?" *Aljazeera*, March 30, 2019, URL: https://www.aljazeera.com/indepth/opinion/kazakhstan-nazarbayev-transition-plan-190331061032825.html/, Accessed 7 February 2021.
15. Mukhtor Nazirov, "The Conceptual Basis of Contemporary Political Processes in Uzbekistan", *Contemporary Central Asia*, Vol. XVIII (2&3), 32-46, 33.
16. *National Statistical Committee of the Kyrgyz Republic*, at www.stat.kg/en/statistics/naselenie/, Accessed 11 February 2021.
17. "Population by Nationality", Ibid.
18. World Bank, URL: https://datahelpdesk.worldbank.org/knowledgebase/articles/906519-world-bank-country-and-lending-groups, Accessed 12 February 2021.
19. "Poverty Data: Kyrgyz Republic", Asian Development Bank, URL: https://www.adb.org/countries/kyrgyz-republic/poverty#:~:text=Poverty%20Data%3A%20 Kyrgyz%20 Republic,day%20is%200.3%25%20in%202019, Accessed 12 February 2021.
20. John Anderson, *Kyrgyzstan: Central Asia's Island of Democracy*, Taylor & Francis, 1999.
21. "Story", *President of the Kyrgyz Republic*, official portal, URL: http://www.president.kg/ru/kyrgyzstan/istoriya, Accessed 12 February 2021.
22. Ibid.
23. Andrew R. Bond and Natalie R. Koch, "Kyrgyzstan, Interethnic Tensions, and Relations with Uzbekistan: A Political Geographic Perspective", at www.nataliekoch.com/docs/Bond_Koch_2010, Accessed 13 December 2017.
24. Michael Caster, "Re-visiting Kyrgyzstan's Bloody Summer", *The Diplomat*, 13 June 2014, URL: https://thediplomat.com/2014/06/revisiting-kyrgyzstans-bloody-summer/, Accessed 8 February 2021.
25. Ibid.
26. Mallinson, Kate, "Kyrgyz Election Shows There is Another Way Forward in Central Asia, *Chatham House*, 17 October 2017, URL: https://www.chathamhouse.org/expert/comment/kyrgyz-election-shows-there-another-way-forward-central-asia, Accessed 6 February 2021.

27. Rashmini Koparkar, "Presidential Elections in Kyrgyzstan: More Continuity than Change", Vivekananda International Foundation, 13 November 2017, URL: https://www.vifindia.org/article/2017/november/13/presidential-elections-in-kyrgyzstan-more-continuity-than-change, Accessed 7 February 2021.
28. Bruce Pannier, "Won't Fade Away: Former, Current Kyrgyz Presidents on Collision Course", Radio Free Europe, 4 April 2018, URL: https://www.rferl.org/a/qishloq-ovozi-kyrgyzstan-atambaev-jeenbekov-collision-course/29144713.html, Accessed 7 February 2021.
29. "Former Kyrgyz president sentenced to 11 years in prison for release of crime boss", *CGTN*, 23 June 2020, URL: https://news.cgtn.com/news/2020-06-23/Former-Kyrgyz-president-sentenced-to-11-years-for-crime-boss-release-RyJEVcE6t2/index.html, Accessed 7 February 2021.
30. Pravesh Kumar Gupta, "Post-election crisis in Kyrgyzstan", Vivekananda International Foundation, 9 November 2020, URL: "https://www.vifindia.org/article/2020/november/09/post-election-crisis-in-kyrgyzstan, Accessed 6 February 2021.
31. Matteo Fumagalli, "Kyrgyz electoral fiasco involves familiar faces" East Asia Forum, 20 October 2020. https://www.eastasiaforum.org/2020/10/20/kyrgyz-electoral-fiasco-involves-familiar-faces/, Accessed 6 February 2021.
32. "CEC of Kyrgyzstan approves results of referendum on form of government", *Kabar News Agency*, 20 January 2021, URL: http://en.kabar.kg/news/cec-of-kyrgyzstan-approves-results-of-referendum-on-form-of-government/, Accessed 8 February 2021.
33. Matteo Fumagalli, "Kyrgyz electoral fiasco involves familiar faces" *East Asia Forum*, 20 October 2020. https://www.eastasiaforum.org/2020/10/20/kyrgyz-electoral-fiasco-involves-familiar-faces/, Accessed 6 February 2021.
34. M. K. Bhadrakumar, "Another colour revolution fails in Kyrgyzstan", *Asia Times*, 16 October 2020. https://asiatimes.com/2020/10/another-color-revolution-fails-in-kyrgyzstan/?fbclid=IwAR1StcPxnbhdHNBX8QWLBfUX05AIgDMeYszfMPp5EXML%E2%80%A6, Accessed 11 February2021.

14

Situating India in Regional Security and Connectivity in Central Asia

Dr. Pravesh Kumar Gupta

ABSTRACT

Since the collapse of the Soviet Union, Central Asia has emerged as a critical geopolitical space. At the crossroads of East, West, South, and Central Asia, its strategic location has often resulted in the spill over of challenges beyond the region's immediate periphery. The core security issues concerning terrorism, extremism and smuggling of drugs and weapons from Afghanistan affect India and Central Asia. In Central Asia, Tajikistan, Uzbekistan, and Turkmenistan share around 2,500 kilometres of long porous borders with Afghanistan. Given the cross-border terror linkages, the Central Asian region remains particularly vulnerable to the unfolding situation in Kabul. This, therefore, demands a greater focus on regional security. India shares similar concerns about Afghanistan, and Kabul is crucial for India's connectivity to Central Asia. This research paper will focus on how India and the Central Asian republics can find convergence in the regional security and connectivity in the region. Based on the findings, the paper would also suggest some recommendations.

Introduction

India shares a long history with Central Asia. In the ancient and medieval periods, there existed a great process of mutual cultural enrichment between India and Central Asia.[1] The findings of excavations at Harappa reveal direct testimony of this mutual relation. Besides the civilization and geo-cultural connections, the role of various empires, such as the Greco-Indian Kingdom, accentuated the historical linkages. The Central Asian region was at the crossroads between Greeks and Indians, which had infused the cultural interactions between the two regions. The Saka rulers (Indo-Scythians), who belonged to Central Asia, have influenced the western parts of India.[2]

Buddhism was the largest source of interaction between India and Central Asia, which the Mauryan kings spread. During Asoka's reign, Buddhist missionaries expanded the network of Buddhist monastic institutions throughout the Mauryan Empire and in Sri Lanka, Kashmir, Gandhara, and the Swat Valley. Archaeological remains of stupas and monasteries established during the Mauryan period show that Buddhist centres in these regions functioned as bases for the transmission of Buddhism to Southeast Asia and Central Asia.[3] The Kushana kingdom had settled its monarchy in India and Central Asia and enjoyed common social interactions. The Kushana period had the most substantial impacts on Indian technology, military, art and culture, pottery, religion, economy, etc.[4] In medieval times, the Mughal connection between the two regions proved another milestone of cultural amalgamation.

India had friendly relations with the Soviet Union and had diplomatic ties with the region, which have helped maintain relations after the dissolution of the Soviet Union in 1991. After the Soviet disintegration, the newly-independent CARs considered India as one of the genuine stakeholders to balance the differing forces in the region. This proved to be true when the leaders of post-Soviet Central Asian states chose India to be the first country outside the former Soviet bloc for their State visits in 1992. Uzbek President Islam Karimov visited India in August 1991, while Kazakh President Nursultan Nazarbayev paid his first official visit to India in 1992.[5]

The opening of Indian missions in all the five capitals of CARs was a good initiative on India's part to win the confidence of these republics. Prime Ministers Narasimha Rao, Atal Bihari Vajpayee, and Dr. Manmohan Singh visited the region in 1993, 2002, and 2006, respectively. Consistent bilateral visits of high levels from both sides have helped sustain the ties. It has also created goodwill amongst India and Central Asia's political elites and local populations. Still, it is crucial to examine how India-Central Asia ties remained below their potential despite having close historical relations and a convergence of interests.

India's interest in Central Asia is multi-fold. With the disintegration of the USSR, New Delhi aspired to play a constructive role in Eurasian political, economic, and security settings. However, due to a lack of political will and the absence of direct land connectivity, India's efforts in this direction were thwarted. In 2015, with PM Modi's visit to the five Central Asian countries, India-Central Asia relations gained momentum. It was the first-ever visit of any Indian prime minister to the region in one go. In 2017, India became a permanent member of the China-dominated Shanghai Cooperation Organization (SCO). It was seen as a critical step in strengthening multilateral cooperation with CARs. India's role in the SCO is a matter of critical assessment about how India can make more use of this platform.

In January 2019, the first India-Central Asia Dialogue at the foreign ministers' level was held in Samarkand, Uzbekistan. Smt. Sushma Swaraj, former External Affairs Minister (EAM) of India, led the Indian delegation to the summit. The EAM described Central Asia as the natural partner of India. She underscored the need for building a modern and comprehensive partnership between the two regions. Several initiatives were adopted during the Samarkand Dialogue to enhance G2G cooperation. The setting up of an 'India-Central Asia Developmental Group' was announced. The group is expected to develop concrete proposals for expanding developmental partnerships between the two regions. The second India-Central Asia Dialogue was held virtually in October 2020. New Delhi recently hosted the Third India-Central Asia Dialogue in December 2021. This multilateral mechanism has the potential to build a stronger partnership between India and Central Asia.

India's trade with Central Asia is much below its true potential. Economic cooperation will remain limited until it fully connects with the region by railways, roads, or air corridors. India needs to shift the focus from an import-oriented approach to establishing a manufacturing base in Central Asia. Also, Indian industries need to be incentivized to invest in Central Asia. Along with this, India needs to mull over speeding up the progress of its connectivity projects, such as the Chabahar and International North-South Transport Corridor (INSTC).

China is the dominant player in Central Asia. It has moved beyond trade and investments to the security domain in Central Asia and conducted joint military exercises with Tajikistan, Kazakhstan, and Kyrgyzstan. The last two are significant as they are members of the Russia-led Collective Security Treaty Organization (CSTO). It remains to be seen whether this creates friction with Russia, the leading security provider in the region so far. India needs to explore ways to cooperate with significant stakeholders in Central Asia, such as the USA, European Union, Japan, and especially Russia, to counter Chinese influence as Russia leads both the Eurasian Economic Union (EAEU) and the CSTO.

India-Central Asia share security concerns arising from neighbouring Afghanistan. This is another common aspect where India can collaborate with CARs. Uzbekistan and Turkmenistan, having greater strategic interests in a stable Afghanistan, have provided developmental support and contributed to the progress of trade and transport corridors in Afghanistan. However, having been present in the region for a long time and with around US$ 333 billion investments in Afghanistan, India's achievements in the region seem inadequate. With the Taliban government back in power in Kabul, a closer partnership between India and Central Asian nations is required to deal with the challenges. The hosting of the Delhi Regional Security Dialogue on Afghanistan by India in November 2021 is a useful outcome of India-Central Asia cooperation concerning Afghanistan.

Trade and Economic Cooperation

India began emphasising its links with Central Asia to defend its geo-economic and geopolitical interests in the region.[6] As a result, policies such as the "Look North Policy",[7] "Extended Neighbourhood Policy", [8] and "Connect Central Asia Policy" have been implemented.[9] Through commodity and services trade, foreign investment, joint ventures, banking, insurance, agriculture, pharmaceutical goods, and technical training, India hopes to enhance its primary economic interests in Central Asian countries.

The level of economic cooperation between India and Central Asia is far below the potential (only 0.17 per cent of the total Indian trade). The total official trade between India and Central Asia in 2015-16 was US$ 819.37 million, which reached US$ 2,700 million in 2019-20, the highest in a decade. In India's overall trade with Central Asia, trade with Kazakhstan accounts for US$ 2,450 million in 2019-20.[10]

The lowest level of trade with other Central Asian Republics is a significant economic setback for India.

Fig. 1: India-Central Asia Trade (in US$ million)

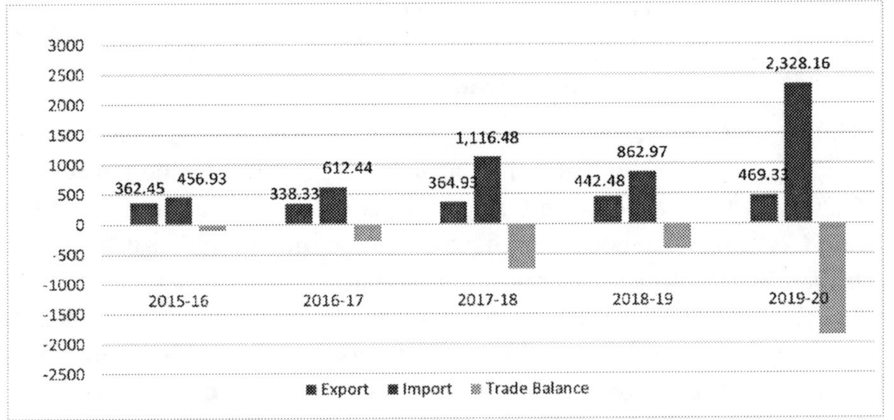

Central Asian exports to India are diverse (mineral fuels, salts, vegetables, fruits, aluminium, ores, chemicals, cotton, fertilizer), while imports from India consist mainly of pharmaceutical products.[11] The Indian export market relating to Central Asia needs to be expanded. India's total trade with the Central Asian region is quite insignificant. An apt framework and future-oriented policies can change the current trade scenario between the two regions. To facilitate trade and investment with the region, Indian policymakers have fashioned an institutional framework. The government set up intergovernmental commissions (IGCs) for trade, economic, scientific, and technical cooperation with all the CARs. Although these IGCs have been meeting regularly, the outcome has been minimal. Joint Working Groups (JWGs) have further institutionalized these relations in various fields, such as information technology, science, technology, hydrocarbons, military-technical cooperation, etc.[12] As proposed during the first India-Central Asia Dialogue, the 'India-Central Asia Business Council' was launched in February 2020 with the participation of apex commercial bodies of respective stakeholders, which can be seen as a stimulus to the economic engagement.[13]

For both India and CARs, energy is a significant motivation to cooperate, as it is in the interest of the latter to diversify their economies and multilateral cooperation.[14] India's energy security in Central Asia is distressed by two significant factors: lack of connectivity and Chinese influence in the region. However, the balancing approach adopted by the Central Asian countries towards the major power competition in the region has some hope for an assertive Indian involvement. However, smoothing out the progress of connectivity initiatives to achieve energy security goals needs to be a priority for Indian policymakers.

How to Improve Bilateral Trade?

- The 'India-Central Asia Business Council' (ICABC), which was proposed during the first India-Central Asia Dialogue, was established in February 2020 with the participation of leading commercial institutions of India and Central Asian countries. This might be interpreted as a stimulus to India-Central Asia economic engagement.
- The ICABC has decided to form four JWGs in energy (oil, gas, and renewable energy), agriculture, food processing, textiles, tourism, air corridors, pharmaceuticals, life sciences, and healthcare.[15]
- India is also working with its Central Asian partners to form an India-Central Asia Development Group. New Delhi would provide technical assistance and finance to the Central Asian countries through Lines of Credit and Buyers' Credit facilities through its EXIM Bank for development projects.
- Connectivity is necessary for realizing the real potential of India-Central Asia economic cooperation. Therefore, New Delhi has accelerated attempts to bring interested Central Asian countries onboard for connectivity projects like Chabahar and INSTC.
- The discussions to negotiate a Free Trade Agreement (FTA) with the Eurasian Economic Union are still progressing. This agreement can increase India's trade and commerce with Russia and other Eurasian countries.[16]

Promoting Regional Security and Connectivity through Multilateral Cooperation

Shanghai Cooperation Organization (SCO)

Proper connectivity with the CARs has been a key impediment for India, particularly given China's influence and huge investments via the Belt and Road Initiative. As a result, new strategies were required to allow India to extend its market share in Central Asia. In 2017, India obtained full membership of the Shanghai Cooperation Organization (SCO), a regional organization dominated by China. India's membership in SCO opened up new avenues to outline its ties with the CARs. The SCO also serves as a medium of keeping vigilance on Pakistan, which became a full member in 2017.[17]

India has offered several significant initiatives by participating in the SCO summits. India is the world's third-largest tech start-up country. New Delhi has proposed that the SCO form a special working group on innovation and start-ups. Furthermore, India requested that the SCO countries promote collaboration in traditional medicine and that a joint working group in this sector be established. Appropriate measures to foster cooperation in the agricultural, energy, education, medicines, and information and communication technology sectors on the micro, small and medium-levels can offer more development to participating nations. India also advocated that tourism should be promoted based on the Buddhist connections that SCO members share.[18]

India also emphasised that through the SCO Business Council, a detailed discussion on a trade and investment development agenda is required. As a result, on 23 November 2020, the FICCI hosted the SCO Business Conclave, which is a significant development. In addition, India underscored that adopting English, along with Chinese and Russian, as a working language in the SCO will ensure that communication is simple and documentation easily accessible. On the sidelines of SCO summits, India took advantage of engaging with representatives from Central Asian countries.[19]

On 17 September 2021, Prime Minister Modi participated in the 21st SCO Summit via video conferencing. In his address, he took a firm position against radicalization and extremism, and asked for the creation of a comprehensive plan to combat terror financing and cross-border terrorism. PM Modi also emphasised India's commitment to improving connectivity with Central Asia. He stressed that any connectivity initiative, including China's BRI, should respect territorial integrity.[20]

Apart from India's existing degree of participation with the SCO, New Delhi's position in the organisation can be expanded. For example, Indian businesses and industries need to be promoted on the SCO platform for greater cooperation with member-countries. The SCO can also be a crucial stage for promoting India's cultural heritage (Yoga) and educational potential.

Connectivity: Challenges and Prospects

Connectivity projects such as the Chabahar port, the International North-South Transport Corridor (INSTC), and the Ashgabat Agreement should be given significant consideration because they can help boost trade and economic cooperation between the two regions.

INSTC

In the last five years, India has invested in projects such as the International North-South Transport Corridor (INSTC) to accelerate connectivity initiatives. The INSTC made considerable progress after India joined the 'Customs Convention on International Transport of Goods' under the TIR Convention in June 2017.[21] INSTC is a multi-modal transportation route linking the Indian Ocean and the Persian Gulf to the Caspian Sea via Iran and to northern Europe via St. Petersburg in Russia. Russia, India, and Iran initiated the INSTC in September 2000 in St. Petersburg. The agreement was signed on 16 May 2002. Once fully realised, the INSTC will provide India with direct access to Central Asia, Russia, and Europe. At the same time, it will allow Iran and Azerbaijan to become regional transit hubs.

According to a study by the Federation of Freight Forwarders Association of India (FFFAI), INSTC will reduce the distance from the JNPT port in Mumbai to Moscow via the current route from 8,700 nautical miles to 2,200 nautical miles and 3,000 km (over-land). In terms of cost, this will reduce the freight cost of a 20foot container from US$ 1400 to US$ 1250. The transit time will be reduced from 32-37 days to 19 days. INSTC will also bring enormous savings in time and cost for transit to CIS countries through Iran. Existing routes go eastward to China or loop back westward to CIS countries. The alternative route through the Georgian port of Poti is also too long. Even though INSTC is a cost-effective mode for the India-Eurasian transport link, there has been a consistent delay in making INSTC fully operational. The absence of a direct route is one of the factors behind the rather small trade volume between India and CIS countries.[22]

Bandar Abbas port is connected to three points on Iran's northern borders by rail—Amrirabad port on the Caspian, Inchebarun on the land crossing between Iran and Turkmenistan, and Mashad/Saraks on Iran's tri-junction with Turkmenistan and Afghanistan. In addition, Astara port in Iran is connected by road from Bandar Abbas. Thus, considerable infrastructure exists for movement along the INSTC. There is, however,

Map 1

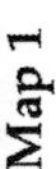

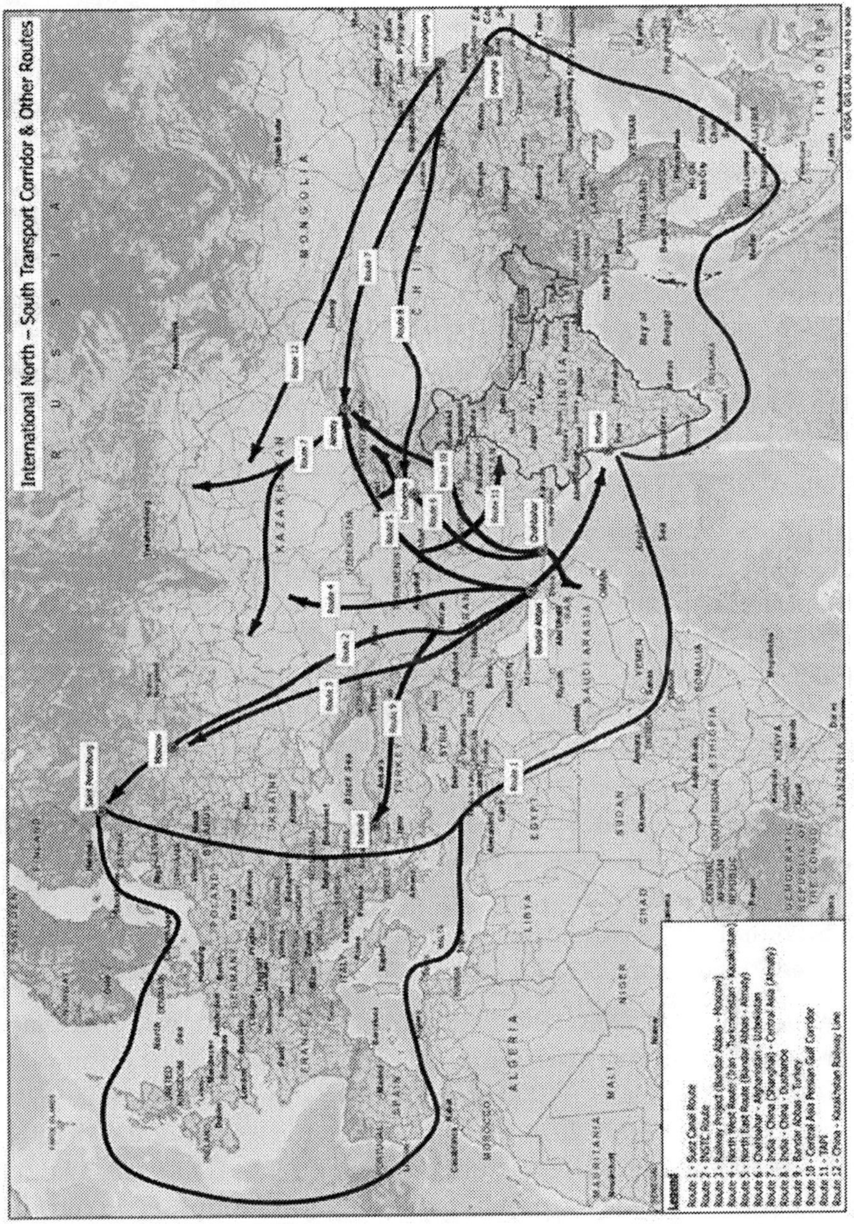

Source: https://i2.wp.com/www.silkroadbriefing.com/news/wpcontent/uploads/2020/03/instc.jpg?quality =90 & strip =all&ssl=1

some apprehension on the part of banks to accept documents. While Bandar Abbas port is the main port serving the International North-South Transit Corridor, Chabahar port could also be linked to this route once the Chabahar-Zahedan rail line is built. The CARs are in support of integrating the Chabahar port into the INSTC. In the first India-Central Asia Summit, Turkmenistan has also volunteered to integrate the Turkmenbashi port into the INSTC, which will help to accelerate connectivity plans.[23]

Chabahar Port

India and Iran signed an agreement to develop Chabahar port during Prime Minister Modi's visit to Tehran in 2016. This port is vital for India since it bypasses its thorny neighbour, Pakistan, which has hampered India's access to Afghanistan and other landlocked nations in the Central Asian Region (CAR). Chabahar is frequently compared to Pakistan's Gwadar Port, which is managed by China.[24]

An Indian company, India Ports Global Limited, took over port operations of Shahid Beheshti Port in Chabahar in December 2018 and has since handled 12 lakh tons of bulk cargo and about 8,200 containers. In the recent past, there has been a rise in transit cargo for Afghanistan through Chabahar. India's assistance of 75,000 tons of wheat to Afghanistan, of which eight consignments have already been shipped, is being supplied via Chabahar.[25] The port has handled over 53,000 tons of India's wheat bound for Afghanistan since 2020. Afghanistan's exports to India are also routed via Chabahar Port. Kabul sent its first consignment to India through Chabahar Port in February 2019. Subsequently, it has sent four more consignments to India through Chabahar Port. As part of the Agreement, India is committed to extending grant assistance of nearly US$ 85 million and a credit facility of US$ 150 million for Chabahar Port development.[26]

On December 11, 2020, the first bilateral virtual summit took place. The proposal of a trilateral dialogue between India, Uzbekistan, and Iran to discuss the shared use of Chabahar port was supported by India. As an outcome, on 14 December 2020, a trilateral dialogue was held, which might be considered a good result of 'Quick Diplomacy.' The CARs are in favour of integrating the Chabahar port into the INSTC. As proposed in the First India Central Asia Summit held in January 2022, a Joint Working Group on Chabahar Port will assist in identifying and addressing challenges relating to India-Central Asia trade and economic relations.[27]

Developments in Afghanistan: A Common Concern

The problem of terrorism, extremism, international crime and drug trafficking, cyber, and narcotics are critical to the collective security of India and Central Asia. As stakeholders, India and Central Asia need to uphold frequent communication and work together to ensure that Afghanistan does not become a hotbed of international terrorism again.[28] Tajikistan, Turkmenistan, and Uzbekistan are three Central Asian nations that share a direct border with Afghanistan and face security challenges due to instability in Afghanistan. New Delhi has also been a strong supporter of the reconstruction of war-torn Afghanistan. India invested billions of funds in the developmental progress of Afghanistan. However, with the fall of the democratic government in Kabul, Afghanistan was again taken over by the Taliban. The Taliban posed a serious threat to both India and Central Asia. On bilateral and multilateral fora, India has promoted a comprehensive approach to strengthen international cooperation to restrain this menace.

With the Taliban's return to power, India's Afghanistan policy was expected to be substantially hampered. India adopted a tough position against the Taliban, requiring a stable Afghanistan with an inclusive government before engaging with it in any way. New Delhi organised a regional security dialogue on Afghanistan on 10 November 2021, as part of its active diplomacy in Afghanistan. This Dialogue was attended by the National Security Advisers (NSAs)/Secretaries of Security Councils of Central Asian republics, Russia, and Iran. This was a major accomplishment of India's proactive diplomacy on Afghanistan. The 'Delhi Declaration on Afghanistan' was adopted after this security dialogue. All representatives from the participating countries agreed to work together to maintain peace and stability in Afghanistan, as well as to combat terrorism and illicit drug trafficking. Furthermore, the NSAs of the participating nations agreed to form an inclusive administration in Kabul and stressed that Afghan territory should not be utilised against another country.[29]

Afghanistan was the focus of discussion during the Third India-Central Asia Dialogue, which India hosted in December 2021. The foreign ministers of the Central Asian countries reiterated their commitment to a peaceful, safe, and stable Afghanistan, emphasising the need to maintain its sovereignty, unity, and territorial integrity. They also resolved to keep providing Afghans with emergency humanitarian assistance. The foreign ministers also emphasised the importance of UN Security Council Resolution 2593 (2021), which states unequivocally that terrorists cannot use Afghan land for refuge, training, planning, or fundraising, and calls for coordinated action against all terrorist organisations. They decided to continue collaborating closely on the Afghan situation.[30]

Uzbekistan has been proactive in its diplomatic engagement with the Taliban administration. Tashkent has also requested that humanitarian aid be sent to Afghanistan and release of Afghan assets. This was largely prompted by the assumption that the Taliban would ensure that extremist organisations did not utilise Afghan territory. Recent reports, however, indicate that ultra-radical terrorist groups such as the Islamic State-Khorasan (IS-K) have gained strength in Northern Afghanistan and have initiated attacks on Uzbekistan and Tajikistan, undermining Taliban rule. Although the Central Asian governments have denied ISK's allegations, it has led to a better understanding of the Taliban's inability to hold control and influence.[31] No country has acknowledged Taliban rule to date, and incidents like these would further discourage regional countries from recognising the Taliban leadership.

During the first India-Central Asia leaders Summit, a Joint Working Group (JWG) on Afghanistan was proposed to be established. This JWG is intended to provide an institutional structure for India and CARs' cooperative efforts to stabilise Afghanistan.[32] All of India's efforts to establish an understanding with Central Asian nations on Afghanistan demonstrate that New Delhi is regarded as an important factor in the regional security settings of South and Central Asia.

Strategically, the India-Central Asia relationship has been challenged by various powerful nations that seek to control the region. China and its Belt and Road Initiative and Russia's attempts to retain influence in the region increase both risks and opportunities for India. Thus, India's attempts to rebuild its relationship with Central Asia are often viewed as an endeavour to counter China's presence in the region.[33] Moreover, as the competition between India and China intensifies, India could also push to gain the support of the Central Asian nations to attain a permanent seat in the United Nations Security Council (UNSC). This could also help build a more constructive India-Russia partnership in Central Asia to balance Chinese influence.[34]

Ideas for Strengthening India-Central Asia Cooperation

- Given the direct access through the Iranian port of Chabahar and rising Sinophobia amongst the region's population, India can use its soft diplomacy to strengthen its position in the Central Asian region.
- It is in India's interest to strategically finalise the long due Free Trade Agreement (FTA) with the Eurasian Economic Union (EAEU). Armenia, Belarus, Kazakhstan, Kyrgyzstan, and Russia are the current members of the grouping. It covers a vast Eurasian landmass with a population of 183 million and a GDP of approximately 5 trillion US$.[35] If finalized without delay, the FTA with EAEU will give India direct access to the region's enormous hydrocarbon resources. It will also open the doors to Eurasian markets for Indian products.
- The agreements signed between India and Central Asia should be given priority in India, especially that on counter-terrorism, the supply of chemical products, defence and military technology, pharmaceutical industry, health and medical sciences, innovation, and science and technology.
- The Indian government should give tax rebates to Indian investors who are willing to explore the Central Asian markets and are interested in investing in the strategic Chabahar port with some sureties and guarantees.
- Besides, the tax rebates can play an accelerating role in reviving the close cultural and economic bonds between India and Central Asia.[36]

Conclusion

A review of existing relations between India and Central Asia indicates that India shares close historical ties with the region tracing back to the ancient Silk Road and even before that age as well. However, attempts to promote these ties to gain strategic benefits are absent. Since Central Asia is not India's immediate neighbour, regional connectivity is paramount for both the regions. The shortest route for India to reach CARs is via Pakistan and Afghanistan. Due to India's hostility with Pakistan over dozens of issues, overland connectivity remains vexed. The safety and security of goods and transport of energy resources are crucial as it involves both the government and private sectors. Because of this, to date, progress in important projects like the TAPI pipeline is in a limbo. However, PM

Modi's refreshed diplomacy towards India's extended neighbourhood is presented as a stepping stone for it to nurture its long-lost relations with Central Asia. Besides, it is an excellent opportunity to improve trade and commerce by expediting connectivity initiatives. Increased economic relations will give the required strategic substance to India. Additionally, India must use its soft power in its favour to gain required leverage in the region. The continuation of the first India-Central Asia leaders' summit has the potential to take forward India's multilateral cooperation with Central Asian countries.

REFERENCES

1. Joshi, N. (2010), "Reconnecting India and Central Asia: Emerging Security and Economic Dimensions", Monograph, Central Asia-Caucasus Institute & Silk Road Studies Program. URL: https://www.silkroadstudies.org/resources/pdf/Monographs/2010_03_MONO_Joshi_India-Central-Asia.pdf
2. Banerjee, Gauranga Nath, "Hellenism in ancient India", Munshi Ram Manohar Lal, Delhi, 1961, pp. 76-77.
3. Joshi, N. (2010), "Reconnecting India and Central Asia: Emerging Security and Economic Dimensions", Monograph, Central Asia-Caucasus Institute & Silk Road Studies Program. URL: https://www.silkroadstudies.org/resources/pdf/Monographs/2010_03_MONO_Joshi_India-Central-Asia.pdf
4. Menon, Rhea and Sharanya, Rajiv (2019), "Realizing India's Strategic Interests in Central Asia", Seminar, Carnegie India. URL: https://carnegieindia.org/2019/12/01/realizing-india-s-strategic-interests-in-central-asia-pub-80576
5. Stobdan, P. *'India and Central Asia: The Strategic Dimension'*, KW Publishers. 2020pp.. 20-21.
6. Laruelle, M. and Peyrouse, S. (2013), *'Mapping Central Asia: Indian perceptions and strategies'*, Farnham: Ashgate Publishing.
7. Pradhan, Ramakrushna, 'India's Soft Power in Central Asia: Why it Must Act on the Look North Policy', *Mainstream*, Vol. III, No. 29, 11 July 2015, http://www.mainstreamweekly.net/article5792.html.
8. Wadhwa, Anil, 'Keynote address at 6th IISS-MEA Dialogue on 'India's extended neighbourhood: Prospects and Challenges', IDSA, 4 March, 2014, https://idsa.in/keyspeeches/6thIISSMEADialogue_secretaryeast.
9. Ahamed, E. 'Keynote Address by MOS Shri E. Ahamed at First India-Central Asia Dialogue', 12 June 2012, https://www.mea.gov.in/Speeches-Statements.htm?dtl/19791/.
10. Export-Import Data, Department Of Commerce, Ministry of Commerce & Industry, Government of India. https://commerce-app.gov.in/eidb/
11. 'India-Central Asia Trade: Roots of Strong Economic Relationship', Research Bureau, PHD Chamber of Commerce and Industry, August 2017, https://www.phdcci.in/wp-content/uploads/2018/12/India_Central-Asia-Trade_Roots-of-Strong-Economic-Relationship-August-2017.pdf
12. Pradhan, Ramakrushna, 'India's Soft Power in Central Asia: Why it Must Act on

the Look North Policy', *Mainstream*, Vol. III, No. 29, 11 July 2015. http://www.mainstreamweekly.net/article5792.html

13. Gupta, Dr. Pravesh Kumar, 'India-Central Asia Business Council: Reinvigorating India-Central Asia Economic Engagement' VIF Commentary, 10 February 2020, https://www.vifindia.org/2020/february/10/india-central-asia-business-council
14. 'Hon'ble PM launches drilling at Satpayev in Kazakhstan', ONGC India. 14 July, 2015, https://www.ongcindia.com/wps/wcm/connect/en/media/press-release/honblepm-launches-drilling-kazakhstan.
15. "India-Central Asia Business Council", FICCI, https://ficci.in/Desk-details.asp?Deskid=54537
16. Gupta, Pravesh Kumar, "India-Central Asia Relations: From Traditional to Strategic Partnership", in *Changing Dimensions of India Foreign Policy* (ed.) Prof Saroj Kumar Verma, Victorious Publishers, New Delhi, 2022.
17. Wani Ayjaz "India and China in Central Asia: Understanding the New Rivalry in the Heart of Eurasia," *ORF Occasional Paper* No. 235, February 2020, Observer Research Foundation. https://www.orfonline.org/research/india-and-china-in-central-asia-understanding-the-new-rivalry-in-the-heart-of-eurasia-61473/
18. Bhatia, Rajiv, "How India can benefit from SCO", *Hindustan Times*, 25 November 2020, https://www.hindustantimes.com/analysis/how-india-can-benefit-from-sco/story-lvHNVzB99Asw6EPcgfE6NK.html
19. Singh, Gunjan, 'India and SCO Summit 2019: An Overview', ICWA, 26 June 2019, https://www.icwa.in/show_content.php?lang=1&level=3&ls_id=4313&lid=3192
20. "At SCO Summit 2021, a message from Modi on Afghanistan", *Dailyo,* 17 September 172021, https://www.dailyo.in/variety/modi-sco-2021-speech-afghanistan/story/1/34744.html
21. Bhashkar, Utkal, 'India ratifies TIR Convention to access transnational multi-modal connectivity', 20 June 2017. https://www.livemint.com/Politics/dqvNmMJGbqQAC8pYZPAYdI/India-ratifies-TIR-Convention-to-access-transnational-multi.html
22. Srivastava, D. P., "International North-South Transit Corridor: VIF Article, 24 October 2016. https://www.vifindia.org/article/2016/october/24/international-north-south-transit-corridor
23. Gupta, P. K., "First India-Central Asia Summit: Some Major Takeaways", VIF, 31 January 2022. https://www.vifindia.org/article/2022/january/31/first-india-central-asia-summit-some-major-takeaways
24. "Question No. 189: Status of Chabahar Project", Lok Sabha Questions, 10 December 102021. https://www.mea.gov.in/lok-sabha.htm?dtl/34624/QUESTION+NO+189+STATUS+OF+CHABAHAR+PROJECT
25. Ibid.
26. Ibid.
27. "Delhi Declaration of the 1st India-Central Asia Summit" MEA Documents, 27 January 2022, https://www.mea.gov.in/bilateral-documents.htm?dtl/34773/Delhi+Declaration+of+the+1st+IndiaCentral+Asia+Summit
28. Gupta, P.K. (2020), 'Summary of Discussions, VIF Roundtable on India-Central Asia Relations', January 2020. URL: https://www.vifindia.org/sites/default/files/VIF-Roundtable-on-India-Central-Asia-Relations.pdf
29. 'Delhi Declaration on Afghanistan', Ministry of External Affairs, Government of India. 10 November 2021, https://mea.gov.in/bilateral-documents.htm?dtl/34491/Delhi_Declaration_on_Afghanistan

30. Joint Statement of the 3rd meeting of the India-Central Asia Dialogue', Ministry of External Affairs, Government of India, 19 December 2021, http://www.mea.gov.in/bilateral-documents.htm?dtl/34705/Joint+Statement+ of+the+3rd+ meeting+of+the+IndiaCentral+Asia+Dialogue
31. Siddique, Abubakar, "IS-K Ramps Up War Against The Taliban By Attacking Central Asian Neighbors", RFE-RL, Gandhara, 11 May 2022. Available at https://gandhara.rferl.org/a/islamic-state-khorasan-taliban-central-asia-attacks/31844898.html
32. "Delhi Declaration of the 1st India-Central Asia Summit" MEA Documents, 27 January 2022, https://www.mea.gov.in/bilateral-documents.htm?dtl/34773/Delhi+Declaration+of+the+1st+IndiaCentral+Asia+Summit
33. Jiang, Y. (2020), "Russia's Strategy in Central Asia: Inviting India to Balance China", *The Diplomat*, 23 January 2020. URL: https://thediplomat.com/2020/01/russias-strategy-in-central-asia-inviting-india-to-balance-china/
34. Ibid.
35. Stobdan, P., 'India's Economic Opportunities in Central Asia', IDSA Policy Brief, 17 September. 2018. https://idsa.in/policybrief/indias-economic-opportunities-in-central-asia-pstobdan-170918
36. Wani, Ayjaz, "India and China in Central Asia: Understanding the New Rivalry in the Heart of Eurasia," *ORF Occasional Paper* No. 235, February 2020, Observer Research Foundation. https://www.orfonline.org/research/india-and-china-in-central-asia-understanding-the-new-rivalry-in-the-heart-of-eurasia-61473/

15

Impact of COVID-19 Pandemic on Food Security in Kyrgyzstan

Dr. Raj Kumar Sharma

Introduction

Due to the outbreak of the COVID-19, pandemic and various economic, social, political, and cultural problems associated with it, the year 2020 will be remembered as one of the worst for humanity around the globe. Food security was a common concern amidst this pandemic and a number of countries faced problems on this front, Central Asia and Kyrgyzstan being no exceptions. The director of the World Food Program (WFP), in April 2020, had warned of famines of 'biblical proportions' if corrective measures were not taken. Incidentally, WFP has been also awarded the Nobel Peace Prize for the year 2020 for its efforts to combat hunger around the world. It had warned of a hunger pandemic and estimated that by the end of 2020; nearly 265 million people could be pushed towards starvation.[1] Further, the UN estimated that between 720 and 811 million people faced hunger due to COVID-19 in 2020. The corona virus had directly impacted food security by disrupting food supply chains as countries resorted to border closures and food export restrictions. Lockdowns slowed down the harvest season while the following sowing season had been delayed.[2] In an indirect impact of the corona virus on food security, millions lost their jobs that affected not only them but also the food security of their families. Apart from the pandemic, other threats to food security include events like locust invasions, drought, and conflict. In Central Asia, food insecurity is one of the perennial problems but also which is least discussed and debated. The genesis of food security issues in Central Asia may be traced back to the time after the region came under Tsarist Russia's control in the second half of the 19th century. Central Asia, due to its hot climate, used to grow cotton for the Tsarist empire and later, for the Soviet Union. This gave rise to a cotton monoculture in the region while food supplies came from other regions to Central Asia. Later, this model was disturbed when the Soviet Union disintegrated and ensuring food security became difficult for countries like Kyrgyzstan and Tajikistan, which mainly have a mountainous terrain. Before examining the impact of the COVID-19 pandemic on the food security situation in Kyrgyzstan, it is pertinent to highlight the concept of food security and the relationship between food security and national security on the one hand and food security and political stability on the other.

Food Security, National Security, and Political Stability

In 1996, during the World Food Summit in Rome, food security was defined as:

> "Food security exists when all people, at all times, have physical, social, and economic access to sufficient, safe, and nutritious food that meets their dietary needs and food preferences for an active and healthy life".[3] This definition emphasizes the multidimensional nature of food security, which includes availability, stability, access, and utilization of food. It must be mentioned that in international security studies, food security is seen as a part of human security. There are two major components of human security, according to the UNDP Human Security Report 1994 as shown in Figure 1. The first focuses on 'freedom from want', which focuses on human needs in economic, food, health, social, and environmental terms. The second focuses on 'freedom from fear' and seeks to remove use or threat of force from the daily lives of people.[4]

Figure 1

Human Security

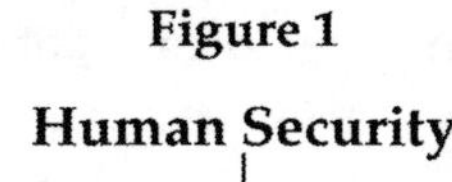

Freedom From Want
- Economic Security
- Food Security
- Health Security
- Environmental Security

Freedom From Fear

(a) Personal Security
(b) Community Security
(c) Political Security

Food security forms an important part of a country's national security, although this is a new idea as national security is mainly seen in military terms around the world. However, COVID-19 could induce a paradigm shift and force many countries to take a holistic view of their national security, including food security. Hunger is one of the causes leading to conflict while terrorist organizations recruit members using food as a tool. Food security forms an important element of national security, according to the ancient Indian political thinker, Kautilya, as mentioned in his book, *Arthashastra*. Classic realist Hans J. Morganthau had identified food production as an element of national power and all states try to achieve maximum food production in order to survive under international anarchy.[5]

Concerns over political stability due to food insecurity shot into the headlines in 2007-08, when there was a big increase in global food prices leading to food riots in as many as 48 countries. Food prices were also one of the grievances that led to the Arab Spring that started in 2010 with a revolution in Tunisia. In some cases, there were serious political consequences of food price increases. The President of Madagascar, Marc Ravalomanana, faced a coup in 2009 as he was negotiating for leasing half of the arable land of his country to a South African firm.[6] Conflict and hunger reinforce each other. Conflict damages infrastructure and displaces people leading to food insecurity while hunger plays an important part in creating conflict and instability. Repressive regimes do not tolerate dissent and suppress protests but democratic governments that allow freedom of expression remain vulnerable to unrest and protests during times of high food prices. If other problems like unemployment, high poverty, and corruption are also present, food insecurity could add to peoples' problems forcing them to come out on to the streets. Access to basic needs like food and water are the essentials to hold a society together. The famous American journalist, Alfred Henry Lewis, had said in 1906 that nine meals separate mankind from anarchy. During the corona pandemic, there were reasons for governments around the world, especially in developing and least developed countries, to ensure the food security of their citizens, which could otherwise put their survival at stake. These issues have been further exacerbated by the Russia-Ukraine conflict as both the countries are one of the largest exporters of wheat and the ongoing conflict would affect their agricultural production and exports.

COVID-19 and Food Security in Kyrgyzstan

Like in all countries, the COVID pandemic had created certain difficulties for people in Kyrgyzstan. In the landlocked country, arable land is only 7 per cent of the total land area, which limits food production and makes it dependent on food imports from Russia and Kazakhstan. Kyrgyzstan imports half of its wheat consumption. There was no food shortage in the global food market when COVID-19 began, but certain countries had resorted to food export bans. Kazakhstan had announced such a ban in March 2020 while it fixed an export quota in April 2020. Such restrictions were lifted in June 2020 allaying fears that Kyrgyzstan may face food availability issues due to them. Russia, the world largest wheat producer, also suspended the export of grains from late April 2020 to 1 July 2020, but Moscow made exceptions for fellow members of the Eurasian Economic Union, which includes Kyrgyzstan. Although the Kyrgyz government had maintained in March 2020 that there was no shortage of food, yet the Russian media had highlighted that Bishkek had requested Russia to supply wheat and cooking oil.[7] Kyrgyzstan had also sought help from Kazakhstan for food supplies and had received assistance from Nur-Sultan in April 2020.[8] During the pandemic, the WFP, with support from Russia, had been providing food aid to vulnerable families in Kyrgyzstan. Due to a below-average domestic wheat output, wheat imports for Kazakhstan needed to be increased by 10 per cent in 2020-21.[9] Kyrgyzstan's membership of the Eurasian Economic Union has been beneficial for its food security as two fellow members, Russia and Kazakhstan, are wheat exporters and the Union has established a green trade corridor to supply essential commodities by simplifying customs procedures, including for food products.[10] The Union also decided that in case of a food crisis, members would provide humanitarian assistance to each other.[11] In March 2022, Russia had banned export of grains and sugar to EEU countries following its conflict with Ukraine; however, the ban was lifted later.

At the domestic level, the lockdown and associated restrictions had created a number of issues that impacted food security in Kyrgyzstan. There were disruptions in domestic food supply chains while loss of incomes and remittances had created food security concerns for a number of people in the country. As of 1 May 2020, nearly 500,000 people in Kyrgyzstan needed direct food assistance while it was estimated that around 1.83 million people would need food or cash assistance. Almost 400,000 small farmers needed support to sustain their agricultural season.[12] Around 184,300 schoolchildren did not receiving meals due to closure of schools. By May 2020, nearly 700,000 people in Kyrgyzstan lost their jobs, which impacted their food security by limiting their access to food.[13] Kyrgyzstan witnessed an economic recession in 2020, losing almost 10 per cent of its GDP due to COVID-19-induced economic problems, according to a study by the Asian Development Bank and the UNDP published in August 2020. This resulted in a budget deficit not seen in Kyrgyzstan since the 1990s. About 22 per cent (1.5 million) people survived on less than US$ 1.3 per day and ended up spending 60 per cent of their income on food.[14] During the pandemic, these people were at risk of food insecurity and needed government assistance as any rise in food prices impacted them directly. Kyrgyzstan's landlocked status also plays a part in determining its food prices. Food prices in landlocked states are three times more volatile compared to coastal countries, as trade costs in these countries are higher due to longer shipment time, higher transport costs, and delays at borders.[15] There has been an increase in prices of potatoes, oil, sugar, and meat from seven to eight per cent in September-October 2020 in Kyrgyzstan. There is a need to focus on food insecurity in Batken province, Jalal-Abad province (Bazar-Korgon and Aksy districts), Osh province (Alay and Aravan districts), Bakay-Ata in Talas province, and Yssyk-Ata and Chuy districts in Chuy province due to high poverty rates in these areas, which hinders access to food.[16]

Another important aspect related to people's food security in Kyrgyzstan is remittances, which play an important part in helping families to afford their basic needs including food. According to World Bank estimates, Europe and Central Asia would witness the highest fall in remittances (27.5 per cent) due to the economic fallout of the corona virus.[17] Remittances represent 30 per cent of Kyrgyzstan's GDP, helping it not only to manage balance-of-payment constraints but also ensure the food security of many households. Even a ten per cent decline in remittances can create a significant balance-of-payment crisis for landlocked developing countries like Kyrgyzstan.[18] In April and May 2020, remittances fell by 39 per cent in Kyrgyzstan compared to the previous year.[19] The importance of remittances to the people of Kyrgyzstan is evident from the fact that without them, the poverty rate in the country would risen to 31.2 per cent in 2019, while with the remittances the poverty rate reduced to 20.1 per cent.[20] The Western sanctions on Russia after the Ukraine conflict have had a major impact on its economy, which in turn, would negatively impact the flow of remittances to countries like Kyrgyzstan. Reduced remittances would particularly impact rural households where this money plays an important role in ensuring their food security. Following the Russia-Ukraine conflict, food prices have increased in Kyrgyzstan while the expected drop in remittances from Russia was 33 per cent.[21]

Landlocked developing countries like Kyrgyzstan have less arable land and less agricultural land under irrigation, making them vulnerable to climate change and adverse natural events.[22] There were locust attacks in 2020 in Africa, West Asia, South Asia, and Central Asia. According to the Kyrgyz Ministry of Agriculture, the locust attacks impacted 120,000 hectares of land that year.[23] If these locust attacks dealt a blow to cereal crops, it would decrease domestic food production. Late frost has already impacted the cultivation of fruits and vegetables in southern Kyrgyzstan.[24] Another important factor to impact food security in Kyrgyzstan is political uncertainty. It has seen political unrest after the Presidential election in October 2020 in which the government's mishandling of the pandemic and associated problems like hunger have been important factors that forced the people to protest. Powerful clans have been competing to control resources while there is a North-South divide in Kyrgyzstan.[25] Frequent political instability would be unfavourable to policy making, while at the same time, there would be no one to claim responsibility to respond to any public crisis, like hunger. A stable government is needed in the country to objectively assess the situation and respond as per the needs of people. In this regard, there are some recommendations, which can help in ensuring food security in Kyrgyzstan during a pandemic in the future.

- Mobile food and health facilities for the poor and marginalized sections.
- Digitalize the system to issue benefits.[26]
- Investments in the health sector and upgradation of medical infrastructure to contain the pandemic.

- Support value addition in agriculture sector, including livestock breeding.[27]
- Relevant engagement with all international donors to secure assistance for food security.
- Food and nutritional assistance should be the core of all the social safety net programmes initiated by the government.
- Since food insecurity is one of the perennial problems in Central Asia, there is a possibility to establish a regional food bank under the Eurasian Economic Union. Food reserves in this bank can be used by the regional countries during a humanitarian crisis in any of the member-states.

India-Kyrgyzstan Cooperation

India is the world's second largest wheat producer. The country has a vast experience in ensuring the food security of its citizens. India has been extending its helping hand to countries around the world in fighting hunger and COVID-19. Agriculture is an important area of cooperation between India and Kyrgyzstan. The two countries have been cooperating in areas like agro-processing, greenhouse technology, water conservation, and agricultural research so as to increase productivity and ensure value addition to the agriculture output.[28] The other areas to cooperate could include greenhouse cultivation of vegetables, horticulture, organic farming, hydroponic farming, poultry, and storage technology.

Conclusion

The corona virus pandemic is not going to severely threaten food security in Kyrgyzstan but there are some areas of concern. Food availability is unlikely to be a problem as food production in Russia and Kazakhstan, the main suppliers of grains to Kyrgyzstan, will be stable. However, economic recession, loss of jobs, reduction in remittances, and disasters like locust attacks and political instability could impact food security in Kyrgyzstan. Hunger and mismanagement of the COVID-19 pandemic are the main reasons that led people to protest after the Presidential election in October 2020. Being relatively an open and free country compared to its other Central Asian counterparts, Kyrgyzstan remains prone to public protests against failure to provide basic amenities to its citizens. The government should be ready for all eventualities, and put food and nutritional security at the core of its social welfare policies.

REFERENCES

1. WFP Chief warns of hunger pandemic as COVID-19 spreads (Statement to UN Security Council), 21 April 2020, URL: https://www.wfp.org/news/wfp-chief-warns-hunger-pandemic-covid-19-spreads-statement-un-security-council
2. United Nations (2020), "The Impact of COVID-19 on Food Security and Nutrition", URL: https://unsdg.un.org/resources/policy-brief-impact-covid-19-food-security-and-nutrition
3. Food and Agriculture Organization (2006), "The State of Food Insecurity in the World, 2006, Eradicating World Hunger – Taking Stock Ten Years after the World Food Summit", URL: ftp://ftp.fao.org/docrep/fao/009/a0750e/a0750e01.pdf
4. United Nations Development Program (1994), "Human Development Report", URL: http://hdr.undp.org/sites/default/files/reports/255/hdr_1994_en_ complete _ nostats.pdf.
5. Naylor, R. L (2014), *"The Evolving Sphere of Food Security"*, Oxford: OUP.
6. Brinkman, H. J. and C. S. Hendrix (2010), "Food Insecurity and Conflict: Applying the WDR Framework" URL: https://openknowledge.worldbank.org/bitstream/.../WDR2011_0025.pdf
7. Timur Toktonaliev (2020), "Coronavirus Tests Central Asia's Strength", URL: https://iwpr.net/global-voices/coronavirus-tests-central-asias-strength
8. Kazakhstan provides humanitarian aid to Kyrgyzstan, Tajikistan, 16 April 2020, URL: https://www.euractiv.com/section/central-asia/news/kazakhstan-provides-humanitarian-aid-to-kyrgyzstan-tajikistan/
9. Country Briefs – Kyrgyzstan, 6 August 2020, URL: http://www.fao.org/giews/countrybrief/country.jsp?code=KGZ
10. EEC Council approved set of urgent measures to control coronavirus, 3 April 2020, URL: http://www.eurasiancommission.org/en/nae/news/Pages/03-04-2020-3.aspx
11. Usenov, Arsen (2020), "Problems of Ensuring the National Security of Kyrgyzstan amidst the Current Crisis", URL: https://cabar.asia/en/problems-of-ensuring-the-national-security-of-kyrgyzstan-amidst-the-current-crisis
12. Disaster Response Coordination Unit Kyrgyzstan: COVID-19 Response, Weekly Situation Update, 1 May 2020, URL: https://reliefweb.int/sites/reliefweb.int/files/resources/Weekly%20situation%20update%201%20May%20V1.pdf
13. WFP Kyrgyz Republic Country Brief, May 2020, URL: https://reliefweb.int/report/kyrgyzstan/wfp-kyrgyz-republic-country-brief-may-2020
14. UN WFP Profile – Kyrgyzstan, URL: https://www.wfp.org/countries/kyrgyzstan
15. Landlocked states face unique food challenges, 5 January 2015, URL: http://www.fao.org/europe/news/detail-news/en/c/273889/
16. WFP Price Monitoring for Food Security in the Kyrgyz Republic, 23 September-20 October 2020, URL: https://reliefweb.int/sites/reliefweb.int/files/resources/WFP-0000120282.pdf
17. World Bank Predicts Sharpest Decline of Remittances in Recent History, 20 April 20 2020, URL: https://www.worldbank.org/en/news/press-release/2020/04/22/world-bank-predicts-sharpest-decline-of-remittances-in-recent-history
18. UN Policy Brief (2020), "COVID-19 poses grievous economic challenge to landlocked developing countries", URL: file:///C:/Users/Geetanjali/Downloads/PB_76.pdf
19. IMF (2020), "COVID-19: Without Help, Low-Income Developing Countries Risk a

Lost Decade", URL: https://blogs.imf.org/2020/08/27/covid-19-without-help-low-income-developing-countries-risk-a-lost-decade/

20. ADB and UNDP (2020), "COVID-19 in the Kyrgyz Republic: Socioeconomic and Vulnerability Impact Assessment and Policy Response", URL: https://www.adb.org/documents/covid-19-kyrgyz-republic-socioeconomic-vulnerability-impact
21. Pryde, Ian (2022), "Russia's Economic Doldrums Causing Hardship In Kyrgyzstan", URL: https://www.rferl.org/a/kyrgyzstan-economic-hardship-russia-sanctions-ukraine/31838787.html
22. Landlocked states face unique food challenges, 5 January 2015, URL: http://www.fao.org/europe/news/detail-news/en/c/273889/
23. Locust plague forecast in Kyrgyzstan,9 June 2020, URL: https://24.kg/english/155345_Locust_plague_forecast_in_Kyrgyzstan/
24. ADB and UNDP (2020) op. cit.
25. Dzyubenko, Olga and Olzhas Auyezov (2020), "Coronavirus lit fuse in Kyrgyzstan, spreading unrest in Putin's back yard", URL: https://in.reuters.com/article/us-kyrgyzstan-protests-pandemic-analysis/coronavirus-lit-fuse-in-kyrgyzstan-spreading-unrest-in-putins-back-yard-idUSKBN26T2ML
26. Usenov, Arsen (2020) op. cit.
27. ADB and UNDP (2020) op. cit.
28. Speech by the Ambassador at Round Table on Agriculture Cooperation (2015), URL: https://indembbishkek.gov.in/pages.php?id=334

16

Cultural Heritage of India and Kyrgyzstan in the Eurasian Region

Dr. Kadyrkulova, A.S.

ABSTRACT

This article examines the cultural heritage of India and Kyrgyzstan in the form of ancient Indian religious and philosophical thought—"Bhagavad Gita" and the Kyrgyz epic, "Manas". An attempt is made to substantiate the role and significance of the "Bhagavad Gita" and the epic "Manas" for Eurasia. Indian philosophical thought has become widespread in the world thanks to Mahatma Gandhi in affirming "soft power" in the strategies of Indian leadership. The Kyrgyz epic is presented as an ideology and encyclopaedia of the life of the Kyrgyz people.

Key words: *Cultural heritage, India, Kyrgyzstan, "Bhagavad Gita", Mahatma Gandhi, "Manas", Eurasian region.*

Cultural heritage, in our view, is the connecting thread of the past with the present, opening the way to the future. While cultural heritage does not include resources and military and economic potential it contains ideological potential, and is capable through the power of words written in national legends as the Kyrgyz epic "Manas" and the ancient Indian religious and philosophical thought, the "Bhagavad Gita" ("Bhagavad-Gita", or simply "Gita"; Skt. - भगवद्गीता, Bhagavad Gita "The Song of the Lord"[1]) to unite society for both further beneficial development and for the national liberation struggle. It should be noted that the Eurasian region is very rich in cultural heritage, uniting all three world religions: Buddhism, Christianity and Islam, with significant potential of national, ideological epics, and literary masterpieces. Therefore, the consolidation of humanitarian cooperation[2] through intergovernmental educational contacts in the Eurasian region will be the driving force behind the spread of national and world cultural wealth, promoting a positive lifestyle among the younger generation.

The Eurasian region,[3] one way or the other, is a source of dissemination of ideological knowledge of all ethnic groups inhabiting this rich region. Thus, the literary masterpieces of Kyrgyzstan and India are able to bring their national knowledge, to one degree or another, to contribute to the development of the internal potential of the states of the Eurasian region. This statement is, in our opinion, relevant, which is explained by the fact that the influence of the Bhagavad Gita on the internal political processes in India, and the epic Manas as the main ideological concept expressed in the Seven Testaments of Kyrgyzstan (Kyrgyz Manastinzheti osuyat[4]) on Kyrgyz society.

In the light of the above, let us turn to the consideration of the monument of ancient Indian religious and philosophical thought, the "Bhagavad Gita". It (a heavenly poem) is a monument of ancient Indian religious and philosophical thought in Sanskrit, a section of the Mahabharata which has 700 poems in its composition. The Gita is considered one of the sacramental literary sources of Hinduism, which contains some of the most significant texts from the philosophy of Hinduism. The Gita is capable of assisting effective guidance in both the spiritual and material areas of life. For the most part, the Bhagavad-Gita is considered one of the most revered and valuable sacred and philosophical works not exclusively in the traditions of Hinduism, but also in the traditions of the philosophical doctrines of the whole world.

The poems, using meaningful allegory, are set out in the classical Sanskrit structure of poetic speech, which is often sung, transformed as a divine song. The Bhagavad Gita is truly a unique phenomenon in the history of world culture. The dignity of the Gita lies in its unique divine gift to influence the spiritual development of the personality, which is embodied in ethical, social and psychological terms. By defining the problem "who am I?" the Gita provides the correct answer to the verbal address "what to do?" and reveals the ways of acquiring a special intimate disposition, in which it is permissible not only to study spiritual riches that do not lose their strength, but also to bring them to life. The Bhagavad-Gita provides a definition of the problems of the importance of human existence, the disagreement between individual and social concepts of morality. The concept of the Gita affects the most diverse areas of life, ranging from ordinary, everyday, and to metaphysical, spiritualized.

The Bhagavad-Gita stresses on selfless activity, self-purification, high acquisition of knowledge, and getting rid of shortcomings: anger, passion, greed and illiteracy. It opens the way to liberation from negative qualities and vices, and opens the way to universal harmony, which is the embodiment of the Supreme Reason[5]. It focuses on the right attitudes and provides us with a chance to live with reality, and not exclusively dream about it.

A prominent historical figure, Mohandas Karamchand Gandhi was an Indian jurist, political and public figure, and a writer who led nationalist activities against British rule in India. That is why, by right, Indians began to recognize him as the Father of the Nation. Mahatma (Great Soul) is the name of Gandhi, which was given to him by Rabindranath Tagore[6], the eminent writer of India. Gandhi has received international respect for his own doctrine of nonviolent opposition (satyagraha) with the aim of gaining political and social enhancement through development. The religious and philosophical work, the Bhagavad Gita, played an important role for him. In the Gita, Gandhi acquired his own ideas for political battle. "If you are faced with an enemy, defeat him with love",[7] he said. Charged with such persuasive views, in 1919 he joined a vigorous struggle for Indian sovereignty.

In modern times, in our interpretation, the ideas of the Bhagavad Gita are fundamental in creating "soft power" in the strategies of Indian leadership[8]. Thus, the unique character and degree of participation in the politics of "soft power" have the worldview principles of peaceful development that the country is capable of presenting. India as the birthplace of non-violent politics evokes the image of Mahatma Gandhi and his ideas, which to this day have not lost their importance and their demand.

As such, the idea of nonviolence (ahimsa) is sacramental in all respects to Indian culture on the grounds that it played an enormous role in

Hinduism, Buddhism, and Jainism. In the latter, the role of ahimsa is more significant. At the same time, in fact, "in the hands of Gandhi, features that once seemed to be an element of Indian vulnerability suddenly turned out to be an element of Indian strength. Gandhi accomplished this feat using the non-linear dynamics of national identity".[9]

The foundation of the spiritual conversion found in the Bhagavad Gita is ahimsa *parmodharma*[10] (Sanskrit), which is understood as the principle of nonviolence in the form of the basic duty of each individual. Classically, this principle was perceived as not to act evil, and not to turn to force in relation to other people. At the same time, according to Gandhi, precisely because of this consideration and perception, Ahimsa missed its own primordial essence—the renunciation of the use of violence not exclusively in physical design. In this understanding, the broadest explanation of violence presented by Gandhi is of obvious interest. Saying that everyone uses violence on a daily basis, he emphasized two of its areas: physical violence itself and passive violence. The manifestation of physical violence[11] in the world is represented by wars, robberies, murders, etc., since the use of physical power in this particular case is manifested by a forced situation. In the passive form of violence, there is no direct use of force. An example is racism and any other discrimination and verbal humiliation. As a result, "through anger and hatred, it reaches its highest point in physical violence",[12] which leads to an environment of violence in the world.

Thus, the cultural sources of India, presented by us through the main ideas of the Bhagavad Gita, are able to bring the ideological orientation of the policy of non-violence to the Eurasian region in different orientations.

It provides a reference point aimed at a student audience and young scientists and therefore there is a desire to borrow the ideas of the Bhagavad Gita in order to achieve academic potential through excellent educational success.

Next, let us look at our greatest cultural heritage—the epic "Manas". "Manas" is the main Kyrgyz epic and the name of its main winner—the hero (Kyrgyz baatyr), who rallied the Kyrgyz. The epic is included in the UNESCO[13] register of intangible cultural heritage of humanity and included in the Guinness[14] Book of Records as the largest epic poem in the world.

The epic "Manas" involuntarily draws us to the definition of the exact origin of our main cultural heritage. So, modern scholars do not have a unanimous position on the period of the appearance of the epic "Manas". There were suggestions that its foundation was connected with the phenomena of the history of the Kyrgyz people of the ninth century. Zhirmunsky, V.M.[15] believed that the historical conditions of the epic poem in the aggregate correspond to the events of the 15th-18th centuries, despite the fact that it also contains more ancient views. E.M. Meletinsky[16] clarifies that the heroic period in the epic is not legendary (in contrast to most of the epic poems of the Turkic ethnic groups of Siberia), but historical. The earliest reports of an epic poem date back to the 16th century. They are in a semi-mythical composition, Majmu at-Tavarikh. In this composition, Manas appeared as a historical personality, in collaboration with the real-life Tokhtamysh[17], Khorezmshah Muhammad,[18] etc.

In the light of the above, it can be figuratively assumed that the epic "Manas" is somehow connected with the events of the distant past. So, its impressive volume serves as a justification for the addition of the ideological concept of the Kyrgyz Republic, formulated in the Seven Lessons of Manas.[19] At the same time, following the main position of consideration of this article, we should make efforts to substantiate the significance of the epic "Manas" in world culture. Based on such a significant fact, we, for our part, will try to substantiate the importance of the cultural heritage of Kyrgyzstan in the Eurasian region.

In modern times, the epic "Manas" is gaining more and more value, primarily as an ideologically consolidating mechanism of Kyrgyz society and sovereignty, in a continuously globalizing world. The erection of the Manas monument on the central square of Ala-Too in Bishkek[20] and the approval of the Resolution on the epic "Manas" on 28 June 2011[21] confirm the fact of the beginning of the process of forming a unification of the people in terms of their development and prosperity. On 24 February 2012, a monument to Manas[22] was erected in Moscow, which is located in the planted grove "Friendship"; the development belongs to the artistic organization of KadyralievZh.

In June 2012, during the current council of the General Assembly in Paris, Kyrgyzstan, based on the results of a successful elected society, in the entire history of its own cooperation with a public association was for the first time appointed to one of the leading collegial bodies of UNESCO,[23] the Interstate Collegial Body for the Protection of Intangible Cultural Heritage.

On 5 December 2013, in Baku, the capital of Azerbaijan, the Kyrgyz epic "Manas" was unanimously added to the representative register of masterpieces of the intangible cultural heritage of mankind by a resolution of the 8th meeting of the Interstate Collegial Body for the Protection of the Intangible Cultural Heritage of UNESCO.[24]

Further, it is necessary to highlight the significance of the epic "Manas" in the context of knowledge on history, ethnography, philosophy, language, diplomacy, military affairs, folk pedagogy[25] and a large number of other areas in the life of the Kyrgyz people.

So, let us now focus on the historical and ethnographic information of the epic legend. The epic "Manas" embodied knowledge about the economy and trade of the Kyrgyz in its pages. The epic contains most of the directions of the Great Silk Road. In support of this fact, reviews of the epics, a significant number of names of fabrics, including a variety of silk fabrics, are indicated. Thus, the merchant and the tubar[26] were directly identified as Chinese silk. In addition, the names of various precious stones, gold and silver works observed in it at the same time confirm the actual phenomenon of familiarization of the Kyrgyz people with the Great Way.

The notions of the epic about the culture of the Kyrgyz are significant in relation to material culture, the types of dwellings, different types of clothing, equestrian equipment, food, etc. Its uniqueness highlights information of the epic on military activities, weapons and military clothing. The epic "Manas" covers a wide range of information on spiritual culture, the totality of folk information (mostly folk medicine), myths, religious teachings, folk games and amusements, musical instruments,[27] etc.

With regard to traditional medicine, it should be noted that medicinal plants are used for healing according to the epic "Manas". Medicines are used that have an animal source, such as internal fat. Further, the remedies of mineral springs are used by people of traditional medicine. The epic "Manas" refers to surgical instruments, herbal medicine, organotherapy.[28] Thus, herbal medicine has the main types of most ancient epic medicines[29] contained in the epic "Manas": apy, apy-p¯, meaning apiyim (opium), barpy, which has a rejuvenating effect, kainatma kara dary (boiled black medicine) to cover a wound or fracture. Further, medet and sebep for the treatment of wounds were used as pain relievers and haemostatic drugs, cantemirdary, which has a mineral origin with the likelihood of forming as a meteorite[30] splinter.

In light of the above, the epic "Manas" is an encyclopaedia of the life of the Kyrgyz people. So, the epic legend focuses on knowledge about rituals, customs, traditions, ethnic, philosophical views, language, and the mentality of the people for many centuries towards education and development of the Kyrgyz as a nation. The epic legend reflects the knowledge of the ancient Kyrgyz on geography, architecture, and astronomy and contains lyrics on love, social and everyday moral and ethical[31] prescriptions.

* * *

This article examines the author's subjective ideas regarding the significance of the cultural heritage of the Republic of India and the Kyrgyz Republic for the Eurasian region, for its development and prosperity. India is widely represented in its own religious and philosophical sources. One of them is the "Bhagavad Gita", which became more widespread thanks to Gandhi and his non-violent policy. The Kyrgyz Republic is a country with a relatively small territory and population, at the same time with such a large-scale epic poem in the world. The epic poem "Manas" is presented as the National Idea of the republic and an encyclopaedia of the life of the Kyrgyz people.

REFERENCES

1. Kochergina, V. A. Sanskrit-Russian dictionary. (ed.) V. I. Kalyanova. With the appendix "Grammatical sketch of Sanskrit" A. A. Zaliznyak, 2nd edn., revised and supplemented—M: Russian language, 1987.
2. Savin L. Eaeu: Social and Humanitarian Cooperation. https: //www. geopolitica.ru/ article/eaes-socialnoe-i-gumanitarnoe-sotrudnichestvo
3. Culture in the Eurasian Space: Traditions and Innovations. Collection of materials of the II International Scientific and Practical Conference, Barnaul, May 12-13, 2016, Part 1. http: //www.spsl.nsc.ru/fulltext/sotr/ collection%20eurasian.%20vol. %20i.pdf
4. Manastinzheti are perceived. https://tyup.net/page/manastyn-zheti-osujaty
5. Kamenskaya, A. Bhagavad-Gita (briefly). https://gitak.ru/induizm/ svyashchennye-pisaniya/bkhagavad-gita.html
6. The great genius is Mahatma Gandhi. https://indiya-land.ru/history/makhatma-gandi.
7. "If you want a change in the future, become this change in the present." https:// www.znak.com/2020-03-11/kak_pobedit_vlast_bez_primeneniya_ nasiliya_ opyt_mahatmy_gandi.
8. Emelyanova, N. Soft charm of India: advantages and limits. http:// www.perspektivy.info/oykumena/azia/_magkoje_obajanije_ indii_ preimushhes tva_i_predely_2016-03-21.htm.

9. Hymans, Jacques E.C., pp. 234-265.
10. Andrews, C.F. p. x.
11. Emelyanova, N. Soft charm of India: advantages and limits. http://www.perspektivy.info/oykumena/ azia / _magkoje_obajanije_indii_preimushhestva_i_predely_2016-03-21.htm
12. Nanda, B. R., p. 264.
13. Intangible cultural heritage, https://ru.unesco.org/themes/nematerialnoe-kulturnoe-nasledie
14. The Guinness Book of Records. http: //www.guinness-records.ru/
15. Manas. Book 1.—M., 1984, p. 430; Meletinsky, E. M., Kyrgyz epic about Manas, History of World Literature, T. 3-M., 1985.—S. 583
16. Meletinsky, E. M. The origin of the geoic epic.—M., 1963, —S. 369;
17. Tokhtamysh, https:// dic.academic.ru/dic.nsf/ruwiki/30750;
18. Ala ad-Din Muhammad II. // https://arboblar.uz/ru/people/ala-ad-din-mukhammed-ii
19. Akayev, A., Kyrgyz statehood and the folk epic "Manas".—B., 2004;. Chapter XIV. —Epic "Manas" and Kyrgyz statehood. Seven lessons of Manas.—S. 402.
20. A monument to Manas the Magnanimous was unveiled on the Ala-Too square, https: //knews.kg/2011/08/31/na-ploschadi-ala-too-otkryit-pamyatnik-manasu-velikodushnomu/
21. Law of the Kyrgyz Republic, dated 28 June 2011 [1]. 59.—About the epic "Manas". http: // cbd. minjust.gov.kg/act/view/ru-ru/203303
22. Kuchenko, A. A monument to Manas the Magnanimous was unveiled in Moscow. https://rg.ru/2012/02/24/manas-site-anons.html.
23. Mamontova, D. Kyrgyzstan became a member of the UNESCO Committee for the Safeguarding of Intangible Cultural Heritage, https: //knews.kg/2012/06/12/kyirgyizstan-stal-chlenom-komiteta-yunesko-po-ohrane-nematerialnogo-kulturnogo-naslediya/
24. The Kyrgyz epic "Manas" was included in the cultural heritage of UNESCO, 13.12.2013., http: //www.sary-kol.ru/stati/pamir/kirgizskii-epos-manas-vnesli-v-kulturnoe-nasledie-iunesko.html
25. Moldobaev, I. B. Epic "Manas" and its significance in world culture, Epic "Manas" and the epic heritage of the peoples of the world.—Abstracts of the international scientific symposium dedicated to the 1000th anniversary of the epic "Manas", August 27-28, 1995—B., 1995—S. 3-5.
26. Moldobaev, I. B. Epic "Manas" and its significance in world culture, Epic "Manas" and the epic heritage of the peoples of the world.—Abstracts of the international scientific symposium dedicated to the 1000th anniversary of the epic "Manas", August 27-28, 1995—B., 1995.—S. 3-5.
27. Moldobaev, I. B. Epic "Manas" and its significance in world culture; Epic "Manas" and the epic heritage of the peoples of the world—Abstracts of the international scientific symposium dedicated to the 1000th anniversary of the epic "Manas"—August 27-28, 1995—B., 1995—S. 3-5.
28. Beksultanova, Ch. D. K. f. D., senior lecturer, Zhunushalieva G. I. Manasology. https: //www.kgma.kg/pdf/ manasovedenie-dlya-studentov.pdf
29. Aalieva, G. K. and Tentigulkizi, N. Evolution of Folk Medicine and its Place in the Social Structure of Kyrgyz by the "Manas" Epos,. https: //docplayer.ru/55987615-

G-k-aalieva-n-tentigul-kyzy-evolyuciya-narodnoy-mediciny-i-ee-mesto-v-socialnoy-strukture-kyrgyzov-po-eposu-manas.html.

30. Aalieva, G. K. and Tentigulkyzy, N. Evolution of Folk Medicine and its place in the Social Structure of Kyrgyz by the "Manas" Epos, https: //docplayer.ru/55987615-G-k-aalieva-n-tentigul-kyzy-evolyuciya-narodnoy-mediciny-i-ee-mesto-v-socialnoy-strukture-kyrgyzov-po-eposu-manas.html.
31. Epic "Manas" and its significance in world culture, https://pravo.bobrodobro.ru/14979

17

Modern Trends in the Development of Intellectual Property Management

(International and National Aspects)

Dr. Alybaev, S.T.

ABSTRACT

This article provides an analysis of modern trends in the development of intellectual property management from the perspective of the international experience of Kyrgyzstan; a volume of statistical data is considered.

Keywords: *intellectual property, foreign experience, patent, trademark, intellectual property management system*

In modern conditions of development of global markets, access to effective legal remedies not only in their own country but also abroad is of great importance for economic agents. Protection of intellectual property is the basis for making a decision by rights holders to enter foreign markets and transfer their rights to other countries.

Overall investment is shrinking in areas where IP protection is inadequate. The protection of intellectual rights at the international and national levels is closely related to global development in general, the creation, dissemination, and use of existing and new technologies that protect these rights. At the same time, the modern world intellectual property market, created with the active participation of the World Intellectual Property Organization (WIPO) and the World Trade Organization (WTO), creates uniform conditions for the circulation of IP rights (unified concepts of objects of protection and types of transactions), the main way to organize and maintain international financial flows. The tools of the modern intellectual property (IP) system—patents, trademarks, industrial designs, geographical indications, copyright and others—ensure that these IP objects appear on the market as goods and services that improve human life in their country and in the world as a whole.

The current state of the international intellectual property market is characterized by a number of significant development trends.

First, there is an increase in geographic coverage due to the accession of new states to the international IP protection system. There are currently 193 members representing all regions of the world. Most of the new acceding parties are developing countries.

Currently, the four main WIPO treaties (the WIPO Convention, the Paris Convention, the Berne Convention, and the Patent Cooperation Treaty) have more than 100 signatory states. We also note the increased use of the global IT databases, systems and platforms managed by WIPO, the expanded range of services they offer, as well as the range of participating offices and other users.

For developing countries and countries with an average level of development, the attractiveness of international IP protection systems lies in the fact that such systems allow them to achieve the level of protection of intellectual rights necessary to stimulate foreign investment.

Secondly, there is an increase in the demand for registration of intellectual property objects. There is a general increase in the number of applications for inventions, trademarks, and industrial designs [1. Ñ.7]:

Table 1

IP rights	*2018*	*2019*	*Growth (%)*
Number of patent applications	3,325,400	3,224,200	–3.0
Number of classes cited in trademark applications	14,314,000	15,153,700	5.9
Number of industrial designs indicated in applications for registration of industrial designs	1,343,800	1,360,900	1.3
Number of applications for registration of plant varieties	19,880	21,430	7.8

The analysis of the data provided by WIPO reflects the fact that in 2019 there was an increase in the world in the field of registration of plant varieties, trademarks, and industrial designs. At the same time, the number of patent applications decreased slightly, which was caused by the weakening of demand in China, one of the centres of IP creation. Trademark and industrial design activities increased by 5.9 per cent and 1.3 per cent respectively. The 3 per cent drop in global patent filings, for the first time in a decade, was driven by a decline in the number of applications from Chinese residents. Excluding China, the number of patent applications in the world increased by 2.3 per cent.

Indicators 2019, i.e., in the period leading up to the COVID-19 pandemic, confirm that there is a long-term growth in demand for intellectual property tools that are driving the development of an increasingly global and digital world economy.

The active use of intellectual property tools indicates a high level of innovation and creativity at the end of 2019, which coincided with the onset of the COVID-19 pandemic. The pandemic has reinforced long-standing trends by stimulating the use of new technologies and accelerating the digitalization of everyday life, because IP is closely related to technology, innovation and the digitalization of human activities.

Third is the uneven distribution and multi-directionality of patenting activity across countries and regions. The top five patent offices (IP5—USA, EU, Japan, China, Korea) file 84.7 per cent of national applications and 95 per cent of applications under the PCT international patent system.

Let us note an important trend, which is the shift of patenting activity to Asia. The share of China is perceptible and is increasing every year. China is the current leader among countries in terms of the number of applications filed. In 2019, China's IP Office received 1.4 million patent applications—double the number of US authorities with the second highest number of patent applications (621,453). This was followed by Japan (307,969), the Korean Intellectual Property Office (KIPO, 218,975) and the European Patent Office (EPO, 181,479).

A feature of this phenomenon is that industrially developed countries are aimed at transferring technologies to developing countries, and therefore the activity of inventors in the USA, Japan, and Germany is aimed at foreign markets; the number of patent applications in foreign offices is higher than domestically. Applicants' activity in developing countries, including China, is mainly directed towards the domestic market.

In terms of filing overseas applications, reflecting the drive to expand into new markets, US residents continued to lead with 236,032 patent applications in 2019. The USA was followed by Japan (206,758), Germany (104,736), China (84,279), and the Republic of Korea (76,824).

In 2019, the global number of patents in force increased by 7 per cent and reached 15 million. The USA had the largest number of patents in force (3.1 million), followed by China (2.7 million) and Japan (2.1 million) More than 50 per cent of all patents in force in the USA are of foreign origin, while in Japan about 80 per cent of all patents in force were granted domestically.

Fourthly, it is possible to trace the tendency of strengthening the protection of intellectual property and the development of mechanisms to restore the balance of interests and prevent abuse by rights holders.

The policy of strengthening the protection of IP rights within the framework of global and regional protection systems is in the interests of developed countries and especially TNCs. Expansion of the scope of protection, an increase in the terms of protection, types of powers in relation to existing objects and the inclusion of new objects in the number of protected (for example, biotechnology, methods and results of genetic engineering), the possibility of which is provided for in Article 27 TRIPS (Agreement on Trade-Related Aspects of Intellectual Property Rights) that restricts technology transfer.

This enhanced protection situation is beneficial for technology rights holders and is negatively perceived by stakeholders in obtaining technology, as it limits access to innovation in the context of limited R&D budgets. Along with positive effects on economic growth in general, intellectual property rights have negative effects when abused. So in Article 8 of the TRIPS Agreement, it is noted that when developing or changing their laws and regulations, members may take appropriate measures, provided that they comply with the provisions of this Agreement that may be necessary to prevent abuse of intellectual property rights by rights holders, or resorting to practices that unreasonably restrict trade or adversely affect international technology transfer.

In particular, there is an acute issue for developing countries to strengthen the system of guarantees at the international level to prevent the abuse of monopoly rights in the international transfer of technologies. In this regard, not only flexible mechanisms (regimes of restrictions and exemptions) are taking on increasing importance to balance the interests between rights holders and users, to resolve the contradiction between IP rights and the right to access technology, as well as to copyright objects related anti-trust and free use regulation.

The study allows us to conclude that the issues of statistical accounting of IP objects remain one of the important points in the derivation of the rating of activity in the IP sphere by countries and regions. North America and the European Union occupy unregistered objects—know-how, objects of copyright and related rights—for which there is no statistical information due to its confidentiality.

Most statistical reports and analytical materials consistently describe trends in registration activity in relation to patents (as a rule, inventions and utility models in the jurisdictions where they are registered are combined), trademarks and industrial designs (designs), but do not raise questions about the relationship between these trends.

When based on the number of applications registered by the patent office a conclusion is made about the country's ranking in the global world, the following should be noted:

- The number of applications filed with the national patent office characterizes the economy of this country not in terms of its science intensity, but in terms of investment attractiveness. If the market is interesting, the patent owner wants to be able to work on it, having the opportunity to exercise his ownership rights;
- An alternative to patenting or any other protection of intellectual property is control over the market in other ways: natural monopoly, technological uniqueness, inaccessibility, etc. It is recommended to obtain a patent only if other control methods are unavailable. Therefore, the state of patenting reflects, in some aspect, the civilization of relations in the market;
- More realistically, innovation potential needs to be assessed by the number of domestic, foreign and PCT applications filed by national applicants in the country and around the world. It is also advisable to use specific criteria: the ratio of the number of submitted and registered applications, the ratio with the number of employees, with costs, with income or added value.

In the Global Innovation Index (GII), Kyrgyzstan ranks 90th among 196 countries reviewed in the annual publication of WIPO [2. Ñ.1].

The following table shows the rankings of Kyrgyzstan over the past three years.

Table 2: GII Rating of Kyrgyzstan in 2017–2019

	2019	*2018*	*2017*
Global Index Innovation (GII)	90	94	95
Contribution of innovation	78	85	86
An innovative result	111	101	10

In Kyrgyzstan, the indicators of the contribution of innovations are higher than the innovative result (product). In 2019, Kyrgyzstan ranks 78th in terms of the contribution of innovations, which is better than the previous year and compared to 2017. According to the results of innovative activity, Kyrgyzstan takes 111th place. This situation is worse than in 2018 when compared to 2017.

Table 3 provides an overview of the strengths and weaknesses from the perspective of the Global Innovation Index 2019.

Table 3: GII Rating of Kyrgyzstan's Strengths and Weaknesses in 2019

Strong sides		*Weak sides*	
Indicator	*Rating*	*Indicator*	*Rating*
Ease of starting a business*	32	Top 3 global research and development companies	43
Education spending (% of GNP)	9	Ranking of universities QS, average score top	78
Teacher-student ratio (high school)	35	Environmental certifications ISO 14001	124
Gross capital formation (% of GNP)	19	Cluster development state	123
Complexity (diversification) of market	36	Patent families 2+ offices	93
Credit	30	PCT patents by origin	99
Loan availability	29	Cited documents H-index	125
Microfinance loans (gross) (% of GNP)	7	ISO 9001 quality certificates	124
Firms offering formal training (% of firms)	6	High-tech and medium-high-tech industries, %	100
Net inflow of FDI (% of GDP), on average over 3 years	17	Intangible assets	125
Origin patents	18	ICT and business model creation	124

Analysis of the above data shows that Kyrgyzstan has good prerequisites for business development, a simple procedure for registering enterprises, and a highly qualified workforce. There is a formed legislative framework in the field of IP, and until 2019 there was a significant inflow of foreign direct investment in the country; there were more than 25 commercial banks and microfinance companies, which determines the availability of borrowed funds for doing business.

However, along with strengths, there are also weaknesses, such as insufficient number of research companies, insufficient use of potential in the field of ICT, low level of use of IP objects as intangible assets of a company, few high-tech and medium-high-tech industries, low level of environmental certification of goods, average rating level of universities of the country, lack of development of cluster orientation of the economy and others.

The place and role of Kyrgyzstan in the world IP market is determined in terms of export by its low potential, which, moreover, is not realized in the field of IP; in terms of imports, the relatively small volume of protected commodity markets; from the point of view of jurisdiction for making transactions—low predictability and instability of the judicial and political system as a whole. All this determines the current state of IP management in our country.

REFERENCES

1. World Intellectual Property Indicators 2020. URL: http://www.wipo.int/wipo_pub_941_2020.pdf (accessed 20.02.21)
2. Global Innovation Index 2020 URL: https://www.wipo.int/global_innovation_index/en/2020/ (accessed 20.02.21)

18

Development of Kyrgyz-Indian Relations in the Field of Science

Dzhumaliyeva Ryskul Sardarbekovna

ABSTRACT

This article considers the ways of developing science in two countries—Kyrgyzstan and India—in the context of mutually beneficial cooperation. The main areas of the development of science are analyzed, as well as their beneficial use for the opposite side. The two countries, moving at different levels of development, find common ground and profitable use of available resources.

Keywords: *Kyrgyzstan, India, education, science, cooperation in the field of science, internationalization.*

The long history of Indian civilization, from the Mauryan dynasty to the arrival of the Great Mughals, from British colonization to independence on 15 August 1947, has always meant that India was open to the outside world. The young Indian state inherited civilizational traditions, using the language of diplomacy to build relations with the world community. When it comes to New Delhi's actions on the world stage, it is appropriate to recall the statement of Jawaharlal Nehru: "India is a geographical and economic whole, a cultural unity amid diversity, a pile of contradictions linked by strong but invisible threads". This is how the state of Hindustan is perceived by the people and elites, this is how the country projects itself to the outside world.

As you know, over the past years, India has retained a stable third place in terms of GDP growth of more than 7 per cent and is an advanced country in the development of information technologies, not to mention huge human resources.

As foreign policy resources grow, India's influence will expand in neighbouring regions, including in the Central Asian region. Currently, the importance of the countries of Central Asia for India lies not only in the civilizational, cultural, and historical aspects. More and more attention is paid to the geopolitical and economic context of cooperation.

Today, India's policy in Central Asia has gone through the stages of formation, institutionalization and some transformation due to external and internal factors. The intensification of India's policy in the region is due to its close proximity to Afghanistan and the presence of potential security threats such as drug trafficking, terrorism and religious extremism that could spread in the region. The Indian establishment is also prompted to pursue a more active policy in Central Asia by fears associated with the steady growth of China's economic and military power and political weight. In addition, in the context of a growing economy and energy needs, it is important for India to look for new sources of hydrocarbons.

In addition to bilateral opportunities for cooperation, India can take advantage of some useful mechanisms to increase its influence in the Central Asian region, including in Kyrgyzstan. In particular, interaction within the SCO provides India with an opportunity to become part of the process of regional cooperation. In this regard, the study of the strategic goals, main directions, and priorities of India's policy in Central Asia, as well as the key instruments and mechanisms for their implementation in general, are becoming the subject of particular importance.

The specifics of Indian foreign policy during the formation of the state laid the foundation for further foreign policy strategy. The Indian leadership had to proceed from the fact that the country existed in the colonial model of the economy and did not have an independent international political experience. Based on the aforementioned initial conditions, Delhi, firstly, focused on the state economy, including foreign economic activity, and, secondly, refused to join any military-political alliances. Thus, according to the Indian sociologist, D. Gupta, on the one hand Nehru, through Foreign Minister S. Bajpai, reassured Washington about India's lack of intentions to follow the socialist path of development, and on the other hand, he refused to participate in the so-called Manila and Baghdad Pacts in 1954 and 1955, which bore an obvious anti-Soviet orientation.

When speaking about India, you need to keep in mind that modern India is one of the largest states in the world with a population of over 1.3 billion people. The prevailing multi-party system and political culture of the population confirms the country's established reputation as one of the largest democracies in the world. India plays a major role in the global economy and ranks among the six largest economies in the world, with a gross domestic product (GDP) of US$ 2.69 trillion. Analysts predict that by 2025, India could become the third largest country in the world by GDP after China and the USA. The Government of India is actively implementing a whole range of measures and programs aimed at stimulating the country's economic development, including improving public administration and national legislation, and improving the business and investment climate. Many of them, such as Make in India, 100 Smart Cities, Affordable Housing for All, Digital India and others, are in consonance with programs we are running in Kyrgyzstan. The country is at the forefront as a centre of vast financial resources, as well as a source of innovation and scientific and technological development, and represents a huge export market for foreign goods, including oil and uranium, while acquiring the status of a major investor and supplier of advanced technologies, primarily IT.. The Republic of India is one of the key political, trade, economic and investment partners of Kyrgyzstan in the region. Relations between our peoples have ancient traditions and are rooted deep in the past, when the Saka tribes from the territory of modern Kyrgyzstan went to India and established a powerful empire there. Some sources attribute the Saka origin to the spiritual teacher and founder of Buddhism, Gautama Buddha, who had the title "Shakyamuni" (Sakyamuni), meaning "the wisest of the Sakyas (Sakyas)".

India can be considered the centre of education. Since ancient times it was from India that trigonometry, algebra and the basic concept of calculus came to us, the ancient game of chess, astronomy and some of the basics of chemistry, medicine (surgery was very well developed).

The modern education system was formed in India after gaining independence in 1947.

Today Kyrgyzstan and India are multi-ethnic, multi-religious, multilingual and secular societies. Bishkek and Delhi share similar positions on the problems of regional and global cooperation. The countries closely interact at multilateral platforms such as the United Nations (UN), and the Shanghai Cooperation Organization (SCO). India became an observer of the SCO, and then a full member of the organization. The main achievement of cooperation between Kyrgyzstan and India is the absence of any political problems. Moreover, today there is a high level of mutual trust.

Frankly, until 2015, Indian society did not know enough about the economic opportunities of our state. Cooperation was focused more on the political component. The official visit of Narendra Modi to Kyrgyzstan and negotiations at the highest level put the economic bloc in priority positions. Now we have felt a real interest in our economy, in the development of trade, economic and investment cooperation.

Considering the Kyrgyz-Indian relations at the present stage, it should be noted that the relations between Kyrgyzstan and India go far into the past. The Silk Road, which ran through Kyrgyzstan, ends in India. Already in those days, there was an exchange of goods and ideas between our states. The ideas of peace and development transmitted through Buddhism at that time are still relevant today. For centuries, the Indian people, just like the people of Kyrgyzstan, have always accepted people of various faiths in their land. Such communication gave results—enrichment through ideas, knowledge and perception of the world. This combination of cultures and different religions has given our peoples inner strength and a unique national character.

Kyrgyzstan and India are developing bilateral cooperation in the field of science, technology and education, since it is those that can accelerate the development of countries and, accordingly, improve people's lives.

Cooperation in science and technology supports the development of industries based on scientific research, encourages investment in the infrastructure of science and education, and promotes the development of international trade and dialogue on global, regional and national security issues.

In 2003, the Indian government awarded a grant for the creation of a mini-hydropower plant in Kyrgyzstan, and the "Kyrgyz-Indian Information Technology Centre" was established in Bishkek.

For Kyrgyzstan, one of the reasons for the dynamic and broad cooperation with India in the field of science and technology is that India has taken a very important place on the new scientific map of the world.

The share of India accounts for about 10 per cent of all research spending in Asia, and the number of internationally ranked scientific publications has grown by 45 per cent over the past five years. However, compared to developed countries, India still lags behind in science and technology. In India, there are only 140 researchers per million population, compared with 4,651 in the USA.

In 2018, India invested US$ 50.1 billion in science and technology. In comparison, China invested about US$ 451.2, and the USA invested 511.1 times more than India. Despite this, five Indian institutes of technology have been named among the top ten in Asia by *Asiaweek* magazine.

The number of publications by Indian researchers is growing at one of the fastest growing rates among the major countries. India, along with China, Iran and Brazil, are the only developing countries among 31 with 97.5 per cent of all scientific production in the world. India's share in scientific publications is 3 per cent. However, in chemistry this figure is 5.7 per cent, pharmacology 4.3 per cent and physics 3.7 per cent. The share of Indian publications in organic chemistry (8.3 per cent) and medicinal chemistry (6.5 per cent) is even higher. India is ranked fourth in the world (after the USA, Japan and China) for R&D in information technology and communications.

India was one of the first countries to establish diplomatic relations with Kyrgyzstan after gaining independence. Since then, there has been close cooperation along with development of bilateral mutually beneficial relations between our countries in the widest and most diverse areas. During this period, an Agreement was concluded between the Kyrgyz Republic and the Republic of India on cooperation in the field of trade and economic relations, science and technology and another Agreement on cooperation in the field of culture, art, education, science, media, and sports.

The Kyrgyz Republic, as a sovereign state during its independence, has built very close and friendly relations with many countries of the world. According to the Ministry of Foreign Affairs of the Kyrgyz Republic, as of 1 January 2019, our country has diplomatic relations with 164 countries of the world, including India [5].

The peoples of the Kyrgyz Republic and the Republic of India have had historical and cultural ties since time immemorial and there has been an upward trend in expanding cooperation in various fields in recent years, since the establishment of diplomatic relations between the two countries reaffirming our commitment to strengthening relations in all spheres of life on the basis of mutual respect, close cooperation for the benefit of peace and prosperity of the peoples of the two countries.

The basis for cooperation in the scientific and educational sphere is the Intergovernmental Agreement on cooperation in culture, education and research activities, as well as a number of bilateral interdepartmental and inter-university agreements.

After the establishment of diplomatic relations in 1992 between our countries, the embassy of Kyrgyzstan was opened in New Delhi in 1993, and in 1994 of India in Bishkek. India was one of the first countries to recognize the independence of Kyrgyzstan. We have cultural and civilizational ties that are closely related to each other.

Cooperation has intensified in the areas of trade, economics, education, and medicine. Relations between Kyrgyzstan and India have also strengthened on security issues due to India's entry into the Shanghai Cooperation Organization.

The cooperation between the two countries has strengthened and has taken a big leap forward in the Kyrgyz-Indian partnership. Visits are held both at the highest level and at the level of foreign ministers.

Our bilateral relations are steadily developing. Last year, 16 agreements and memoranda were signed during Narendra Modi's visit.

Former President of Kyrgyzstan S. Jeenbekov proposed to declare 2021 the Year of Indian-Kyrgyz Friendship and Cultures. He said that Kyrgyzstan and India were entering a new level of strategic partners, initiating the announcement of 2021 as the Year of Indian-Kyrgyz friendship and culture.

Kyrgyzstan is a popular country among Indian students for medical education. More than a thousand Kyrgyz civil servants have completed courses under the Indian Technical Cooperation Program (ITEC).

Kyrgyzstan and India have achieved mutual recognition of higher education diplomas. On the initiative of the Kyrgyz side, Ambassador of Kyrgyzstan to India Asein Isaev and Director of the Indian Council for Cultural Relations Dinesh Patnaik met in New Delhi. During the meeting, the parties agreed on the following issues:

- increasing the quota for Kyrgyz students to study through ICCR programs;

- the possibility of choosing a specialization according to the request by Kyrgyz;
- mutual recognition of higher education diplomas of the two countries;
- the possibility of holding a joint Kyrgyz-Indian art exhibition;
- mutual invitation of teachers and professors from India and Kyrgyzstan to conduct lectures on the basis of the faculties of international relations of universities of the two countries; and
- exchange of experience in the field of general education schools.

The quotas in the ITEC program have also increased from 85 to 100 for Kyrgyz citizens. India and Kyrgyz agreed to work on expanding the Kyrgyz-Indian information centre at KSUCTA and to consider the possibility of opening similar centres in other large cities of Kyrgyzstan on the basis of an Indian grant.

India has invested in joint research work in high altitude biology and medicine. On this industry, 20 business forums were held in the Kyrgyz Republic. It should be noted that the project is aimed at further developing and strengthening Kyrgyz-Indian relations in the field of science and medicine.

Scientific research is carried out by the National Centre for Cardiology and Therapy under the Ministry of Health of the Kyrgyz Republic and the Organization for Research and Development in the Field of Defence of the Ministry of Defence of India on the basis of the Kyrgyz-Indian Mining Biomedical Research Centre, established in 2011, under the NCCT of the Ministry of Health of the Kyrgyz Republic. Equipment for scientific research, infrastructure development and maintenance of a scientific station at the Too-Ashuu Pass and a new scientific station at the Seok-Ashuu Pass were purchased.

Kyrgyz-Indian relations occupy a special place in the foreign policy of both countries. Over a short period, bilateral cooperation in various forms has made an invaluable contribution to the development of both countries. If we add to this the fact that never in all the past decades have relations between the Kyrgyz Republic and India been burdened by any conflicts or insoluble contradictions, then there is every reason to call them a reliable partnership.

Kyrgyzstan and India also consider each other as promising scientific partners and note that today there is a fairly wide space for the implementation of joint projects in the field of innovation and modernization.

Historically, India has close ties with Central Asia, but during the Soviet era, there were limited political, economic and cultural ties between India and Kyrgyzstan (as one of the Soviet republics). Rajiv Gandhi, former Prime Minister of India, visited the city of Frunze (Bishkek) and Lake Issyk-Kul in 1985. After the Kyrgyz Republic gained independence in 1991, India, in 1992, was among the first countries to establish diplomatic relations with it, and the Permanent Mission of India to the Kyrgyz Republic was established in 1994.

Relations between Kyrgyzstan and India are developing in many aspects, which are important not only for Kyrgyzstan, but also for India. Among the priorities for the development of interstate relations between India and Kyrgyzstan, along with diplomatic, trade and commercial relations, the sphere of science occupies an important place.

Kyrgyzstan and India are reliable partners in the field of science and education. Bilateral cooperation in the field of science of the Kyrgyz Republic and the Republic of India is developing progressively and systematically. In addition, the Kyrgyz-Indian partnership has a good reputation and is an example to follow: congresses and forums between the Kyrgyz Republic and the Republic of India are held on an ongoing basis, which are widely covered in both republican and regional media.

Within the framework of the Program of Scientific and Technical Cooperation between the two states, the practice of regular scientific contacts has developed, and prerequisites have been created for intensifying our joint efforts in this area. The most promising and strategically important areas for the two countries for further interaction are the medical sector, agriculture, pharmaceuticals, as well as environmental protection.

Kyrgyz-Indian cooperation in the field of education and science began on 18 March 1992 with the signing in Delhi of the "Agreement between the governments of the Kyrgyz Republic and India on cooperation in the field of culture, arts, science and education, sports and mass media". There is also, between the two countries, an Intergovernmental Commission on Trade, Economic, Scientific, Technical and Cultural and Humanitarian Cooperation.

There is a law "On the ratification of the Memorandum of Cooperation between the Government of the Kyrgyz Republic and the Government of the Republic of India on joint research work on high mountain biology and medicine, signed on 14 June 2019 in the city of Bishkek".

Scientific research is carried out by the National Centre for Cardiology and Therapy under the Ministry of Health of the Kyrgyz Republic (NCCT MH KR) and the Defence Research and Development Organization (DRDO) of the Ministry of Defence of India on the basis of the Kyrgyz-Indian Mountain Biomedical Research Centre under the NCCT of the Ministry of Health of the Kyrgyz Republic.

Thus, it should be concluded that currently the Kyrgyz Republic and the Republic of India are partners in the field of science and technology. Both sides express interest in joint cooperation in this promising direction. Relations between the countries have made significant progress: the leaderships of both countries have developed a common opinion that these should be strong and friendly relations.

Taking into account the potential and experience of India in the implementation of projects in the field of new technologies, such as Digital India, Electronic Government, and StartUp Village, Kyrgyzstan calls on Indian companies to take an active part in the implementation of high technologies on mutually beneficial terms in such priority areas as IT technologies, mining and agricultural industries, transport and logistics communications, textile and processing industries, education, medicine and pharmaceuticals. Free economic zones of Kyrgyzstan are also ready for cooperation with India: where there is a favourable investment climate, tax incentives and customs conditions for domestic and foreign entrepreneurs.

The state and prospects for the development of Kyrgyz-Indian relations show that we have chosen the right vector for the development of cooperation. The existing opportunities for interaction are large and practically unlimited.

REFERENCES

1. Internationalization of higher education: challenges and realities, Accreditation in education: electron. zhurn. 23.08.2013. URL: http://www.akvobr.ru/inter nacionalizacia_vysshego_obrazovania.html (accessed 02.05.2016).
2. India: scientific and technological development and innovation. URL: http://

www.lawinrussia.ru/ internacionalizacia_vysshego_obrazovania.html (accessed 11/ 22/2019).
3. "Kyrgyz-Indian cooperation in the field of education", Ala-Too 24, studio "It's not evening", 2019. [Electronic resource].—Access mode: https://www.youtube.com/ watch?v=WhntrCmath8.
4. Torkunov, A.V., Education as an instrument of "soft power" in foreign policy, Vestnik MGIMO, 2018, No. 4 (25).
5. Sheregi, A.F.; Dmitriev, A.L. and Arefiev, A.L. Scientific and pedagogical potential and export of educational services of Russian universities (sociological analysis). M., 2017, p. 110.

Literature and Electronic Resources

1. Current international agreements on scientific and technical cooperation. URL: http://window.edu.ru/catalog/ pdf2txt/933/66933/39709 (accessed: 02/08/2016).
2. Declaration on strategic partnership between the Russian Federation and the Republic of India. URL: http://archive.kremlin.ru/text/docs/2000/10/ 80628.shtml (accessed 09.02.2016).
3. Maltseva, O.D. Russia-India. Vladivostok: Publishing house of the Far Eastern University, 2014.
4. Scientific and technical cooperation between Russia and India. URL: Fr.: // minobrnauki.rf/news / 5731 (accessed: 02/11/2016).
5. Protocol on scientific cooperation between the Russian Academy of Sciences and the Department of Science and Technology of the Government of India. URL: http:/ /www.ras.ru/news/ shownews.aspx? Id = e543eaf1-db40-4205-8871-507c227f7147 & print = 1 (accessed 15.02.2016).
6. Agreement on scientific cooperation and exchange of scientists between the Russian Academy of Sciences and the Indian National Academy of Sciences. URL: http:// www.conventions.ru/ view_base.php? Id = 1431 (accessed 03.02.2016).

19

Expansion of Economic Diplomacy of Kyrgyzstan in the World Community: Prospects for Regional Cooperation

Ryskulov, I.A. and Alybaeva, G.D.

ABSTRACT

This article reveals the problem of regional integration of Central Asian countries, gives a brief country profile of the national economies of Uzbekistan, Kazakhstan, Tajikistan, Turkmenistan, and Kyrgyzstan and identifies prospects for the development of regional cooperation

Keywords: *national economy, economic resources, country advantages, economic diplomacy, regional integration, and cooperation, regional economic unions.*

Regional integration of the countries of Central Asia is the imperative of the times. The understanding of the need to unite the republics has existed since the collapse of the Soviet Union. In 1994, the Central Asian Union (CACU) was formed; then in 1998 the Organization of the CACU and in 2002 the Central Asian Economic Union (CAEC) was established. But all of them turned out to be unviable and in 2005 the CAPS ceased to exist, joining the EurAsEC.

This association is beneficial to all neighbouring countries. At present, favourable integration prospects have been created and there exists cooperation within the framework of the CA-EU, CA-Japan, and CA-US dialogue. The first summit of the heads of state of the Central Asian countries was held on 15 March 2018 in Astana, the second in November 2019 in Tashkent. The third was planned to be held in Bishkek in 2020, but was postponed to 2021 due to the ongoing spread of the corona virus pandemic.

This format of consultative meetings can be the beginning of the formation of a full-fledged union. There is a mutual interest of states based on the economic resources of each of them.

For example, Uzbekistan, by Central Asian standards, has a relatively large population, limited area for agricultural use, and significant unemployed labour resources in rural areas. In terms of gold reserves, the republic ranks fourth in the world, and in terms of its production, it ranks seventh (about 80 tons of gold annually); in terms of copper reserves, it ranks tenth; uranium is in the twelfth place, and in its production, the eighth place.

A powerful mineral resource base exists in Uzbekistan, which is one of the main items of foreign exchange earnings in the country's economy. Today, this base is made up of more than 1,800 deposits and about 1,000 prospective occurrences of minerals, 118 types of mineral raw materials, of which 65 are being developed. Mineral resources of Uzbekistan are estimated by experts to be worth about 3.5 trillion dollars.

The production of cotton is developed, as well as the cotton market. The country ranks third in the world for exports and sixth for cotton production. The most important agricultural products of Uzbekistan, in addition to cotton, are fruits, vegetables, and grain (wheat, rice, and corn).

There are significant untapped reserves of oil and gas. Current gas production makes a decisive contribution to electricity generation. Uzbekistan also has experience in the production of agricultural machinery and the only aircraft building plant in Central Asia. There is a large GM Uzbekistan plant in the city of Asaka, which produces cars under licences from Daewoo and Chevrolet. The national company Uzbekneftgas, ranks 11th in the world in terms of natural gas production (annual gas production is 60-70 billion cubic metres.)

In the structure of GDP, the weight of agriculture is significant—38 per cent; industry accounts for 26 per cent, and services 36 per cent. Uzbekistan exports cotton, gold, uranium ore, natural gas, mineral fertilizers, metals, textile and food industry products, and cars. Uzbekistan has a positive trade balance. Gold and foreign exchange reserves amount to more than US$ 131.5 billion.[1]

Kazakhstan is a country with a huge territory by Central Asian standards and various rich resources that must be industrially developed, and a small population in relation to the territory. The birth rate in Kazakhstan is lower in comparison with Uzbekistan, Tajikistan, and Kyrgyzstan; agricultural land (compared with Uzbekistan, Tajikistan, and Kyrgyzstan) for growing agricultural crops is limited, because significant territories are deserts and semi-deserts, and therefore the crops grown are not so diverse in comparison with Uzbekistan and Tajikistan.

Taking into account the above-mentioned features of development, Kazakhstan could attract labour resources from Uzbekistan, Tajikistan, and Kyrgyzstan. At the same time, agricultural products from Uzbekistan could be widely and easily sold in the markets of Kazakhstan, Tajikistan, Kyrgyzstan, and contribute to the food supply of the population of Kazakhstan.

Kazakhstan possesses a variety of minerals. Of the 105 elements of the periodic table, 99 have been identified in the bowels of Kazakhstan; 70 have been explored, more than 60 elements have been involved in the production.

In terms of mineral reserves, Kazakhstan ranks first among the CIS countries for chrome ores and lead, second for reserves of oil, silver, copper, manganese, zinc, nickel, and phosphorus raw materials, and third for gas, coal, gold and tin.

The volume of proven oil reserves amounted to 39.6 billion barrels, or 6.5 billion tons, which is 3.2 per cent of the world's total reserves. Projected oil reserves in the fields located in the Kazakh sector of the Caspian Sea alone are more than 17 billion tons. Proved gas reserves of Kazakhstan amount to 1.82 trillion cub. m, which is 1.7 per cent of world reserves.

Explored reserves of uranium deposits in Kazakhstan amount to 1.69 million tons, or 21 per cent of world reserves (2nd place in the world).[2]

Leading industries: non-ferrous and ferrous metallurgy, chemical, mechanical engineering, light, and food. Oil refining and production of building materials are also developed. As a "grain king", Kazakhstan can provide all the republics of Central Asia with grain in the requested volumes.

Tajikistan is a country with a high birth rate and large reserves of unemployed labour resources that could be used not only in Kazakhstan, but also outside Central Asia. There is a variety of products grown by villagers in Tajikistan, especially fruits and vegetables. They could find their legal markets in Kazakhstan and Kyrgyzstan, that is, become an additional source of income for the rural labour resources of Tajikistan and a product of consumption by the populations of Kazakhstan and Kyrgyzstan.

In the north of Tajikistan, in the Sughd region, there is one of the world's largest silver deposits—Bolshoi Konimansur. Also, Tajikistan is rich in deposits of precious stones, uranium (according to some sources 16 per cent of world reserves), gold, coal, and aluminium and polymetallic ores.

The advantage of the economy is its large hydropower potential. Primary aluminium, agricultural products, dried fruits, and carpets are produced.

The weak side is the instability of the economy—a high level of unemployment, dependence on commodity exchange, and little or weak diversification of agriculture, for which only 6 per cent of the land is suitable.

According to UNDP, 63 per cent of Tajikistan's population lives on less than two dollars a day (in purchasing power parity). The prolonged war, the associated destruction, and human losses led to a sharp decline in the economy. However, in recent years of peace, the economy and living standards have improved significantly. Agriculture accounts for 18.9 percent of GDP, industry 21.9 per cent, and the services sector 59.2 per cent.[3]

Aluminium exports account for half the export earnings. In second place is the export of cotton. The main agricultural crops are cotton, silk, grain, tobacco, vegetables, fruits, and dried fruits.

The country has significant potential in the field of hydropower, which is still poorly realized. The bulk of electricity in Tajikistan is produced at the hydroelectric power station. The total volume of hydropower resources is estimated at 527 billion kWh, including 202 billion kWh that are technically feasible for use, and 172 billion kWh that are economically feasible for construction. This makes the state one of the most secure in terms of this renewable energy source in the world (eighth place in terms of absolute generation potential.[4] Among the CIS countries, the country is second only to Russia in this indicator.

Possessing large reserves of natural gas (15–20 trillion cubic metres) and oil (1.5–2.0 billion tons), Turkmenistan is one of the most important exporters of fuel resources. However, transportation and exploration problems complicate the development of this sector of the economy, which forms about 70 per cent of the gross national product. At the same time, industry accounts for 34 per cent, agriculture 10 per cent, and services sector 56 per cent of GDP.

Limited privatization has taken place in Turkmenistan, mainly in the services sector. Industry, agriculture, energy, transport, and communications continue to be predominantly public sector. As a result, many government services remain free and dependent on subsidies.

Agriculture employs 48 per cent of workers, industry 14 per cent, and services 38 per cent.

The main industries include the refining and processing of oil and natural gas, the production of glass, textiles (mainly cotton) and clothing, and the food industry.

For the supply of energy resources, various types of transport are used, the main of which is the Central Asia-Centre gas pipeline, built during the Soviet era. An agreement was signed for the construction of the Trans-Caspian gas pipeline. At various stages of development are gas pipeline construction projects to Afghanistan, India and other Asian countries. The construction of a gas pipeline to China has been completed. Turkmenistan was interested in transporting gas to Europe bypassing Russian territory under the Nabucco project, which has not been taken forward.

The main place in the export is occupied by gas, oil and oil products, cotton goods, carpets and rugs. The main buyers are Ukraine (51.6 per cent), Poland (10 per cent), and Hungary (8 per cent).

Industrial products, foodstuffs, chemicals, and medicines are imported. The main suppliers are Russia (16.8 per cent), China (16.7 per cent), Turkey (13.8 per cent), Ukraine (7.8 per cent), and Germany (5.5 per cent).[5]

Kyrgyzstan is a country that, like Uzbekistan and Tajikistan, differs, albeit to a relatively lesser extent, in labour surplus.

The advantages of the economy are as follows: there is a fairly developed agriculture. Gold (Kumtor deposit) and mercury are exported. There are reserves of uranium and the possibility of its enrichment (Kara-Balta Mining Combine (KGRK)) for use in nuclear power plants, sufficiently large reserves of antimony and rare earth metals. The country is rich in natural resources for the development of tourism (Issyk-Kul and Sary-Chelek lakes, Dead Lake, Dzhety-Oguz gorge, etc.). The country really has great hydropower potential.

According to the results of 2019, the industry produced 20 per cent of the GDP of Kyrgyzstan. About 40 per cent of industrial production comes from gold mining, one of the few actively developing industries in the republic.

Exports reach about US$ 2 billion: they include cotton, wool, meat, milk and dairy products, gold, mercury, uranium, antimony, garments, and footwear. The main buyers of exports are Switzerland (26.2 per cent), Russia (17.2 per cent), Uzbekistan (2.7 per cent), Kazakhstan (2.2 per cent), and UAE (20.3 per cent).

Imports amount to about 4 billion US dollars: they include oil and gas, machinery and equipment, chemicals, and food. The main import suppliers are Russia (33.6 per cent), China (20.7 per cent), Kazakhstan (11.9 per cent), and CIIIA (5.9 per cent).[6]

Thus, Kyrgyzstan, Kazakhstan, Uzbekistan, Tajikistan, and Turkmenistan, possessing huge resources and economic potential, are priority political and economic partners for each other. In addition, each country has certain difficulties in its development. Of course, given the approximately same level of development, historical past, the presence of many similarities in the economy, cooperation with both developed and developing countries would be more effective if the CA countries were a single whole, that is, a union.

Economic diplomacy of the Central Asian countries is aimed at reducing imports, increasing exports and increasing trade with non-CIS countries. The integration of the countries of the region will make it possible to move away from the ongoing policy of self-sufficiency and focus on a mutually beneficial division of labour, which will reduce the consumer price of products, and increase employment and export opportunities in the region.

For the countries of Central Asia, it is a very important task to successfully solve the problem of the deadlock in the region. Joint efforts to promote the construction of a trans-Asian railway, participation in the implementation of the TRACECA project (highway from Central Asia to China, etc.) will lead to a breakthrough in the geographical isolation of the region and its transformation into one of the constituent parts of the global system.

Kyrgyzstan and Tajikistan are rich in water resources. Given the projected data on the shortage of clean drinking water in the 21st century, Kyrgyzstan and Tajikistan will have real opportunities for mutually beneficial cooperation with neighbouring countries in the use of water resources.

The presence of colossal reserves of coal, oil, gas and other resources in Kazakhstan, Turkmenistan and Uzbekistan allows these countries not only to fully meet their own needs and needs of the region, but also to export energy resources to other countries.

The analysis showed that according to official statistics, trade between the countries of the Central Asian region is growing more slowly than with foreign countries and even other CIS countries. At the same time, the results of many studies carried out by international organizations suggest the opposite. According to their data, the volume of foreign trade between the countries of the Central Asian region is quite significant, but the actual exchange of goods is not reflected in the official data.

An important argument for the integration of the Central Asian countries is the complementarities of their economies that have existed since the times of the Soviet Union. The transition from a planned economy to a market economy in all the Central Asian countries has been implemented with the end of which barriers to integration have been removed and real prerequisites for regional unification have been created.

An active use of diplomacy, including economic, is required to settle, first of all, issues of delimitation and demarcation of borders between neighbours to ensure the successful development of cooperation.

The development of this Central Asian economic association can go in two directions. The first is its formation, the basis of which can be the issue of a joint solution of common regional problems, for example, water use. The second direction is through joint participation in economic associations of countries, for example, in the EAEU.

An important circumstance in favour of the development of integration of the countries of one region is also the fact that the population of the countries of the same region, as you know, most often has similar languages, customs, mentality, and social relations that are well developed between such countries, which also favour the development of economic relations.

In addition, as the history of independent management of Central Asian entities has shown, the prerequisites for the economic unification of countries should mature and become obvious.

REFERENCES

1. Statistical collection "Uzbekistan in figures, 2018-2019." https://stat.uz/ru/publikatsii/3684-uzbekistan-v-tsifrakh, p. 23.
2. Statistical collection. Balances of resources and use of the most important types of raw materials, industrial and technical products and consumer goods in the Republic of Kazakhstan 2015-2019 Nur-Sultan 2020, p. 15.
3. Labour Migration, Remittances and Human Development in Central Asian Countries Human Development Policy Briefs Series for Central Asian Countries, 2015. https://www.eurasia.undp.org/content/, p. 12
4. Statistical collection "Tajikistan in figures". Agency for Statistics under the President of the Republic of Tajikistan, 2018, pp. 37, 85.
5. Statistical compilation Industry in the countries of the Commonwealth of Independent States 2015-2019. http://www.cisstat.com/rus/sod_promCIS2020.pdf, p. 23.
6. Statistical Yearbook of the Kyrgyz Republic 2015-2019. National Statistics Committee of the Kyrgyz Republic. B.2020. http://www.stat.kg/ru/publications/statisticheskij-ezhegodnik-kyrgyzskoj-respubliki/, p. 237.

Index

A. Kazantsev, 84
ADM Hospitality & Services LTD, 42
Afghanistan, 51, 55-56, 65, 71, 76, 78, 109, 145, 179
    Developments, 179
    ISKP Activities, 47
    Taliban-AQ Ties, 148
Afghan-Tajik Border, 99
Africa, 190
Agriculture, 191, 224
Akromiya, 88
Al-Azaim, 146
Albeit, 99
Al-Furqan, 130
al-Ikhwan al-Muslimin, 82
al-Naba newsletter, 145
Al-Qaeda (AQ), 45, 49, 86, 128, 130, 148-49, 152
Ansarulloh (Ansarull Allah), 88
Anti-Terrorism Centre of the member-states of the Commonwealth of Independent States (ATC CIS), 86, 91
Armed Islamic Group, 81
Armenia, 27
Ashgabat Agreement, 23, 142
Asian Development Bank (ADB), 34
At-Takfir Wal-Hijra, 88
Azerbaijan, 60

Bakay-Ata in Talas Province, 189
Bakshi, Jyotsna, 139
Bandar Abbas Port, 176
Bangladesh, 37
Batken Province, 189
Bay of Bengal Initiative for Multi-Sectoral Technical and Economic Cooperation (BIMSTEC), 116
Belt and Road Initiative (BRI), 23-24, 29, 140
Bhabatron-2, 40
Bhagavad Gita, 194-97, 200
Bilateral Economic Ties, 19
Bilateral Investment Treaty (BIT), 21
Bilateral Trade, 41
Bishkek, 8, 13-14, 21-22, 25, 34, 58, 62, 86-90, 111, 114-15, 134, 217-18
Bolshevik Revolution, 159
Bolshoi Konimansur, 223
Border Cooperation Component, 112
Border Crossing Points, 112
Border Liaison Offices, 112
Brand India, 29
Brothers-Muslims, 82
Buddhism, 170
Business Ombudsman, 19

C+C5 Format, 69
C5 + European Union, 33
C5 + Japan, 26, 33
C5 + Republic of Korea, 33
C5 + USA, 26, 33
CA-EU, Dialogue, 221
CA-Japan Dialogue, 221
CASA-1000, 67
CAS-Afghanistan Relationship, 154
CA-US Dialogue, 221
Central Asia, 16, 25, 28, 33, 51, 56, 65, 69-70,

78, 81, 89, 128-29, 157-59, 169, 171-72, 181, 186, 189, 190, 225
ISKP Activities, 47
Political Processes, 158
Raising, 62
Security Situation, 45
Central Asia-Afghanistan ISKP's Footprints in, 46
Central Asian Economic Union (CAEC), 220
Central Asian Regional Information and Coordination Centre (CARICC), 112
Central Asian Republics (CARs), 76, 134, 146, 157-61, 165, 170, 178
Central Asian Union (CACU), 220
Central Intelligence Agency (CIA), 47
Chabahar Free Trade Zone, 29
Chabahar Port, 142, 178
China, 5-6, 24-25, 29, 54, 56, 59-60, 68-70, 72, 76-77, 78, 96, 128, 133, 139, 171, 205-06, 224-25
China's
Belt and Road Initiative, 65
Customs Service, 24
Education Ministry, 25
Interests in Central Asia, 68
Xinjiang, 65
China-Central Asia Trade, 69
China-Pakistan Economic Corridor, 57
Chinese Communist Party, 68
Chinese Impact on Regional Economic Environment, 23
Chinese Language International Council, 25
Chinese Ministry of Commerce, 24
Chinese products enter Central Asia, 23
Chinese threat, 24
CIIIA, 225
Civil War, 159
Clinton, Hillary, 128
CNN, 130
Cold War, 53, 134, 139, 142
Collective Security Treaty Organization (CSTO), 140
Commission on Narcotic Drugs, 104
Commonwealth of Independent States (CIS), 45, 83, 86
Comtrade Database, 2-3, 6
Confucius Institute, 25
Connect Central Asia Policy (CCAP), 33, 61, 135, 172
Constructive Strategic Partnership, 59
Cooperative Framework of Inclusive engagement, 56
Counter Narcotics Service (CNS), 104, 112, 114
Counter Narcotics Service of the Kyrgyz Ministry of Interior, 113
COVID-19, 64-65, 67, 108, 134, 185, 187, 191, 205
Crime and Terrorism, 107
Cs—Commerce, Connectivity, Consular and Culture, 61

Defence Research and Development Organization (DRDO), 218
Deguang, 137
Delhi Declaration on Afghanistan, 179
Double Taxation Avoidance Agreement (DTAA), 21
Dr. Jaishankar, External Affairs Minister of India, 22, 141
Drug Law Enforcement Systems for Criminal Intelligence Collection, Analysis and Exchange and Pilot Intelligence-Led Policing initiative (ILP), 113
Drugs, 102-04
Money, 103
Trafficking, 102, 106-07
Durand Line, 153

Economic and Social Council (ECOSOC), 111
Energy Club, 60
Envall and Hall 'Security Governance', 54
Eurasian Economic Union (EAEU), 6, 13, 16, 23, 26-28, 41, 72, 140, 172, 181, 195
Regional Economic Development, 27
Europe, 189
European Patent Office, 205
European Union, 19, 27, 30, 128

Strategy on Central Asia, 26
European Union GSP+, 15
Extended Neighbourhood Policy, 172

Facebook, 130
FDI, 20
Federation of Freight Forwarders Association of India (FFFAI), 176
Federation of Indian Chambers of Commerce and Industry (FICCI), 15-16, 23, 175
Fergana Valley, 47, 97, 100, 128
Financial Action Task Force (FATF), 151
Financial Intelligence Unit, 116
Food Security, 186-87, 189
Foreign Policy Concept, 32
Foreign Service Institute (FSI), 38
Foundation for Tolerance International (FTI), 112
Fractured Polity, 149
Free Trade Agreement (FTA), 23, 181
Free Trade Area, 41
Front al-Nusra, 88

Garbyal, S., 34
Germany, 205, 206
Ghazwa-e-Hind, 49
Global Terrorism Index 2017, 92
Greater Central Asia, 72
Greater Eurasia, 140
Gupta, D., 211

Haqqani Network (HQN), 148
Heart of Asia, 35
Hizbut-Tahrir al-Islami, 80, 82-83, 85, 87, 130
Hu Jintao, 136
Hungary, 224

IDTV, 85
India, 4-6, 16, 22, 27-28, 32, 36-38, 41, 57, 60, 115, 128, 133, 153, 170, 175, 212, 214, 216-17
  Exports Kyrgyzstan, 5
  ISKP, 49
India Ports Global Limited, 178
India's Connect Central Asia Policy, 26, 211
India's Engagement with Kyrgyzstan, 55
India-CARs, Energy, 173
India-Central Asia Business Council (ICABC), 16, 22, 174
India-Central Asia Cooperation, 181
India-Central Asia Dialogue, 171-72
India-EAEU
  Bilateral Trade, 27
India-Kyrgyz, 115-16
  Civil Aviation, 7
  Computer Software, 7
  Business Forum, 20
  Cooperation, 191
  Project Exports, 7
  Services Sector, 7
  Bilateral Trade, 3, 10, 21
  Economic Ties, 20, 22, 28
India-Kyrgyz Inter-Governmental Commission (IKIGC), 20
Indian Council for Cultural Relations (ICCR), 35
Indian Technical Cooperation Program (ITEC), 21, 28, 215
Information Communication Technology (ICT), 28
Information Technology (IT), 7
Ingrained Sense of Equality, 97
INSTC, 176
Intellectual Property (IP) System, 204, 206, 209
  IP5—USA, EU, Japan, China, Korea, 205
Intergovernmental Commissions (IGCs), 173
International Indian Trade Fair-2017, 42
International Narcotics Control Board (INCB), 110
International North South Transport Corridor, 142, 178
International North-South Corridor, 23
International North-South Transport Corridor (INSTC), 171, 176
International Security Assistance Force (ISAF), 135
International Terrorist Organizations, 79

Iran, 56, 60, 65, 76, 128, 153, 178-79
Islamic Movement of East Turkestan (IDTV), 84
Islamic Movement of Uzbekistan (IMU), 44, 48, 51, 76, 78-82, 85, 106, 146, 149, 152
Islamic State (IS), 44, 84-85, 87, 90, 148
Islamic State Khorasan Province (IS-KP), 45-51, 145-47, 150, 152
  Expansion, 145-46
  Propaganda Countering, 50
Islamic State-Khorasan (IS-K), 180
Israel, 27
Istanbul Process on Afghanistan, 35

Jalal-Abad Province, 189
Jamaat Ansarullah, 45
Jamaat Tauhidva-Jihad, 89
Japan, 117, 205, 206
Jihad Group, 86
Joint Declaration on the Principles and Directions of Cooperation between the Kyrgyz Republic and the Republic of India, 37
Joint Working Groups (JWGs), 50, 173, 180
Jund-al-Khalifat, 88

Kant, K., 34
Kara Darya, 97
Kara-Balta Mining Combine (KGRK), 225
Katib al Imam al Bukhari, 89
Kazakhstan, 15, 19, 22, 26-27, 35, 60, 64-65, 78, 83, 130-31, 133, 171, 222, 225
Khan, Hafiz Saeed, 46
Khanov, Yusuf, 85
Khurshid, S., 34
Korean Intellectual Property Office (KIPO), 205
Kyrgyz "Manas", 16, 194, 197-200
Kyrgyz news site Kloop.kg, 25
Kyrgyz-Chinese Border, 25
Kyrgyz-Indian Cooperation, 217
Kyrgyz-Indian Inter-governmental Commission on Trade, Economic, Scientific and Technical Cooperation, 13, 42
Kyrgyz-Indian Mining Biomedical Scientific Centre, 40
Kyrgyz-Indian Relations, 9, 17, 37, 39, 216
Kyrgyzstan, 4, 6, 15, 18, 22, 25, 28-30, 36, 38-39, 41, 55, 57-58, 64-65, 78, 81, 83, 89, 93, 96-97, 99, 105, 110-11, 115, 117, 124, 130-31, 133, 152, 158, 162-63, 165-66, 171, 188-90, 208-09, 212-13, 215, 217, 224-26
  Countering Spread of Terrorism, 84
  COVID-19 and Food Security in, 188-90
  Drugs Situation, 102
  Export, 3, 12
  GII Rating, 208
  Import, 3
    from India, 11
  Political Process, 161
  Radicalisation, 100
  South-South Cooperation, 28
  Support to Drug Control, 113
  Trade Partners, 2
Kyrgyzstan's GDP, 18
Kyrgyzstan's Strategic Engagements, 58
Kyrgyz-Tajik Border, 100

Law of the Kyrgyz Republic on Investment in the Kyrgyz Republic, 19
Law on State Registration of Legal Entities, Branches and Subsidiaries in Kyrgyz Republic, 20
Lewis, Alfred Henry, 187
Look North Policy, 172
Lt. Gen. Klimenko, 140

Manifestations of Terrorism and Extremism CAR, 77-80
Markaz-e-Shura, 48
Mattuo Fumagalli, 165
Meletinsky, E.M., 198
Middle East, 154
Military-technical Cooperation, 40
Mobile Food, 190
Modi, Narendra, Prime Minister of India, 7, 8, 33-35, 57, 135, 138, 175, 213
Mohan, C Raja, 56-57
Movarounnahr, 147

Muhammad, Khorezmshah, 198
Muslim Brotherhood, 80
Mylnikov, B.A., 78

Narayanan, K.R., 34
Narco Money, 103
Narco-Trafficking, 102-03
Naryn Darya, 97
National Academy of Customs, Excise, and Narcotics (NACEN), 116
National Centre for Cardiology and Therapy under the Ministry of Health of the Kyrgyz Republic (NCCT MH KR), 218
National Resistance Front (NRF), 147
National Security Concept (NSC), 98
NATO, 60, 66, 128
NDA-2 Government, 57
Nepal, 57
New Silk Road, 67, 72
Non-Governmental Organisations (NGOs), 50
Non-Military or Non-Traditional Security Environment, 99
Non-Traditional Threats, 109
North Atlantic Treaty Organisation (NATO), 135
North South Corridor, 62
Nurzhi, 128

Obama, Barack, 66, 137
Odnoklassniki, 130
Olcott, Martha Brill, 141
On Freedom of Religion and Religious Organizations, 124
On the Concept of State Policy of the Kyrgyz Republic in the Religious Sphere for 2014-20, 91
One Belt and One Road, 61, 69
One China Policy, 139
Operation Resolute Support, 66
Organization for the Liberation of Turkestan, 87
Organized Crime and Corruption Reporting Project (OCCRP), 25
Osh Province, 189

Pakistan, 22, 133, 151-52
  ISKP Links, 50
Panjshir, 147
People's Congress of Kurdistan, 87
Pharmaceuticals, 5
Poland, 224
Political Cooperation, 36

Qatar, 128
QUAD, 142

Radicalization Threats, 128
Radio Azattyk (RFE/RL's Kyrgyz service), 25
Raimbek Matraimov (aka Raim-Million), 25
Rao, N., 34
Reddy, Dr. Sangita, 15
Regional Anti-Terrorist Structure, 136
Regional Economic Environment, 18
Republic of Korea, 206
Roggio, Bill, 145
Rome, World Food Summit, 186
Russia, 19, 22, 26-27, 45, 54, 56, 59-60, 68, 70, 76, 83, 117, 128, 133, 153, 179, 224-25
Russia's Interests in Central Asia, 70
Russia's Soft Power, 71
Russia-China Strategic Partnership, 134
Russia-led
  Collective Security Treaty Organization (CSTO), 172
Russian Joint Military Base, 59
Russian-Sponsored CIS anti-terrorist Centre, 58
Russo-Chinese Partnership, 60

Sadieva, Abdul, 104
Saka rulers (Indo-Scythians), 170
Salafit, 128
Security, 97
Seleznev, Andrey, 105
Self-sufficient India, 33
Serbia, 27
Seven Testaments of Kyrgyzstan, 195
Shakyamuni (Sakyamuni), 212
Shanghai Cooperation Organization (SCO),

22, 33, 54-55, 57, 60-61, 72, 116, 133, 135-39, 140-42, 171, 174-75, 213
Challenges, 139
Energy Club, 60
Structures, 136
Silk Road Economic Belt (SREB), 72, 140
Singapore, 27
Singh, Rajnath, Defence Minister of India, 141
Smuggling, 101
South Asia, 190
South Korea's Eurasia Initiative, 26
Soviet Socialist Republics (SSRs), 159
Sri Lanka, 37, 57
Starr, F., 66
Strategy for Sustainable Development, 124
Sufi, 128
Surajkund Mela-2018 International Fair, 42
Swaraj, S., 40
Syr Darya, 97
Syria, Civil War, 129

Tabligavets, 128
Tajikistan, 15, 22, 25, 60, 64, 65, 81, 83, 107, 130-31, 133, 151, 171, 223, 225-26
Tajik-Uzbek border, 100
Takfirist-Jihadist Movement of Salafist Orientation, 88
Takhir Yuldashev, 82
Taliban, 45, 47, 49, 84, 144, 149, 151, 179
Movement, 87
Resistance, 147
Taliban-AQ
Domestic and Regional, 150
Implications for India, 152
Kyrgyz Implications, 151
TAPI, 67, 181
Tehreek-e-Taliban Pakistan (TTP), 44, 46, 153
Terrorist-related Activities, 101
The Institute for Training (Retraining) of Leading Personnel of the Spiritual Directorate of Muslims of Kyrgyzstan, 92
TRACECA Project, 226
Trade and Economic Cooperation, 172
Trans-Caspian Pipeline, 67
Transition Report 2019-20, 30
TRIPS (Agreement on Trade-Related Aspects of Intellectual Property Rights), 206
Trump, Donald, 128
Administration, 67
Turkey, 60, 128, 224
Turkey-based Turkic Council, 26
Turkmenistan, 15, 22, 60, 64-65, 151, 225

Ukraine, 224
Ummat, 147
UN Human Rights Council, 36
UN Office on Drugs and Crime (UNODC), 77
UN Security Council Resolution, 180
UNAMA, 145, 147
UNDP, 189, 223
UNESCO, 197-99
UNIDO, 29
United Nations (UN), 6, 148, 213
United Nations Drug Control Program, 111
United Nations Office on Drugs and Crime (UNODC), 103, 112-14, 116-17
Regional Office for Central Asia (ROCA) Programme, 111
United Nations Security Council (UNSC), 36, 55, 180
United Tajik Opposition (UTO), 78
UNODC-NACEN Cooperation, 116
USA, 30, 45, 54, 58, 65-66, 68, 70, 117, 128, 153, 205-06, 214
Interests in Central Asia, 66
Strategy for Central Asia 2019-25, 68
US-Russia-China triangle, 64, 72
US-China Economic War, 134
US-Taliban Deal, 144-45
Uyghur Diaspora, 78
Uzbekistan, 15, 19, 22, 60, 64-65, 78, 81, 83, 131, 133, 137, 151, 178, 180, 221, 225
Uzbekistan Islamic Movement, 81

Value Added Tax, 14

Vehicle-Borne Improvised Explosive Device, 50
Voice of Hind, 49
Voice of Khurasan, 49

Weapons of Mass Destruction (WMD), 66
West Asia, 190
WhatsApp, 130
Wilayat Khorasan, 46
World Bank, 162, 189
World Bank's Doing Business 2020, 18
World Food Program (WFP), 185
World Intellectual Property Organization, 204-05
World Trade Organization (WTO), 16, 204

Xinjiang Uygur Autonomous Region (XUAR), 25, 77-78

Yakyn Inkar, 89
Yoga, 175
YouTube, 130

Zarb-e-Azb, 46
Zhaish ul Mahdi, 88
Zhannat Oshiklari, 89
Zhirmunsky, V.M., 198

ABOUT THE EDITOR

Dr. Ramakant Dwivedi has a PhD from the Central Asian Studies Division of the School of International Studies, Jawaharlal Nehru University, New Delhi. Dr. Dwivedi was a Visiting Research Fellow at the Al-Beruni Institute of Oriental Studies, Tashkent (1998-2001). He was Associate Fellow at the Institute for Defence Studies and Analyses (IDSA), New Delhi (2003–2007). He has been working with Government of India since last 16 years. He has looked after a variety of domains assigned to him during the service.

His major areas of research are national security, foreign policy, ethnic issues and religious extremism in Eurasian region (Russia, Caucasus and Central Asian countries). He holds a Diploma in the Russian Language from the University of World Economy and Diplomacy, Tashkent and a Diploma in the Uzbek Language from the Tashkent State Institute of Oriental Studies, Uzbekistan. He has widely travelled in the Eurasian region. Dr. Dwivedi was awarded Nehru Memorial Scholarship for Doctoral Studies by Jawaharlal Nehru Memorial Fund, Teen Murti House, New Delhi. He has represented India in 14 countries as domain expert and part of official delegation for scholarly presentations.

His published works include 41 research papers in national/ international journals, edited books. He co-edited *India and Central Asia: Advancing the Common Interest* (IDSA & Anamaya Publishers, New Delhi, 2004), *India-Tajikistan Cooperation: Perspectives and Prospects* (ICAF & Anamaya Publishers, New Delhi, 2007), *India-Kazakhstan Perspectives: Regional and International Interactions* (Al-Farabi Kazakh National University Press, Almaty & Anamaya Publishers, New Delhi, 2007), *India-Turkmenistan Relations* (ICAF & Anamaya Publishers, 2007), *Indo-Uzbek Perspectives on the Environment and Sustainable Development* (ICAF & Anamaya Publishers, 2007), *India-Kyrgyz Relations: Perspectives and Prospects* (ICAF & Anamaya Publishers, 2008), (Russian edition brought out by Diplomatic Academy,

Ministry of Foreign Affairs, Bishkek) and *Contemporary Indo-Uzbek Perspectives on Bilateral and Regional Issues* (ICAF & Anamaya Publishers, 2008)

Dr. Dwivedi is Founding & Life Member of the India–Central Asia Foundation (ICAF), New Delhi; Life Member, United Services Institution of India (USI), New Delhi, Life Member, India Islamic Cultural Centre (IICC), New Delhi and Associate Member, Institute for Defence Studies and Analyses (IDSA), India International Centre (IIC), Press Club of India (PCI), New Delhi.

e-mail: ramakantdwivedi2012@gmail.com